A Traveller's Wine Guide to
GERMANY

A Traveller's Wine Guide to
GERMANY

By Freddy Price
Photography by Janet Price
Text for the original edition by Kerry Brady

Interlink Books
An imprint of Interlink Publishing Group, Inc.
Northampton, Massachusetts

First published in 2013 by
INTERLINK BOOKS
An imprint of Interlink
Publishing Group, Inc.
46 Crosby Street, Northampton,
Massachusetts 10160
www.interlinkbooks.com

Maps: Julian Ramirez
Book design: James McDonald/
The Impress Group
Edited by Laura Brown

Traveller's Wine Guides series
conceived by Philip Clark
Abbotsford, 14 Watts Road,
Tavistock, Devon PL19 8LG, UK

Library of Congress Cataloging-in-Publication Data
Price, Freddy.
A traveller's wine guide to Germany / by Freddy Price.
pages cm. -- (Traveller's wine guide)
"Text for the original edition by Kerry Brady."
Includes index.
ISBN 978-1-56656-893-7
1. Wine and wine making--Germany--Guidebooks. 2. Germany--Guidebooks. I. Title.
TP559.G3P75 2012
641.2'20943--dc23
2012032364

To request our complete 48-page full-color catalog, please call us toll free at 1-800-238-LINK, visit our website at www.interlinkbooks.com, or send us an email: info@interlinkbooks.com

ACKNOWLEDGEMENTS
The author would like to thank Christian Rümmelein of VinTour Wine Experiences for all his help in the preparation of this book, particularly in compiling the lists of hotels and restaurants. He would also like to thank Dr Dirk Richter of Weingut Max Ferd Richter in Mosel, as well as hundreds of German and worldwide friends, too numerous to mention by name, for their help in the preparation of this new edition.

The publishers are grateful to Cheryl Connolly for her help with the maps.

Printed and bound in China

To all the German wine growers who have welcomed us
over many years in their vineyards,
their cellars and their homes

—FP and JP

CONTENTS

North Sea
Hamburg
R. Weser
Hanover
NETHERLANDS
R. Ems
GERMAN
R. Rhein (Rhine)
Köln (Cologne)
Bonn
Mittelrhein
R. Fulda
BELGIUM
Ahr
R. Lahn
R. Ahr
Koblenz
Rheingau
Rheinhessen
Wiesbaden
Bergstrasse
Mosel
Mainz
LUXEM-BOURG
Würzbu
Nahe
Fran
Pfalz
Heidelberg
R. Tauber
R. Mosel
R. Saar
Karlsruhe
Württemberg
R. Rhein (Rhine)
Struttgart
R. Neckar
R. Donau (Do
FRANCE
Baden
Freiburg
Bodensee
Basel
SWITZERLAND
LIECHTEN

ENMARK
Baltic Sea
Rostock
Schwerin
R. Elbe
POLAND
R. Oder
Berlin
R. Elbe
Leipzig
R. Unstrut
Meissen
Saxony
Naumburg
mar
Dresden
R. Saale
CZECH REPUBLIC
nberg
remberg)
München
(Munich)
N
S
E
W
AUSTRIA

How to use this book

This book is about Germany's 13 winegrowing regions and their wines. Each section begins with a brief look at the geographical, historical and cultural developments that have influenced a region's character and that of its wines.

Visits to castles, churches, and museums are integral to a wine tour. These monuments are the legacy of the Church and the aristocracy, which had improved the quality of wines until the 18th and 19th centuries, when many of the vineyards in each village were granted to private estates and winegrowers. Fortunately, after centuries of wars in central Europe and the French invasions by Louis XIV and Napoleon, the market squares, tithe courts, half-timbered buildings, and country houses with vineyards are still there.

The itineraries

The suggested itineraries are designed primarily for the motorist, but hiking or cycling paths (especially through the vineyards) and boat trips are enjoyable alternatives to driving. You can also travel by train to major wine centers, such as Koblenz, Mainz, Würzburg, Stuttgart, Freiburg and Dresden, and by coach to smaller towns, where the steep vineyards and the wonderful views are a great bonus.

Meeting growers and visiting estates

There are wine festivals, "open house" in wine villages, shops at cooperatives and estates, open-air tasting stands and dozens of wine restaurants and *Weinstuben* (wine pubs), where you can meet growers in order to visit estates and taste wines without prior appointment and without being able to speak German. You may be surprised that so many Germans speak English well.

Wherever you see the sign *Weinverkauf*, wine is for sale. If hours are not posted, it is reasonable to stop at a grower's from 8AM–12PM and from 2PM–6PM. Nevertheless, it is greatly appreciated by the growers and estates if you can make appointments in advance.

Organizing visits in advance

If you are interested in visiting a specific estate, email, telephone or write for an appointment (see the sample letter or e-mail on page 301), bearing in mind that most estates are family operations and speak English. Local tourist offices may also be able to help.

If possible, I suggest you tell a good wine merchant that you are planning a trip to Germany's wine country. They should be able to give you useful tips and perhaps help to arrange appointments for you.

If you are an adventurous and independent traveler, you'll relish making your own arrangements and scheduling visits to wine estates yourself. However, and especially if you lead a busy life, you may prefer the peace of mind that comes with having your own personalized trip arranged for you. A wine tourism professional will be able to make all your arrangements in advance, including obtaining tickets to musical or gourmet events, as well as transportation, river cruises and of course winery visits, cellar tours, vineyard walks and accommodations. One such company is **VinTour Wine Experiences**, contact details on page 301.

A group of wine tourists at the Wittmann wine estate in Rheinhessen.

The bridge over the Ahr at Rech dates from 1759.

Where to stay and eat

Each chapter ends with a list of suggested hotels (H) and restaurants (R). Many hotels in Germany have their own restaurants (H/R), and these are often of high quality. In addition, many establishments that are primarily restaurants also have guest rooms. A *Weinstube* (W) is one of the traditional German wine and food establishments. They are local, very friendly, traditional, and some of them have gourmet restaurants. You're more likely to encounter wine bars in large towns and cities, but these do not always provide meals.

Most restaurants offer several *offene Weine* (wines by the glass), so that you can enjoy wines with your meal without having to purchase a whole bottle.

Drinking and driving

Sweet German wines can have as little as 8-10 per cent alcohol, while dry wines can have 12-13.5 per cent alcohol. Don't forget that, if you are driving, the quantity of wine you consume is important. The German laws on drinking and driving are strict and are enforced. Many of the places recommended are hotels or have guest rooms, so you can enjoy several wines with a leisurely dinner without having to worry about driving afterwards.

The regional wine promotion boards have maps, brochures and calendars of events. The addresses are listed under each wine region.

INTRODUCTION

EACH OF THE 13 WINE REGIONS of Germany has beautiful towns, villages, hills, mountains and rivers, plus many other attractions, within a total area of 102,000 hectares (252,047 acres) of vineyards. Eleven of these regions are close to the Rhine, or its tributaries.

The Ahr Valley, Mosel, Franken, Saale-Unstrut and Sachsen are in the north and east of Germany and have a cooler climate, but the vines are protected from cold winds by forest-topped, south-facing slopes, with maximum exposure to the sun. The grapes ripen slowly, retaining their fruit-acidity as the sugar levels increase.

This cold climate effect is less evident in Rheingau and Nahe. Rheinhessen is slightly warmer and the regions in the south – Pfalz, Württemberg and Baden – have almost Mediterranean climates.

Sachsen and Saale-Unstrut are both about 193 km (120 miles) south of Berlin. They suffered terribly from bombing until 1945. Thereafter, the Russians seized the vineyards and the growers became members of agriculture cooperatives. The Russian Zone of Occupation was followed by the German Democratic Republic, until the Berlin Wall came down in 1989. The quality of their wines is now slowly establishing an excellent reputation, greatly helped by the change in the climate through global warming in all the wine regions in Germany.

Almost all of the vineyards in Sachsen overlook the great Elbe river and are centered around Dresden and Meissen. The Saale and Unstrut rivers join at Naumburg, close to Leipzig, to become a tributary of the Elbe, and there the vineyards are more spread out.

In the 1980s, German wine production was stagnating and the focus shifted from sweet to dry wines. At the same time there was a revolution in German cuisine, which encouraged people to enjoy more good wine with good food. As a result Germany has a large number of Michelin-starred and other highly rated restaurants.

The drier German wines in restaurant lists were once mainly from the grapes of Riesling, Weissburgunder (Pinot Blanc), Grauburgunder (Pinot Gris) and Silvaner from Franken. In the 1990s Spätburgunder (Pinot Noir) became Germany's top quality red wine, thanks to a number of talented growers who realized that they needed to learn how the Burgundians make their great wines.

The cheap sweet wines were labelled *Grosslagen* (vast areas of vineyards) such as Niersteiner Gutes Domtal and Piesporter Michelsberg. These labels were misleading, as they exploited the names of the best-known villages in each area (Nierstein and Piesport). Worst of all were the *Liebfraumilch* blends, which included Müller-Thurgau grapes and many "new varieties" (from crossing two or more different grape varieties). Such wines lost their appeal in the 1980s, and from then on there was a greater emphasis on quality.

There used to be only two or three fine vintages in each decade and a couple of poor ones. Since the 1988 vintage, global warming in Germany has meant that there has not been a single poor vintage to date. The climate has changed in all the wine regions and since 1992 there have been no serious spring frosts and only minor local problems with rain and hail at the wrong times. This change has been supported by the increased skills of the recent generation of inspired young growers, and some cooperatives are making better wines. Each vintage is still unique and every wine region has different soils. This is part of the fascination of German wines.

Wine publications provide guidelines on what to expect and a knowledgeable wine merchant can offer advice, but your own tasting impressions are meaningful, especially for wines that are for drinking within two or three years. Make notes about the wines you taste and when and where you tasted them. It is a very special experience to taste wines where the grapes are grown, or, better still, together with the winemaker (note his or her comments about the wines). Some are produced for drinking while they are

Riesling grapes growing in the Mosel's characteristic slatey "soil."

young and fresh and will not develop with age. Such wines may be protected by screw tops, which are far better than cheap corks, or worse, plastic corks. Simple but fine Kabinetts and Spätlesen, and of course the higher-quality wines, tend to develop and mature much better with high-quality traditional corks. It is fascinating to taste the same wine from a good estate after three, five, or more years, and you can compare your recent notes with your original ones.

The Language of the Label

This Dr. Heger label exemplifies the basic requirements of Germany's 1971 Wine Laws.

1. Baden, the Region
2. Germanic Crest of Dr. Heger
3. Vintage 2010
4. Grauburgunder, the grape variety (Pinot Gris)
5. Ihringer, the village, followed by Winklerberg, the vineyard
6. Spätlese, quality of this wine
7. Trocken, dry wine less than 9 grams of sugar per liter
8. Prädikatswein, quality wines from Kabinett to Trockenbeerenauslese
9. AP number, official test of sugar content in the grapes before fermentation
10. Sulphur content (required by USA)
11. Erzeugerabfüllung, bottled by the owner (otherwise Abfüller = bottler, Gutsabfüller = estate bottled)
12. Weingut Dr. Heger, wine estate name
13. Address of producer
14. Produce of Germany
15. Alcohol by volume
16. Wine content in the bottle
17. The logo of the VDP (the Association of Germany Quality Estates). Obligatory for members but not a wine law.

The German Wine Laws of 1971

There were no regulations concerning the origins of the grapes and the blending of sugared water with the wines until 1898, when the top estates in Rheingau founded an association to protect Riesling, called Natur, natural wines with no usage of sugar-water or chaptalization.

In 1971 new German wine laws came into force and included a ban on labeling wine *Natur*. These laws were specifically aimed at benefiting wine cooperatives and large companies that mass-produced wines with brand labels such as Liebfraumilch, while concurrently damaging the vital VDP objective – to produce high-quality wines.

The 1971 laws are the basis for the appellation of origin system and regulate the amount of natural sugar in the grapes at harvest before fermentation. The wines of origin must pass official analytical and sensory tests, and include the test number (AP Nr). But the wines are not tasted for quality.

The lowest categories, which are sold primarily by supermarkets, are *Landwein*, *Bereich*, and *Grosslage*.

Quality Categories

Prädikat (QmP) wines: should have special attributes that come from different levels of sugar in the unfermented grapes.

Kabinett the lightest *Prädikat* wine, but a *trocken* wine tends to have more body and alcohol.

Spätlese generally picked later, and therefore riper, without botrytis. A *trocken* wine tends to have more body and alcohol. The alternative in most wineries is to use industrial yeasts, which means that the winemaker can stop the fermentation before all of the natural sugar is converted. For mass-production he can blend unfermented (still naturally sweet) grape juice with a dry wine to create the desired style (not recommended).

A cold underground cellar, which has natural yeast, can stop the fermentation, leaving high sugar levels and very low alcohol (eg Mosel, with 8 degrees of alcohol and 50 grams per liter of residual sugar).

Auslese very ripe grapes

selected bunch by bunch, and usually including a certain amount of botrytised grapes. Rich, noble wines with more intense bouquet and flavor.

Beerenauslese individually selected botrytised grapes, very sweet and luscious.

Eiswein the most difficult wine to produce in Germany. It resembles the Icewines of North America. Ideally, green bunches of Riesling grapes, deliberately left on the vines until the temperature at around 3AM is -8° C, or lower. The frozen bunches are picked by hand before dawn and immediately pressed. The wines have intense sweetness and very high acidity, in balance, and the total yield from a specialist estate is as little as 100 liters to 500 liters (26-132 gallons) in a very good year, of which there are few in each decade. These *Eisweine* fetch extremely high prices at auction or in the trade.

Trockenbeerenauslese individually selected grapes, dried by botrytis and late autumnal sunshine, giving the wine a fabulous honeyed nectar tone, with extreme richness and longevity.

The German Wine Institute

The *Deutsches Weininstitut* (DWI) is the promotional board for German wine and coordinates with all 13 regional wine promotion boards. It represents all interests involved in wine: the wine laws, exporters, cooperatives, winegrowers, wine companies, wine estates, the German wine market, and, last but not least, wine tourism. The DWI arranges wine tastings and fairs all over the world and these are vital for exporting members of the VDP.

WHAT'S AVAILABLE

• *Deutsche Winzerfeste*/German Wine Festivals: a calendar of events and wine festivals, listed by region – note for US readers: the day precedes the month, eg 10.3 is 10 March, not Oct 3.

• Guides with maps, and books to help you to find wine estates and wine-orientated restaurants, *Weinstuben*, hotels and guesthouses – when ordering, be sure to mention which region(s) you'll be visiting.

Deutsches Weininstitut
Gutenbergplatz 3-5
55116 Mainz, Germany

Tel: 00 49 6131 28 290
www.deutscheweine.de

OFFICES IN USA
www.germanwineusa.org
CANADA
www.germawinecanada.org
UK
www.winesofgermany.co.uk

The VDP

VDP. Prädikatsweingut

The VDP (Association of German Prädikat Wine Estates) was founded in 1910 by wine estates from the four main wine regions – Mosel, Rheingau, Rheinhessen and Pfalz – to protect and guarantee the quality of their wines.

The vital principles of VDP were:

1. Members' wines must be natural (*Naturel*) and genuine, and it is forbidden to use sugared-water or chaptalization.

2. Bottling must be in members' own cellars (*Originalabfüllung*).

3. The VDP logo of a stylized eagle bearing a bunch of grapes must be shown on every label or capsule.

From the beginning, the VDP's aim was to produce fine quality wines, from the simple *Gutswein* for everyday drinking, to those of great wines for their annual auctions.

By the early 1980s, Rheingau members of the VDP had proved that, before 1933, fine dry Rieslings were unusual but very popular with a small clientele. By 1990 the VDP had established regular inspections of each estate for quality standards, developments in ecology and viticulture, and strict maximum yields of grapes. They had realized the benefits of their freedom to use different labels, with simple, clear front labels, and all other details on a small back label. Above all they established a classification "pyramid" with the great vineyards at the top.

This symbol denotes a top-quality classified vineyard. L stands for *Lage*, vineyard in German. For vintages after June 2012 a new symbol with the letters GG is used.

At the time of writing, there are some 200 members of VDP from all 13 wine regions, accounting for about 5000 hectares (12,355 acres), over half of which are planted with Riesling. Today, the members account for 12 per cent of the sales of German wines and they are a bastion of quality in today's globalized world.

VDP quality regulations

Gutswein (estate wine), very good quality, inexpensive wines for restaurants and for drinking at home.

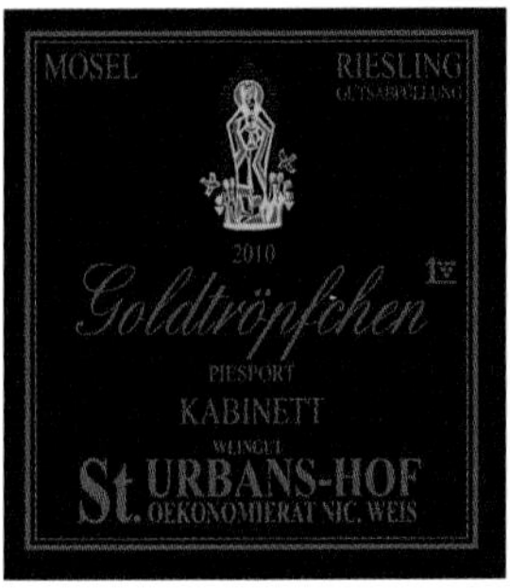

Ortswein from vines belonging to VDP members in a named village.

Erste Lage The umbrella term for wines from classified vineyards, notably for top quality dry and sweet wines, especially from Mosel and Nahe.

Grosses Gewächs (Great Growth), top quality dry white and red wines from classified vineyards.

Erstes Gewächs (First Growth) almost the same regulations above, but only for wines from Rheingau.

Sekt

In the 19th century, Germany imported quantities of champagne, and many Germans set up their own import businesses, such as the well-known names of Bollinger, Heidsieck, Krug, and Mumm among others. Producers in Germany could not compete with champagne, so they concentrated on their own sparkling wines, or *Sekts*. Mass-market brands use 90 per cent cheap French, Italian and other foreign grapes, and produce the sparkle in tanks rather than by the expensive secondary fermentation in the bottle.

However, those *Sekts* labelled *Winzersekt, Deutscher Sekt* or *Deutscher Sekt ba*, (higher quality from a specific area, or vineyard), are produced exclusively from German grapes.

The following estates are considered to be among the best *Sekt* producers. Their priorities are their fine vineyards and wines, so that the quality of their *Sekts* is not heavily marketed or appreciated by most people. They use the traditional champagne method with the secondary fermentation in bottle.

Weingut **Ökonomierat Rebholz** (www.oekonomierat-rebholz.de) produces one of the finest *Sekts* from Pfalz. **The Reichsrat von Buhl** estate (www.reichsrat-von-buhl.de) produces single-grape wines: Riesling, Spätburgunder, and Weissburgunder, the last with zero residual sugar.

Weingüter Wegeler (www.wegeler.com) produces a splendid Geheimrat "J" Riesling Brut, with a fine blend from their own vines in Mosel (elegance), Rheingau (minerality) and Pfalz (power).

Helmut Solter of **Sekthaus**

RIESLING BRUT
Mülheimer Sonnenlay
2008
Deutscher Sekt b.A. Mosel
Weingut Max Ferd. Richter · D-54486 Mülheim/Mosel

Solter in Rheingau (www.sekthaus-solter.de) uses precise champagne methods and has a brilliant range of five *Sekts*.

Sekthaus Raumland in Rheinhessen (www.raumland.de) has a wonderful range of Riesling Brut *Sekts*, from a simple Deutscher Sekt to their Triumvirat Grande Cuvée Brut that has received great accolades in Germany.

Weingut Max Ferd Richter (www.maxferdrichter.com) in Mülheim, Mosel, produces a single vineyard and vintage Mülheimer Sonnelay Riesling Brut, Deutscher Sekt b.A., disgorged by hand. The Mosel character is very pronounced.

Tasting the Wine

Wine festivals and tasting stands

It's very difficult to taste many wines at a wine festival, and if you decide to do so, you should start with the first grower's tables that you fancy. Taste a simple quality (QbA) and then the range of their wines, if you wish to do so, which might end with a great *Auslese*, or an even finer wine. It is not unusual for ten or more wines to be offered. Germans taste red wines before whites, but I suggest you taste white wines first.

The wines are sold by both the glass and bottle. When you order wine you will be asked to pay a *Pfand* (deposit) for glasses and/or bottles. The deposit is refunded on return. You might decide to keep the small tasting glasses, however, as an inexpensive souvenir of your visit. All this is great fun, but it is difficult to make notes, unless you buy some wines, especially if there is no charge for the tasting.

Tasting at estates

It is vital to arrange a visit in advance. The staff at most estates speak English, but those who do not will welcome you anyway. You should be asked what wines you would like to taste from a list. With their advice, you can decide which wines to taste. You will then probably sit together at a table to taste and talk about the wines, and it is very important to note your impressions of each

A cellar tasting at the Bürklin-Wolf estate at Wachenheim, Pfalz.

wine. Don't be embarrassed by pouring away the wine into the empty container on the table. If you are fortunate enough to be offered a rarity (*Auslese*, *Beerenauslese*, *Eiswein* or *Trockenbeerenauslese*), the pride of every grower, it will be a small quantity and it would be a shame to pour it out.

Tasting at cooperatives

The advantage of cooperatives is that they are open for most of the day for tasting, buying and sometimes eating. Sadly, few cooperatives produce fine wines but some smaller ones do succeed. Of these the most successful are **Mayschoss-Altenahr** in Ahr (page 38), **Durbach** in Baden (page 100), **Divino Nordheim** (page 215) and **Winzer Sommerach** (page 214) both in Franken, and **Weinmanufaktur Untertürkheim** (page 224) in Württemberg. More details of these are included in the chapters on their regions.

The large cooperatives buy grapes from their members, most of whom are "hobby vintners" who have just a few rows of vines. They do their best to separate the good grapes from the bad, but this is not easy under the circumstances. Mass-production for supermarkets is their strength and of course both quality and prices tend to be low.

Traveling in Germany

Germany's network of railways and motorways is the densest in the world, and passenger boats cruise the Rhine, Mosel, Main (Franken), Neckar (Württemberg), and the Saale, Unstrut and Elbe rivers in the east, as well as the Bodensee close to Switzerland. The **Eurolines** bus travels famous routes, such as the *Burgenstrasse* (Castle Road) through parts of the Baden and Württemberg winegrowing regions and the *Romantische Strasse* (Romantic Road) through Franken. Last but not least, there is an impressive network of hiking trails and cycling paths in all 13 winegrowing regions. Bicycles may be hired at 150 railway stations or bicycle shops with the *Fahrradverleih* (rental service).

German trains are efficient and comfortable. **The Intercity-Express** (*ICE*) provides a fast service between all the major cities. The slower, frequent-stop trains are called *Regional-Express* or *Regionalbahn*. There is now a high-speed rail link between Cologne and Frankfurt. The journey takes about an hour and there is a connection loop to Cologne-Bonn Airport.

The **German Railway** (DB) and **Köln-Düsseldorfer** (KD) boat company offer many concessions. Ask about *Sparpreise* (Saver Tickets). The KD combines boat trips with coach excursions to famous castles and other sights (*Tagestouren mit Landarrangements*).

If you are traveling on the Rhine, the lower

You get a great view of the Rhine on the Bingen-Rüdesheim car ferry.

Mosel or the Bodensee, rail and boat tickets are often interchangeable (for a supplementary fee). Boat landing stages are often conveniently adjacent to train stations. This facility is useful for round trips, as it saves time and the combination fares are more economical.

Some of the Rhine's most beautiful scenery lies between Rüdesheim and St Goarshausen. You can purchase a round-trip rail ticket in Rüdesheim: take the train to St Goarshausen (30 minutes); pay the *Übergangsgebühr* (transfer fee) at the KD landing stage in St Goarshausen; and board the boat to return to Rüdesheim (three hours in all). A round trip by boat takes 5-6 hours. On your birthday (take your passport as proof) you can travel free of charge on all KD boats except the hydrofoil.

The Autobahn

Most of the itineraries suggested in the book are routed on a *Bundesstrasse* (two-lane highway, abbreviated "B," as in B 9) rather than an Autobahn (motorway, or "A," as in A 3). But you will probably drive on an Autobahn at some stage of your journey and it is worth pointing out that Germany's reputation for fast cars and frustrated drivers is largely justified, even though the practice of flashing headlights to pressure slower drivers to move to the right is illegal.

There are usually three reasons for traffic to come to a halt on the Autobahn: there has been an accident; there is a *Baustelle* (road works); or school holidays have started or ended, when there is a traffic jam of monumental proportions. Thus, from mid-June to mid-September you are likely to arrive at your destination almost as quickly and with less irritation by avoiding the Autobahn, provided that the distance to your destination is less than 300 km (186 miles) or so.

Accommodations

Contact the organizations listed below for details on castle hotels and historic inns. Guest rooms at winegrowers' estates offer an enjoyable, economical alternative. If you plan to visit a village during its wine festival, make your

The landing stage for Mosel riverboats at Traben-Trarbach.

reservation well in advance. However, even on short notice, local tourist offices are extremely helpful in finding rooms.

Tourist information

DZT – Deutsche Zentrale für Tourismus (German National Tourist Office)

GERMANY

Beethovenstrasse 69
60325 Frankfurt am Main
Tel: 069 974640
Email: info@d-z-t.com
www.germany.travel/de

CANADA

480 University Ave
Suite 1410
Toronto M5G 1V2
Ontario
Tel: 416 968 1685
Email: info@gnto.ca
www.cometogermany.com

UK

PO Box 2695
London W1A 3TN
Tel: 020 7317 0908
Email: gntolon@d-z-t.com
www.germany.travel/en

USA

122 East 42nd Street
New York, NY 10168-0072

Tel: 212 661 7200
Email: gntonyc@d-z-t.com
www.cometogermany.com

Köln-Düsseldorfer
Deutsche Rheinschiffahrt (KD)
Frankenwerft 15
50667 Köln
Tel: 0221 2088 318
Email: info@k-d.de
www.k-d.de
(KD boat excursions on the Rhine and lower Mosel; cabin cruises on the Rhine, Mosel, Saar, Main, Neckar and Elbe; details on "The Floating Wine Seminar," a 7-day Rhine cruise with wine tastings and visits to estates.)

Deutsche Touring GmbH
Am Römerhof 17
60486 Frankfurt am Main
Tel: 069 7903 501
Email:
incoming@deutsche-touring.de
www.touring.de
(Details on Eurolines bus service.)

Historic hotels and restaurants

European Castle Hotels & Restaurant
Weinpalais
67146 Deidesheim
Tel: 06326 70000
www.european-castle.com

Romantik hotels and restaurants

Hahnstrasse 70
60528 Frankfurt
Tel: 049 69 66 12340
Email:
info@romantikhotels.com
www.romantikhotels.com

Road maps

Die Generalkarte by Mairdumont is a good choice, available atall Shell gas stations and bookshops spirin Germany. To tour wine country you will need maps 12, 15, 16, 18, 21, 24, 36 and 37.

Useful words

Ausfahrt exit
Autobahndreieck (AB-) Dror-kreuz (AB-Kr) motorway intersection
Benzin petrol (gasoline)
Bleifrei lead-free
Panne breakdown
Polizei police; dial 110
Raststätte (*R*) rest area/ snack shop/restaurant + restrooms
Selbstbedienung (SB) self-service
Tankstelle (*T*) petrol/ gas station
Umleitung detour/diversion
Unfall accident

400m

AHR VALLEY

THE VINEYARDS OF GERMANY'S "red wine paradise" line the valley slopes of the Ahr river from near its confluence with the Rhine south of Bonn to Altenahr, only 25km (15 miles) to the west. There are magnificent views of the striking landscape from the heights of a basalt cone (Landskrone), slate cliffs and castle ruins. The main town is the elegant spa town of Bad Neuenahr-Ahrweiler.

Signposts with a cluster of red grapes signal two well-marked routes through the region: for motorists, the *Rotweinstrasse* (Red Wine Road, B 266 and B 267); and for hikers the *Rotweinwanderweg* (Red Wine Hiking Trail). The second is an absolute must, because you can catch the frequent train, which stops at every village and can take you right up to the start of the trail. Then you can walk down, stopping in any of the villages for a light meal and refreshing wines or even to stay overnight. Cyclists can follow the signs along the *Ahr-Radtour*, a circular route from Remagen/Rhine through the Ahr valley and back to the Rhine. The region is popular for its natural beauty as well as for its wines. In the fall, vineyards and forests are ablaze with color and wine festivals take place every weekend.

The Romans had farms in the Ahr valley and the many Roman vineyards in the Mosel valley a little further south were on similar steep slate slopes, so it is almost certain that wines were made in the Ahr valley in those times. By the 9th century, viticulture was well established there and continued to flourish throughout the Middle Ages, when the Church owned many of the vineyards. The period of decline caused by French invasions in the 17th and 18th centuries, and a series of poor harvests, led to the formation of the first German winegrowers' cooperative, founded in Mayschoss in 1868, where excellent wines are still produced.

‹‹ The vertiginous terraced vineyard of Recher Herrenberg.

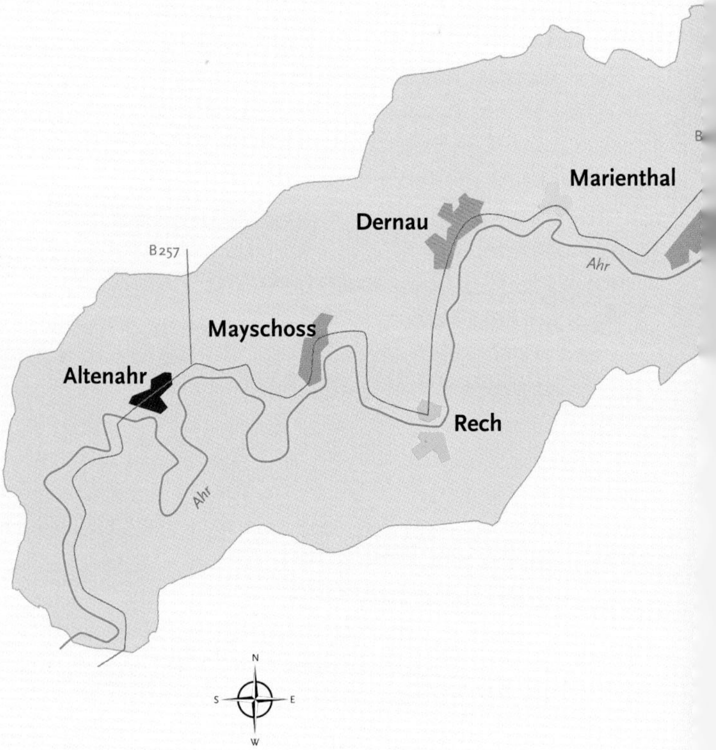
Marienthal
Dernau
B257
Ahr
Mayschoss
Altenahr
Rech
Ahr
N
S
E
W

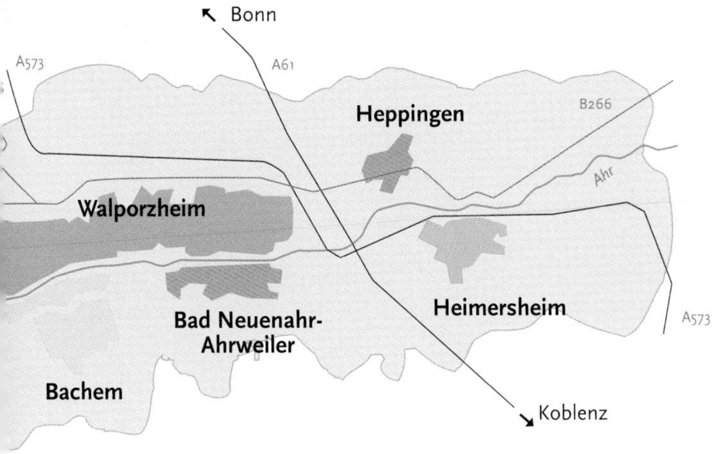
Bonn
A573
A61
Heppingen
B266
Ahr
Walporzheim
Heimersheim
Bad Neuenahr-
Ahrweiler
A573
Bachem
Koblenz

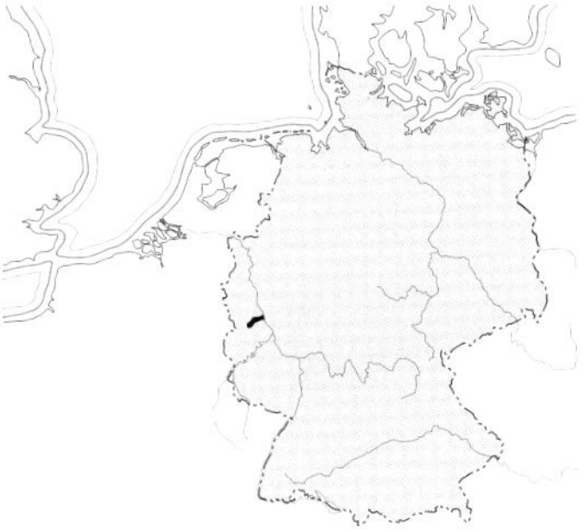

Jean Stodden
2008
Recher Herrenberg
Frühburgunder
Gutsabfüllung
Weingut Jean Stodden D-53506 Rech/Ahr

In 1663 Samuel Pepys wrote in his diary that he drank in London a pretty red "Rheinisch" wine called Bleahard, which was known as *Ahr-bleicherte* (Ahr-Bleached). Spätburgunder wines in Ahr in particular and elsewhere in Germany had no similarity with the wines of Burgundy because the grapes were immediately pressed and kept for a short time in large old oak barrels. Most of them were more rosé than red and many were quite sweet. This process lasted right up to the late 1980s, as Ahr wines were unknown outside this tiny region.

In 1982, inspired by the great wines of the world, Werner Näkel gave up teaching mathematics to return to his father's estate of 1.5 hectares (3.7 acres). He drove to Burgundy to discover how the growers made their great Pinot Noirs and returned with two new Burgundian oak *barriques* (220-liter casks). He followed the Burgundian methods, including long maceration of the grapes with the skins followed by 18 months in the *barriques*. The result was an absolutely new German style of *Spätburgunder* and a revolution for the growers in Ahr.

Red wine paradise

With 506 hectares (1250 acres), the Ahr is one of the smallest and most northerly wine regions. The vineyards are labor-intensive, planted mostly on terraced cliffs of slate, volcanic soil and graywacke (hard sandstone rock). These heat-retaining soils, the tempering influence of the river and the protective Eifel mountain range to the west create an ideal microclimate for Spätburgunder (Pinot Noir).

Spätburgunder and Frühburgunder vines account for 61 per cent of the area planted. Portugieser is a red grape variety, but not apparently from Portugal. It produces extremely large yields of inexpensive wine. The entire Ahr valley produces elegant, velvety Spätburgunder, which is pricier, but the overall quality is excellent. Blanc de Noir, a specialty in Ahr, is Spätburgunder vinified as a delightful, brisk, dry white wine.

Riesling is the most important white grape although it is only planted in seven per cent of the area.

The village of Heimersheim seen from the Landskrone mountains.

The overall quality is excellent and the Mayschoss Cooperative makes some of the best.

Lower Ahr valley

The broad eastern end of the valley has orchards and fields on its lower slopes, with vineyards on the higher ground. The leading vineyard here is **Heimersheimer Landskrone**. With vines planted on loam, loess and basalt soil, its wines have great depth.

Near Heimersheim's market square, the late Romanesque **St Mauritius Church** has the oldest (13th century) stained glass windows in Germany. From the Middle Ages to the early 1800s, landlords collected der *Zehnt* (one tenth of the harvest) as rent from peasant growers at the 13th-century Zehnthof (tithe court). Don't miss the historic wine festival in mid-August.

A short drive plus a 15-minute walk (or a 45-minute walk) from the railway station in Heimersheim (on the north bank of the Ahr) will take you to the top of the Landskrone, where there is a fine view. En route you can see the thousand-year-old chapel and ruins of Burg Landskrone, built in 1205 by Philip von Schwaben as a romantic home for his bride.

The Bunte Kuh vineyard overlooks the village of Walporzheim.

Bad Neuenahr–Ahrweiler

Bad Neuenahr–Ahrweiler is an elegant spa town that is popular with tourists. The heart of town is the **Jugendstil Kurhaus**, with alkaline thermal baths, a casino (opens daily at 2PM) and gardens (one devoted to dahlias) along the banks of the Ahr. Nearby are the **St Willibrordus Church** dating from AD 990, and the Baroque house where Beethoven spent his summers from 1786 to 1792.

Ahrweiler, across the river, has a long history. **The Römervilla**, a magnificent Roman villa (2nd and 3rd

centuries AD) unearthed in the Arweiler Silberberg vineyard testifies to the site's warm, sunny location and today produces beautiful Spätburgunder wines. The villa is a "working" museum as archeologists continue restoration (closed mid-Nov through March). Within the medieval town walls and the four gateways, built in 1248, you can see half-timbered houses near the market square as well as the Gothic St Laurentius Church (1269), and the rococo town hall.

If you prefer a short walk, the *Weinbaulehrpfad* (educational vineyard trail) is a signposted path 4 km (2.5 miles) through the vineyards, leading from the railway halt "Markt" in Ahrweiler to the station.

WINERIES & MORE

HEIMERSHEIM/ BAD NEUENAHR

Weingut Nelles
Göppinger Strasse 13a
53474 Heimersheim/Bad Neuenahr
Tel: 02641 24349
www.weingut-nelles.de

AHRWEILER

Weingut JJ Adeneuer
Max-Planck-Strasse 8
53474 Ahrweiler
Tel: 02641 34473
www.adeneuer.de

Bread and wine

In the Middle Ages, as today, few growers had enough vineyards to make a living from the wine alone. Many grew grain as well, giving rise to the establishment of community bakeries, where growers would bring their flour or bread dough and hire the bakery to bake it. Bachem's 13th-century *Backhaus* (bakery) is now a wine museum.

Romantic Ahr valley

From Walporzheim to Altenahr the valley narrows, the hills are steeper and the landscape is dominated by terraced vineyards and rocky cliffs. The **Walporzheimer Gärkammer** vineyard has a great *terroir* for Spätburgunder and the wines from this grape are rich and memorable.

A huge greywacke-slate cliff called *Bunte Kuh* (Mottled Cow) overlooks Walporzheim. Drive or walk (half an hour) to the top for the view. Try red

The wine estate of Toni Nelles in Heimersheim.

wines from the Kräuterberg vineyard at the *Weinstube* of the same name or from Alte Lay and Domlay (*Lay* means vineyard or site) at **Sanct Peter**, the oldest (1246) restaurant in the region.

The former Kloster Marienthal (founded in 1137) was sold to two private estates and two major cooperatives in the region in 2004, but you can still visit the vaulted cellars (12th-17th centuries), the remains of the monastery church and the cloister. **Marienthaler Klostergarten** is the famous vineyard here.

Dernau, Rech and Mayschoss

Half-timbered houses line Dernau's narrow alleys. On a clear day the view from the Krausberg (400 m/1300 ft) hill on the south side of the river extends all the way to Cologne Cathedral. The great vineyard here is **Derner Pfaarwingert.**

The 12th-century village of Rech straddles the Ahr and boasts the river's oldest (1759) bridge. On the cliffs of weathered slate at this end of the valley, there is an incredibly steep vineyard, **Recher Herrenberg**, with the vines clinging to the rocks. The Spätburgunder wines are superb.

Mayschoss-Altenahr cooperative, the best in the region, lies at the foot of the ruins of the 11th-century Saffenburg fortress, the oldest on the Ahr. Walk up the hill (30 minutes) for a view of the Ahr's largest loop and the great vineyard, **Mayschosser Mönchberg** (Monk's Hill). There are several vantage points and hiking trails on the surrounding hills. The town's church contains the 17th-century black marble gravestone of Countess Katharina von Saffenburg and other art treasures.

WINERIES & MORE

DERNAU

Weingut Kreuzberg
Schmittmannstrasse 30
53507 Dernau
Tel: 02643 1691
www.weingut-kreuzberg.de

Weingut Meyer-Näkel
Friedenstrasse 15
53507 Dernau
Tel: 02643 1628
www.meyer-naekel.de

RECH

Weingut Jean Stodden
Rotweinstrasse 7-8
53506 Rech
Tel: 02643 3001
www.stodden.de

Half-timbered houses on the market square of the medieval walled town of Ahrweiler.

MAYSCHOSS

Weingut Deutzerhof-Cossmann-Hehle
Deutzerweise 2
53508 Mayschoss
Tel: 02643 7264
www.deutzerhof.de

Winzergenossenschaft Mayschoss-Altenahr
Ahrrotweinstrasse 42
53508 Mayschoss
Tel: 02643 93600
www.wg-mayschoss.de

End of the Rotweinwanderweg

The ancestral fortress of the Counts of Are (1100) and 18th-century Kreuzberg castle overlook the village of Altenahr, and below is the amazingly rocky vineyard, **Altenahrer Eck**, with superb Spätburgunder wines. You can get a good view of the wild, romantic landscape from the ruins of Burg Are (30-minute walk or take the cable car to Ditschhardt Höhe). In the town, the 12th-century church has a fine Gothic choir.

Grand Prix fans can visit the famed **Nürburgring and Rennsport-Museum** (historic racing cars). These are 30 km (18 miles) from Altenahr via the B 257.

REGIONAL WINE PROMOTION BOARD

Ahrtal-Tourismus Bad Neuenahr-Ahrweiler e.V.
Hauptstrasse 80
53474 Bad Neuenahr-Ahrweiler
Tel: 02641 91710
Email: info@ahrwein.de
www.ahrtaltourismus.de

REGIONAL WINE GLASSES

The *Römer* wine glass typical of the region is called a *Pokal* on the Ahr. It holds 0.2 liters of wine. For a glass of wine half that size, order a *Spezial*.

EXCURSIONS

About 25 km (15 miles) south of the Ahr via the A61, visit **Maria Laach Abbey** (Romanesque) or from Brohl ride the **Vulkan Express**, a narrow-gauge railway.

Altenahr

Gasthaus Assenmacher (H/R)
Brükenstrasse 12
53505 Altenahr
Tel: 02643 18 48
www.gasthaus-assenmacher.de
Seven rooms, elegant restaurant with classic and international food.

Bad Neuenahr-Ahrweiler

(Ahrweiler is far nicer than Neuenahr as it is an original walled town.)

Hohenzollern an der Ahr (H/R)
Am Silberberg 50
53474 Bad Neuenahr-Ahrweiler
Tel: 02641 9730
www.hotelhohenzollern.com
Twenty-seven rooms, family-owned hotel and excellent separately managed restaurant. Outstanding view from the restaurant terrace.

Rodderhof Hotel (H/R)
Oberhutstrasse 48
53474 Bad Neuenahr-Ahrweiler
Tel: 02641 39 90
www.rodderhof.de
Painstakingly restored hotel with a long history.

Idille I (R/W)
Am Johanissberg 101
53474 Bad Neuenahr-Ahrweiler
Tel: 02641 28429
www.idille.de
Excellent German and Italian dishes, fine wines.

Ahrweinstuben Prümer Hof (W)
Marktplatz 12
53474 Bad Neuenahr-Ahrweiler
Tel: 02641 4757
Showcase for Ahr wines in historic half-timbered house.

Bad Neuenahr-Heimersheim

***Freudenreich* im Weinhaus** Nelles (H/R)
Göppingerstrasse 13
53474 Bad Neuenahr-Heimersheim
Tel: 02641 6868
www.restaurant-freudenreich.de
Comfortable hotel, delicious international cuisine, splendid Weingut Nelles and other wines.

Dernau

Weingut Kreuzberg (W)
Schmittmannstrasse 30
53507 Dernau

Tel: 02643 1691
www.weingut-kreuzberg.de
Weinstube (May-Oct). Fine wines, 5 splendid guest rooms.

Im Hofgarten I (R/W)
Bachstrasse 26
53507 Dernau
Tel: 02643 1540
www.hofgarten-dernau.de
Owned by the Meyer-Näkel family, whose winery is round the corner. This is a beautiful and comfortable restaurant with artistic design elements, and very fine regional food. A splendid wine list with great German wines.

Heppingen

Steinheuers Restaurant (H/R/W)
Zur Alten Post,
Landskroner Strasse 110
53474 Bad Neuenahr-Ahrweiler
Ortsteil Heppingen
Tel: 02641 9 48 60
www.steinheuers.de
Hotel with 11 rooms. Restaurant (two Michelin stars), great wines and fabulous food. Also a second restaurant, Poststuben, with lower prices and very good food and wines.

Mayschoss

Lochmühle (H/R)
Ahr-Rotweinstrasse 62
53508 Mayschoss
Tel: 02643 8080
www.hotel-lochmuehle.com
A very attractive hotel by the river and near the steep vineyards, with 120 rooms and a restaurant.

Zur Saffenburg (H/R)
Ahr-Rotweinstrasse 43
53508 Mayschoss
Tel: 02643 83 92
www.gasthof-saffenburg.de
A good-value, family-run guesthouse with 13 rooms and a restaurant.

Walporzheim

Brogsitter's Sanct Peter (H/R)
Walporzheimer Str 134
53474 Walporzheim
Tel: 02641 97750
www.sanct-peter.de
Hotel with 17 rooms plus 3 suites, and tasting room, Sanct Peter (Michelin-starred gourmet restaurant), *Weinstube* and wine shop.

Bitburger
RESTAURANT PENSION
Am Markttor
Bitburger
Jägerstube
EINGANG
1322 Marktturm 1366
WEINPROBE

MITTELRHEIN

The Mittelrhein includes the spectacular stretch of the Rhine between Bonn and Bingen, also known as the Rhine Gorge. Here the river has carved its course through the stone hills to form a steep, narrow valley with a special microclimate in which vines have existed since Roman times.

It's a region steeped in legend (the Loreley, the Nibelungs) and has long been a source of inspiration to artists, poets and composers. The ancient castle ruins which tower over vine-covered cliffs and medieval villages are reminders of the Mittelrhein's turbulent past. Today, the robber barons are gone but many of their castles are open for visits and offer outstanding panoramic views of the Rhine valley. Visitors can sample the region's wines in the many *Weinstuben* (wine pubs) and garden cafés in the picturesque towns and along the tree-lined promenades.

It is a real challenge to plant, care for and harvest grapes on the steeply terraced cliffs of the Mittelrhein. At 457 hectares (1130 acres) it is one of the smallest and most labor-intensive wine regions of Germany. Nearly all the work is done by hand, and winches are used to pull workers uphill on specially-designed plows. Not surprisingly, the number of vineyards is steadily decreasing. About a quarter of the vines are owned by growers' estates that have improved the quality of their wines with the help of global warming and modern skills, and the rest are "hobby vintners" with a few rows of vines that they care for on evenings and weekends.

Between Koblenz and Bingen vineyards are located on both sides of the Rhine. At first glance, the craggy inclines of clayish slate and greywacke seem like inhospitable sites for growing grapes (or any other crops). Yet the hills protect the vines from cold winds and they thrive on the stony, heat-retaining soils. The Rhine acts as a heat

‹‹ **A gateway in Bacharach's medieval Market Tower.**

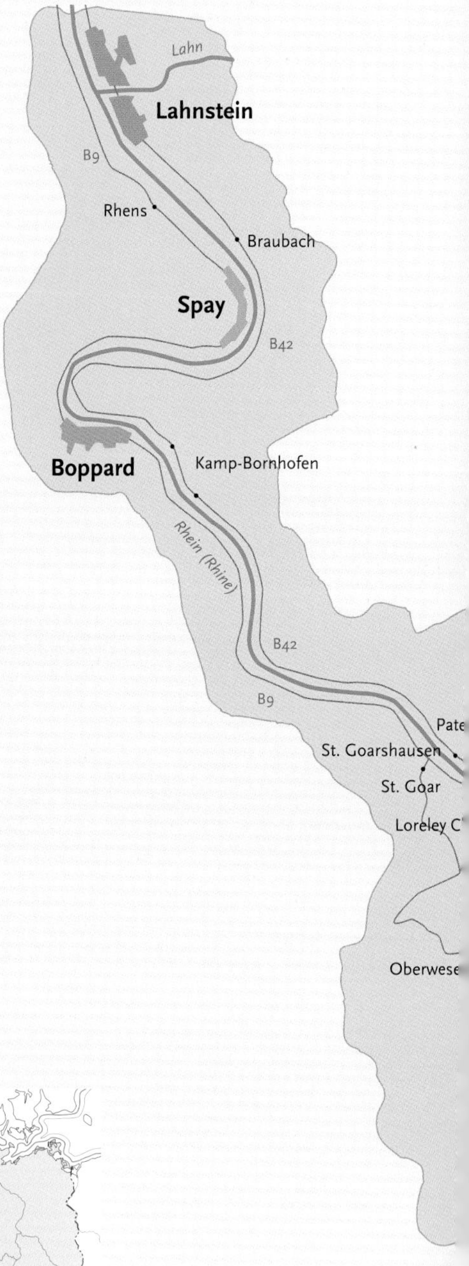
Lahn
Lahnstein
B9
Rhens
Braubach
Spay
B42
Boppard
Kamp-Bornhofen
Rhein (Rhine)
B42
B9
Pate
St. Goarshausen
St. Goar
Loreley C
Oberwese

WEINGUT
TONI JOST
HAHNENHOF
HAHN 1G

MATTHIAS MÜLLER
2010
Bopparder Hamm
Feuerlay
Riesling feinherb
-alte Reben-
Gutsabfüllung - Deutscher Qualitätswein
A.P. Nr. 1 656 110 01811
11.5% vol.
750ml
Enthält Sulfite
Weingut Matthias Müller D-56322 Spay am Rhein
MITTELRHEIN

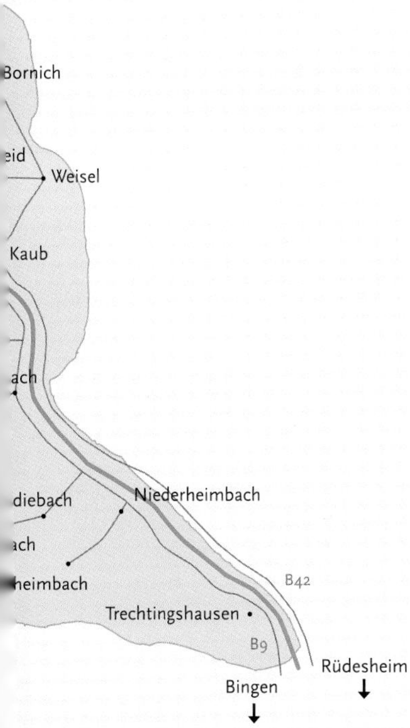
Bornich
Weisel
Kaub
Niederheimbach
B42
Trechtingshausen
B9
Rüdesheim
Bingen

reflector during the day, while at night the mists over the water help to maintain a constant temperature.

Mittelrhein wines are a specialty not often found outside the region. A small amount of red wine, mainly Spätburgunder, is produced ("Dragon's Blood") but the region is best known for steely, elegant Rieslings with fine acidity. This gives them a refreshing character and enables them to age well. The wines are often *Spritzig* (naturally sparkling) and are lighter-bodied than their *Rheingau* counterparts. Try them in a terrace café at one of the castles where knights and nobles once lived, or stop at a historic *Weinstube* inside the old walls of the towns below. Many are run by a grower's family who will be happy to show you their vineyards and cellars.

Wine festivals provide another opportunity to meet growers and sample their wines. Most take place in September or early October.

REGIONAL WINE PROMOTION BOARD

Mittelrhein-Wein e.V.
Am Hafen 2
56329 St Goar
Tel: 06741 7712
www.mittelrhein-wein.com

Upstream from Königswinter to Koblenz

Grapes have been grown on the steep slopes between Königswinter and Koblenz for centuries. Yet the area under cultivation is shrinking, for winegrowing here requires extraordinary dedication and hard work: approximately 2000 hours per hectare (about 2.5 acres).

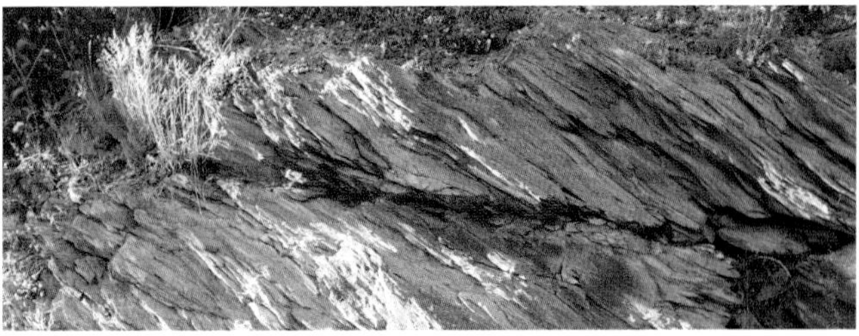

Underlying slate retains the sun's heat and helps the grapes to ripen.

The tombstone of Heinrich Bayer von Boppard, who died in 1376, and his wife. Now in the New Museum in Berlin.

Grapes could not ripen here were it not for the tempering influence of the Rhine and the soil types (slate, greywacke, volcanic stone), which quickly absorb heat in the daytime and gently release it during the night.

The wines

Located mostly on the east side of the Rhine, for better exposure to the sun, the vineyards are planted primarily with Riesling and a small amount of Spätburgunder and Portugieser (red). Over half of the Riesling wines are dry or medium dry in style and, when young, they have a pronounced, refreshing acidity. The red wines are pleasantly light and fruity.

Tasting and purchasing wine

Most of the wines are available only locally. You can sample and purchase directly from a grower's wine estate or in the local *Weinstuben* and restaurants. Even the souvenir shops sell wine. Look for signs that include words such as *Weingut*, *Weinhaus*, *Winzerhof* or

Weinkeller. *Weinverkauf* means wine for sale.

The villages from the north to Koblenz

All the villages on this route remind us of their medieval past. Explore them on foot to discover the Romanesque and Gothic churches as well as the beautiful half-timbered houses on crooked alleyways, usually near the *Markt* or *Marktplatz* (market square). You can enjoy the local wine and scenery at cafés along the riverbank. Nearly all of the tourist attractions are open from April to October, but many close during the winter.

Linz, Erpel and Unkel

These are less important towns in terms of wine production, but are very picturesque and full of inviting *Weinstuben* and little shops. Unkel has manor houses dating from the 17th and 18th centuries, medieval half-timbered houses and a lovely Rhine promenade. The Gothic church is also worth seeing. Opposite Linz, the river Ahr flows into the Rhine. A huge basalt cliff, the Erpeler Ley, soars above Erpel, and the ruins of the famous **Ludendorff Bridge** to Remagen, which was the first crossing of the Rhine by the American Army on March 7, 1945. The bridge collapsed on March 17 and the war against Hitler and the Nazis ended on May 8, 1945.

Rheinbrohl and Bad Hönningen

At Rheinbrohl, the Romans' frontier defence line reached the Rhine. Bad Hönningen is a small health resort, with mineral baths and thermal pools. Its most famous vineyard, **Schlossberg**, is situated on the south-facing hillside below Schloss Arenfels.

Leutesdorf and Hammerstein

Vines have been cultivated for more than 1500 years in Leutesdorf, an important winegrowing town. Riesling is the main variety planted on the volcanic soils and the best vineyard is **Leutesdorfer Gartenlay**. If you are driving on the B 42 from Koblenz, watch for the turning into the *historische Rheinstrasse* (historic part of town) along the Rhine promenade. A 2.5 km (1.5 miles) *Weinlehrpfad* (marked hiking trail through the vineyards) starts at St Laurentius Church.

Bad Honnef and Rhöndorf

These towns lie at the foot of a range of volcanic mountains known as the Siebengebirge. Bad Honnef is an elegant health resort with lush gardens and parks and very attractive manor houses. Konrad Adenauer, first chancellor of the Federal Republic of Germany, lived in Rhöndorf. The **Adenauer Memorial** established in his home on the Bundeskanzlerplatz is open to the public.

Dragon's Cliff and Dragon's Blood

Drachenfels (Dragon's Cliff) is the most famous hill of the Siebengebirge and is the name of the steep vineyard planted below the ruins of the 12th-century Drachenfels fortress.

The red wine produced here is called *Drachenblut* (Dragon's Blood), alluding to Siegfried's battle with the dragon that lived in a cave on this hill (*Song of the Nibelungs*). It is a specialty that one can enjoy in any number of *Weinstuben* in the popular resort of Königswinter.

Rhenish specialties

Backes-Grumbeeren are well-seasoned scalloped potatoes topped with a piece of pork and baked in the oven. *Himmel und Erde* (heaven and earth) is a mixture of mashed potatoes and chunky apple sauce topped with pan-fried slices of blood sausage. *Sauerbraten* is marinated pot roast with a sweet-and-sour raisin gravy. *Spundekäs* is whipped, spiced cheese to spread on slices of buttered bread.

Koblenz

Koblenz, situated at the confluence of the Mosel and Rhine rivers, is the gateway to some of Germany's most dramatic and beautiful winegrowing regions. Founded as a Roman fort, it prospered as the residence of the powerful Electors of Trier (11th-19th centuries), became the provincial capital under

Bopparder Hamm is one of the finest vineyards in the Mittelrhein.

Prussian rule in 1822, and is now a major administrative center for the wine trade.

Koblenz boasts one of the smallest vineyards in Germany, **Schnorbach-Brückstück**, located adjacent to the charming half-timbered houses of the *Weindorf* (wine village) on the *Rheinanlagen* (Rhine promenade) near Pfaffendorfer Bridge. On the other side of the bridge, walk along the Rhine past the Schloss (Electoral Palace), an impressive neo-Classical structure, towards Deutsches Eck (German Corner). Continue walking, parallel to the Mosel, to the 14th-century Balduin Bridge and the Alte Burg (old Electoral Castle), for a glimpse of Koblenz's medieval past.

Koblenz to Bingen

This route is on the west of the Rhine going south to Bingen. The finest wines of Mittelrhein come from this area. Vineyards and castles have dominated the landscape and shaped the history of this area for centuries. Boppard and Bacharach are the most important wine towns, but nearly every village has a tradition of winegrowing.

On the southern outskirts of Koblenz, the first castle comes into view – **Schloss Stolzenfels**, a neo-Gothic castle rebuilt in 1836 for King Friedrich Wilhelm IV of Prussia.

Rhens is known for its sparkling water as well as its wine. In the Middle Ages the powerful Electors of the Rhineland met here to elect German emperors. The **Königsstuhl** (King's Throne), a tall stone structure built in 1308, stands on a hill north of the town. Rhens is a good example of a 16th-century fortified city. Within the town ramparts, the half-timbered houses have intricately carved beams.

The Bopparder Hamm

From Rhens to Boppard, the Rhine makes its longest loop, known as the Bopparder Hamm. Boppard's finest vineyards are on the slopes facing due south, including the famous **Bopparder Hamm, Feuerlay** and **Mandelstein**. For a view of the loop and the **Vierseenblick**, where the Rhine looks like four large lakes, take the chairlift from Mühltal at the northern edge of Boppard (a 15-minute walk from town – www.sesselbahn-boppard.de).

Boppard

Originally settled by the Celts, and later a Roman citadel for the royal court of the Franks, Boppard was a free imperial city in the Middle Ages. Its historic buildings reflect this illustrious past, and include the remains of the 4th-century Roman fort; twin-towered **St Severus Church**; Gothic Carmelite monastery church; and medieval town houses. The Rhine promenade is beautifully landscaped.

The valley narrows as you approach St Goar, founded in AD 570 and named after the patron saint of innkeepers and potters. From Burg Rheinfels, once the mightiest castle on the Rhine, the view across the river is magnificent: the Loreley rock and Burg (fortress) Katz (cat) and Maus (mouse). www.st-goar.de

Ruins of the 12th-century Schönburg fortress overlook Oberwesel, the "town of towers." Sixteen of the original 21 still line the town walls. Visible for miles, the red brick **Liebfrauenkirche** (Church of Our Lady) is one of Germany's finest High Gothic churches. **Oberwesel Oeslberg** is the best vineyard here.

The vineyards of all the fine wine estates are in Boppard or Bacharach on the west side of the Rhine. They are listed from north to south.

WINERIES & MORE

BOPPARD

Weingut Matthias Müller
Mainzer Strasse 45
56322 Spay
Tel: 02628 8741
www.weingut-matthiasmueller.de

Weingut Weingart
Rheinufer 23/24
56322 Spay
Tel: 02628 988610
www.weingut-weingart.de

Weingut Didinger
Rheinuferstrasse 13
56340 Osterspai
Tel: 02627 512
www.weingut-didinger.de

BACHARACH

Weingut Toni Jost
Oberstrasse 14
55422 Bacharach
Tel: 06743 1216
www.tonijost.de

Weingut Ratzenberger
Blücherstrasse 167
55422 Bacharach
Tel: 06743 1337
www.weingut-ratzenberger.de

BENDORF

Garten der Schmetterlinge
Visit the Garden of Butterflies located in the Schlosspark in Bendorf-Sayn. Daily from Mar–Dec. www.sayn.de

MITTELRHEIN MOMENTE

A series of food and wine events, often with music or entertainment, featuring the talents of the region's fine winemakers and chefs.
www.mittelrheinmomente.de

VERANSTALTUNGSKALENDER RHEINLAND-PFALZ

Rheinland-Pfalz Information
Löhrstrasse 103-105
56068 Koblenz
Tel: 0261 915200
www.rlp-info.de
A calendar of events listing hundreds of festivals and wine and food events along the Rhine, Mosel, Nahe and Ahr rivers.

Deinhard Kelle Museum
Deinhardplatz 3
56068 Koblenz
Tel: 0261 91151520
www.deinhard.de
Shows how wine and sparkling wine are made, historic tools, beautiful cellars. Visits weekdays, by appointment only.

Weindorf Koblenz
Julius-Wegeler-Strasse 2

A typical barge on the Rhine passing the wine town of Kaub.

56068 Koblenz
Tel: 0261 1337190
www.koblenz-touristik.de
Just south of the Pfaffendorfer Bridge and the Electoral Palace. This half-timbered winegrowers' village was created in 1925 for a wine exhibition and has 38 buildings, mostly wine shops, and restaurants. Music and dance events.

Ehrenbreitstein Fortress

Excellent view from the terrace. Ferry across from Koblenz, then walk uphill (1 hr) or take cablecars built in 2011, which leave the Deutsches Eck and climb 850 m (2,789 ft) over the Rhine. The museum has history of local industries and river traffic. Mid-Mar to mid-Nov. **www.diefestungehrenbreitstein.de**

Altar of Bacchus

Bacharach (Roman Bacchi ara) became the region's most important shipping center for wine in the Middle Ages because the narrow course of the Rhine used to be desperately fast and dangerous, with underwater rocks. It was safer to transport as much as possible by other means to Bacharach for re-loading there. The steep Riesling vineyards, **Bacharacher Hahn** and **Wolfshöhle**

and Bacharach-Steeg St Jost are among the top sites of the Mittelrhein. Enter the town through one of the town gates and climb the steps to walk along the town wall, just behind the railway line. Historic buildings include Haus Sickingen, Alte Post, Alter Zollhof, Rathaus, Altes Haus and St Peterskirche (church). Next to the chapel ruins of the Wernerkapelle, a gem of High Gothic architecture, take the footpath to the ruins of **Burg Stahleck** (now a youth hostel) for a great view of the river and vineyards.

From Bacharach to Trechtingshausen, vineyards spill into the side valleys. Three castles, with exhibits and period rooms, are open for visits: **Burg Sooneck, Schloss Reichenstein** and **Burg Rheinstein**.

Binger Loch, a very narrow, rocky and shallow stretch of the Rhine, and the Mäuseturm (Mice Tower) on an island in the Rhine, signal the approach to Bingen. There is a *Fähre* (ferry) across the Rhine to Rüdesheim. Continue on the B 42: upstream through the Rheingau or downstream toward Koblenz.

Downstream from Kaub to Lahnstein

This route follows the Rhine to Koblenz from the Rheingau. It also enables you to complete a circular tour of the Mittelrhein if you followed the B 9 upstream from Koblenz to Bingen. From the Bingen-Rüdesheim ferry dock, turn left and drive through the last villages of the Rheingau to Kaub.

Thirteenth-century Burg Gutenfels (now a hotel) overlooks the medieval townscape of Kaub, once the center of the Rhenish slate quarry trade. Today, the slaty hills from Kaub to Dörscheid yield excellent Riesling wines. Walk along **Metzgergasse** to see the historic buildings or visit the **Blücher Museum** (No. 6).

In the middle of Pfalzgrafenstein island, opposite Kaub, is a six-sided fortress shaped like a ship (tours except Mon). Known as the Pfalz, it was built as a toll station in the 14th century.

Near St Goarshausen, the Rhine narrows to about 100 meters (330 ft) and the massive slate cliffs of the Loreley come into view. Justifiably renowned as one

The Pfalz is a six-sided fortress shaped like a ship. It was built on an island in the 14th century to collect tolls from passing vessels.

of the Rhine's most dangerous passageways, the Loreley achieved romantic fame through Heinrich Heine's *Song of Loreley* (1824) about the siren on the rocky cliffs who lured sailors to their death with her singing. Equally treacherous is the reef where a river god turned "seven virgins" into rocks because they resisted his advances. Follow the signs to the Loreleyfelsen for the view and a glass of wine from the vineyard of the same name.

Downstream to Braubach

Patches of vines cling to the slopes of Katz and Maus castles, but from here to Braubach, castles and orchards, not vineyards, dominate the landscape. Braubach has retained

A comfortable guesthouse in Kester, facing the Rhine and a few miles north of Boppard. *Zimmer frei* means Rooms Available.

much of its medieval character. Visit the **Marksburg** fortress (12th-14th centuries) rising above the town. The only castle on the Rhine never destroyed, the buildings, interior and gardens are well worth a visit.

Lahnstein straddles the Lahn river at its junction with the Rhine. There are fine Romanesque and Gothic buildings within the town ramparts. The wild cliffs of the Ruppertsklamm are also worth a visit. The last castle on our route is the 13th-century **Burg Lahneck**, built to protect the nearby silver mines. The view is outstanding.

There are a few vineyards along the river valley near Bad Ems (a spa resort made famous by Bismarck's *Ems' Dispatch*, which sparked off the 1870 Franco-Prussian war) and between Nassau and Obernhof.

"THE RHINE IN FLAMES"

Spectacular fireworks displays on the Rhine.

1st Sat in Jul: Bingen, Rüdesheim, Niederheimbach.

2nd Sat in Aug: Spay, Koblenz.

2nd Sat in Sept: Oberwesel.

3rd Sat in Sept: St Goar

and St Goarhausen. For exact dates visit www.rhein-in-flammen.com

Scenic routes through the hills

The *Rheingoldstrasse* is an alternative route through the Hunsrück Hills, from Rhens to Niederheimbach. Best views: Königsstuhl, Jakobsberg (footpath to Vierseenblick) and Fleckertshöhe. The **Loreley-Burgenstrasse** winds through the Taunus Hills, from Kaub to the Loreley and from St Goarshausen to Kamp-Bornhofen. Best views: Kaub, Loreley, castles near Kamp-Bornhofen.

Wine hiking trails

Rhein-Weinwanderweg between Kaub and Kamp-Bornhofen; *Weinwanderweg* between St Goar and Trechtingshausen.

Rhine cruises

The KD line and smaller local companies offer many boat trips (season: from Easter or May-Oct). If time is short take an hour-long *Rundfahrt* (round trip) or travel one way by boat, return by train. Especially scenic: Bingen/Rüdesheim to St Goar (two hours). www.kdrhine.com

In the Middle Ages Bacharach became a vital port for the wine trade.

Andernach

Hotel-Restaurant Am Helmwartsturm (H/R)
Am Helmwartsturm 4-6
56626 Andernach
Tel: 02632 95 84 60
www.hotel-am-helmwartsturm.de
The Kauffmann family owns the 18-room hotel in the middle of the town, with their son Kaufmann's restaurant, which has elegant Mediterranean-style cuisine.

Bacharach

Altkölnischer Hof (H/R)
Blücherstrasse 2
55422 Bacharach
Tel: 06743 13 39
www.altkoelnischer-hof.de
Family-owned hotel with 19 rooms. Good restaurant. Closed Nov-Dec.

Bacherach-Henschhausen

Landhaus Delle (H/R)
Gutenfelsstrasse 16
55422 Bacherach-Henschhausen
Tel: 06743 17 65
www.landhaus-delle-hotel.com
Eight rooms. Restaurant has a classic menu and excellent wines, but main meals are available only for hotel guests.

Bendorf

Bistrorant Weinhaus Syré (W/R)
Engersport 12
56170 Bendorf
Tel: 02622 2581
www.weinhaus-syre.de

Hotel-Restaurant Villa Sayn (H/R)
Koblenz-Olper-Strasse 111

56170 Bendorf
Tel: 02622 94490
www.villasayn.de
Good classic food.

Boppard

Best Western Bellevue Rheinhotel (H/R)
Rheinallee 41
56154 Boppard
Tel: 06742 1020
www.bellevue-boppard.de
The hotel has 94 rooms. The restaurant Le Chopin has classic food and a view of the Rhine. The Günther hotel has 19 less expensive rooms, but no separate restaurant.

Tannenheim (H/R)
Bahnhof Buchholz 3 (B327)
56154 Boppard-Buchholz
Tel: 06742 2281
www.hotel-tannenheim.de
Nine rooms in a nice house with a beautiful garden and outside terrace. Very good, inexpensive seasonal menus.

Kaub

Zum Turm (H/R)
Zollstrasse 50
56349 Kaub
Tel: 06774 9 22 00
www.rhein-hotel-turm.com
Six excellent rooms. Restaurant serves good seasonal food at very reasonable prices.

Koblenz

Weinhaus Hubertus (W)
Florinsmarkt 6
56068 Koblenz
Tel: 0261 31177
www.weinhaus-hubertus.de
Oldest wine tavern in Koblenz, dating from 1689. Very cozy.

This rocky outcrop shields the vines from the worst of the weather.

Historischer Weinkeller (R)
Mehlgasse 14-16
56068 Koblenz
Tel: 0261 91481420
www.historicher-weinkeller.de
Restaurant and wine bar in 13th-century vaulted cellars in the old town. Classic German food with some Mediterranean dishes. Flourishing under the new owners Rudi Staiger and the Gerber brothers.

Königswinter-Stieldorf

Gasthaus Sutorius (R)
Oelinghovener Strasse 7
53639 Königswinter-Stieldorf
Tel: 02244 912240
www.sutorius.de
In the suburb Königswinter-Stieldorf. Good food, cozy atmosphere.

Oberwesel

Burghotel auf Schönburg (H/R)
55430 Oberwesel
Tel: 06744 93930
www.hotel-schoenburg.com
Spectacular views. Many of the 18 rooms and 4 suites have balconies. The restaurant has a medieval feel, both inside and on the terrace. (Closed Jan 6–Mar 16.)

Römerkrug (H/R/W)
Marktplatz 1
55430 Oberwesel
Tel: 06744 7091
www.hotel-roemerkrug.rhein-castles.de
A remarkable house built in 1458. Seven rooms and a restaurant with regional cooking and a *Weinstube*.

Weinhaus Weiler (H/R/W)
Marktplatz 4
55430 Oberwesel
Tel: 06744 93050
www.weinhaus-weiler.de
Historic hotel with 11 rooms, restaurant.

St Goar

Schloss Rheinfels (H/R)
Schlossberg 47
56329 St Goar
Tel: 06741 8020
www.schloss-rheinfels.de
64 rooms. Restaurants, Burgschänke Der and Landgraf (closed in winter). Excellent wine list. Fabulous view from the terrace.

Boppard has a fine promenade on the Rhine and many historic buildings, including the twin-towered church of St Severus (left).

ERDENER
TREPPCHEN

MOSEL

THE VALLEYS OF THE MOSEL RIVER and its tributaries, the Saar and the Ruwer, are the setting for some of Germany's most beautiful and romantic wine regions. The Saar and the Ruwer flow into the Mosel river to the south and the north, respectively, of the ancient town of Trier. Vines and forests carpet the steep slopes formed millions of years ago, as the Mosel cut a gorge through the Hunsrück and Eifel hills. Spectacular loops mark the sites where the slate has resisted the power of the river.

The best way to see the vineyards of the Mosel region is to paddle downstream in a kayak from Serrig on the Saar river, stopping at Trier and the Ruwer. Then sweep round the Trittenheim 360-degree loop, on the way to Piesport and its amphitheater of vines and, shortly afterwards, medieval Bernkastel. You can then drift along the great steep wall of famous slate vineyards past Graach, Wehlen, Zeltingen, Ürzig, and Erden, carrying on through the countless turns of the Mosel passing unsung vineyards and villages, until you reach Winningen and its extraordinary vineyards perched on cliffs, ending at Koblenz. Alternatively, this trip can be done by steamer, bicycle or on foot, unless you prefer to drive.

The *Mosel Weinstrasse* (Mosel Wine Road) (242 km/150 miles) runs parallel to the river and passes through dozens of famous wine villages. Hikers can enjoy breathtaking panoramas from the heights of the *Moselhöhenweg* trails on both sides of the river. Or you can spend a few hours absorbing the landscape and its wines on a leisurely river cruise.

Viticulture has been the heart and soul of the Mosel-Saar-Ruwer for the past 2000 years. The region was settled as early as 3000 BC by a Celtic tribe, the Treveri, but their Roman conquerors were the first to cultivate vineyards systematically. During their 450 years of supremacy, the

‹‹ The wine-growing area of Ürzig from the Erdener Treppchen vineyard.

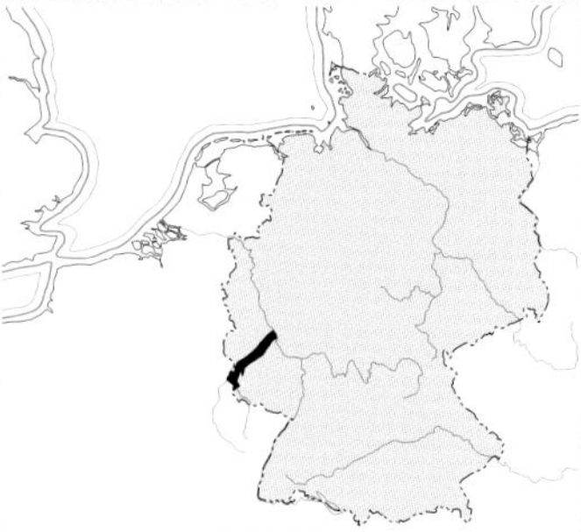

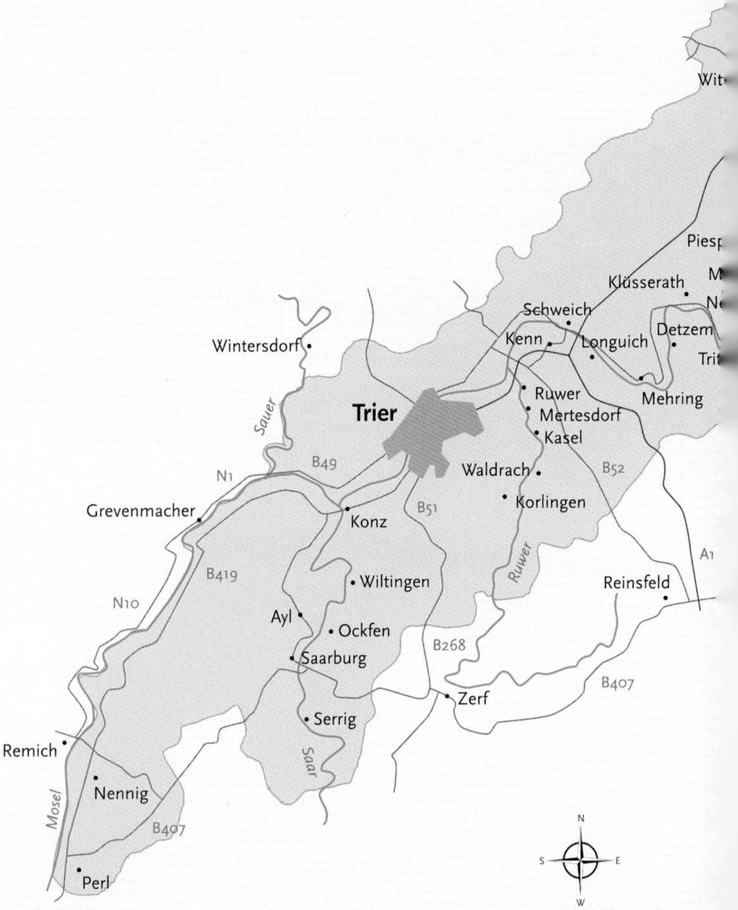
Klüsserath
Schweich
Kenn
Longuich
Detzem
Wintersdorf
Ruwer
Mehring
Trier
Mertesdorf
Sauer
Kasel
B49
Waldrach
B52
N1
B51
Korlingen
Grevenmacher
Konz
A1
B419
Ruwer
Wiltingen
Reinsfeld
N10
Ayl
Ockfen
B268
Saarburg
B407
Zerf
Serrig
Remich
Saar
Nennig
Mosel
B407
N
S
E
W
Perl

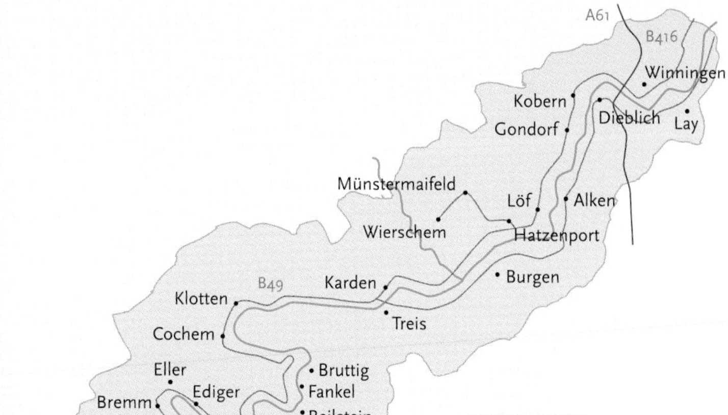

A61
B416
Winningen
Kobern
Dieblich
Lay
Gondorf
Münstermaifeld
Löf
Alken
Wierschem
Hatzenport
Burgen
B49
Karden
Klotten
Treis
Cochem
Eller
Bruttig
Fankel
Ediger
Bremm
Beilstein
St. Aldegund
Senheim
Alf
Pünderich
Reil
Zell-Kaimt
Briedel
Kröv
Enkirch
Erden
Zeltingen
B53
Graach
Traben-Trarbach
Lieser
Bernkastel-Kues

SELBACH-OSTER
Mosel

REICHSGRAF VON KESSELSTATT
2010 SCHARZHOFBERGER
RIESLING SPÄTLESE

MOSEL - SAAR - RUWER
Forstmeister Geltz
ZILLIKEN
2005
Saarburger Rausch
Riesling Auslese

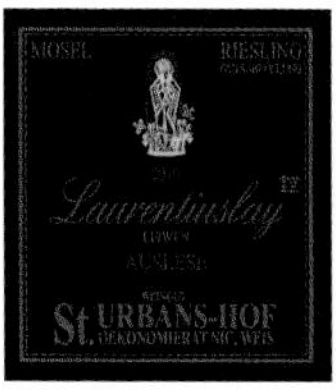
MOSEL
RIESLING
Laurentiuslay
St. URBANS-HOF

2010
JOSEPHSHÖFER
RIESLING KABINETT
REICHSGRAF VON KESSELSTATT

WEGELER
2010
Bernkasteler Doctor
Auslese

Joh. Jos. Prüm
750 ml
Mosel
Riesling
Prädikatswein
Joh. Jos. Prüm
2007
Wehlener Sonnenuhr
Spätlese

DR. LOOSEN
2010
Erdener
Prälat
Riesling
Auslese

Weingut Max Ferd. Richter
D-54486 MÜLHEIM / MOSEL
2010
Mülheimer Helenenkloster
Riesling Eiswein
375 ml
MOSEL-SAAR-RUWER

Romans developed the viticulture and importation of wine that remains the Mosel's most important industry, for the vine is still the only crop to flourish on the steep slate slopes.

Another feature of the landscape dating from Roman times is the use of single stakes to support vines. This method is used on most of the steepest sites, and nowhere else to my knowledge. Rather than stretching the vine horizontally across a wire trellis, the canes of each vine are bowed into a heart shape and tied to an individual stake. The vine benefits from improved air circulation, exposure to the sun and nutrient distribution. The growers work the rows vertically, from the bottom of the hill to the top.

The frequency of wine motifs in Roman works of art and the beautiful objects designed to enhance the pleasure of drinking wine, such as wine jugs and glasses, show that the Romans appreciated fine wines. One of the finest examples of Roman wine culture is the *Diatretglas*, a glass cup ingeniously encircled by delicate glass netting. Such art treasures and other wine-related Roman artifacts are displayed in museums throughout the region, the most notable collection being that in the **Rheinisches Landesmuseum** (Landesmuseum-trier.de) in Trier.

Post-Roman era

During the turbulent reign of the Franks, the successors of the Treveri carried on the wine tradition of the Romans. From the 7th century onwards, vineyards were regularly mentioned in deeds of gift to the Church and its monasteries. In the beginning of the 19th century, when ecclesiastical property was secularized, the Church owned a majority of the region's best sites, a fact also reflected in many of the vineyard names, such as Klosterberg (Cloister Hill), Domprobst (Provost of the Cathedral), Abtsberg (Abbot's Hill), etc. Although a few vineyards were returned to the Church, notably in Trier, most were sold at auction when the Mosel region was occupied by France and Napoleon needed money after the total defeat of his army by the Russians. These sales marked the foundation or expansion of what today are some of Germany's most famous privately-owned wine estates.

Modern times

The Mosel, including Ruwer and Saar, is the fifth largest (9,000 hectares/ 22,240 acres) of Germany's wine regions. Its worldwide reputation for fine wines derives from the steep, south-facing slopes with slate soil, and the Riesling grape, not forgetting the incredible determination of the growers, some of whom have retained their holdings for centuries, despite all the wars.

Many traditional Riesling wines are fermented and developed in large old oak casks (*Fuder*) in cool cellars, where the fermentation tends to stop before the sugar has changed to alcohol. These are the world's lightest and most delicate wines, with about eight per cent of alcohol. Other Riesling wines are fermented in stainless steel tanks and the fermentation is deliberately stopped. Both methods are valid and the wines have a wonderful balance of natural acidity and residual sugar, with great finesse and fragrance. Almost all *trocken* (dry) Mosels are fermented in tanks to about 12.5 per cent of alcohol and do not have this finesse and fragrance. They are mainly produced for German wine lovers to drink with food. The majority of fine dry German Rieslings are from the other regions, where the climate is different and the soils are not slate.

Riesling is king here. The other grape varieties planted in the region are mainly in vineyards where the terroirs are unsuitable for Riesling, or growers want volume rather than quality. Müller-Thurgau (also called Rivaner) is a pale imitation of Riesling, mainly planted in flat vineyards that are some distance from the Mosel valley. Hopefully, Müller-Thurgau will gradually fade away, as it did in New Zealand where it was all pulled up to be replaced with Sauvignon and Chardonnay in the 1980s.

Weissburgunder has a very good reputation in some areas, especially in summer and when the white asparagus is in season, whereas Auxerrois and the ancient white variety Elbling are only grown along the border with Luxembourg, and are of little interest.

The great success and the high prices fetched for Spätburgunder from the Ahr valley have encouraged a few brave growers to follow their example. *Dornfelder*, the relatively new dark red grape variety, is planted on the flat vineyards to fill the gap of a good decent red wine for local customers and restaurants.

Koblenz to Cochem

The lower Mosel extends 90km (56 miles) from Koblenz to Zell. The *Mosel Weinstrasse* (wine road) starts from Koblenz and has dark green signs with a stylized "M" and grape clusters in orange. It usually corresponds to the B 49 and the B 53. Later it crosses the Mosel, and includes most of the important wine towns. Church spires can help you locate historic buildings and town centers.

There is a tall motorway bridge over the valley and ancient castles and Romanesque church towers are silhouetted against the landscape. The vineyards are striking, particularly the terraced sites between Winningen and Gondorf, whose formidable slate cliffs seem to defy gravity as they sweep from the river bank to the sky. Two estates in Winningen produce great Riesling wines, both dry and sweet, with a perfect balance of acidity and natural sugar. The two finest vineyards are **Winninger Rötgen** and **Uhlen** and the quality of their wines is outstanding. In spring and autumn growers and chefs along the **Terrassenmosel** (an area known for its steep, terraced vineyards) host festive events on vine-canopied streets with wine, food and music.

In the 17th century, the area was notorious for its witch-hunts. Imagine the surprise of the Winningen grower who finally caught the "witch" who had been stealing wine from his best barrel, only to discover that she was his wife! In late August, Germany's oldest wine festival is celebrated around Winningen's **Hexenbrunnen** (witches' well). There is a wonderful view from the heights of the **Weinlehrpfad** (educational wine trail) that starts on Am Rosenberg at the edge of town.

WINERIES & MORE

WINNINGEN

Weingut Reinhard und Beate Knebel
August-Horch-Strasse 24
56333 Winningen
Tel: 02606 2631
www.weingut-knebel.de

Weingut Heymann-Löwenstein
Bahnhofstrasse 10
56333 Winningen
Tel: 02606 1919
www.heymann-loewenstein.com

Kobern-Gondorf

Upstream, the ruins of the 12th-century Niederburg fortress come into view. Kobern's other castle, the Oberburg, is notable for its Romanesque **St Matthias Chapel**, reminiscent of the Holy Sepulchre in Jerusalem. Historic houses line Kobern's pretty market square, and one of Germany's oldest (1321) half-timbered houses is nearby, on **Kirchstrasse 1**. Gondorf's Oberburg, formerly a moated castle, suffered a curious fate when the town fathers decided to build a road through its walls.

Excursion to Burg Thurant

Cross the Mosel at Löf and backtrack to the medieval town of Alken. Burg Thurant overlooks the town and the Burgberg vineyard. Built in 1197, the castle was besieged from 1246 to 1248 by the

The start of "Golden October" in the vineyards of Graach.

Archbishops of Trier and Cologne, and thereafter divided by a partition wall, with one keep for Trier and the other for Cologne. It is open daily. Wine is served in the garden.

Löf to Cochem

There are half a dozen wine villages with historic houses, churches and castle ruins between Löf and Cochem. Two sights especially recommended are **Burg Eltz**, in the Elzbach valley, and the **Church of St Castor** in Karden.

Burg Eltz is a dramatically picturesque castle. From Hatzenport, drive through the scenic Schrumpfbachtal (old mills) via the town of Münstermaifeld (the Church of St Martin is notable) to Wierschem, where there are signs to the Burg Eltz car park. You can also drive from Moselkern or Milden to the start of marked trails through the woods to reach the castle (40 minutes).

Restored frescoes, carved tombs, a Stumm organ and Europe's only remaining terracotta altar (1420) are just a few of the treasures in the Romanesque and Gothic Church of St Castor in Karden. The ancient town of Cochem is just past the Mosel's wide bend at Klotten.

Cochem to Zell

At Cochem the Mosel begins its series of scenic loops, with many south-facing slopes. From here to Zell is one of the areas where mass-produced Mosel wines are made. Cochem is a delightful town to explore on foot. From the 14th-century Enderttor (town gate) it is a brief walk up the Hinter Kempeln steps to the Klosterberg and former Capuchin monastery for a view of Old Town and the neighboring heights. Descend the old monastery steps and walk along the town wall to Obergässchen, Balduinstor (town gate) and Branntweingässchen to see **Cochem's historic houses.** The Oberbachstrasse leads to the market square, with the Baroque town hall and half-timbered houses. From here it is a 15-minute walk via Herrenstrasse and Schloss-Strasse to Reichsburg Cochem. For a look at the Elector of Trier's administrative buildings and Cochem's narrowest houses,

The fortress of Cochem, a Frankish manor from AD 866 and rebuilt 1000 years later (1869) as a "classic" German castle, is now a hotel.

follow the Herrenstrasse to Wenzelgasse. A stroll from the Burgfriedentor (town gate) along the beautiful Mosel promenade to St Martin's Church completes the circuit.

Beilstein

After you cross the Mosel at Cochem or Ernst, drive through Bruttig and Fankel to see very fine half-timbered houses with stepped gables and oriels. Beilstein is a medieval gem. Romantic alleys and stairways wind from the picturesque market square up to the castle ruins (Burg Metternich) and the former monastery church, with its Baroque furnishings and a late Gothic "Black Madonna" of Spanish-Moorish origin. The vine-canopied terrace of **Haus Lipmann's Alte Mosel Weinstuben** (Marktplatz 3) is an idyllic setting for a glass of wine from Beilstein's Schlossberg vineyard site.

Ediger-Eller and Bremm

The road crosses the Mosel from Senheim to Nehren. Ediger's narrow cobbled streets are lined with half-timbered houses

The Neumagen Wine Ship is a memorial to a Roman wine merchant. This is a copy: the original is in the Rheinisches Landesmuseum in Trier.

within remnants of the 14th-century fortifications. The church at the top of Kirchstrasse has an interesting mixture of styles. Its exterior is adorned by a Romanesque bell tower, a Gothic spire and gargoyles; inside, a Baroque high altar stands beneath an elaborate vaulted ceiling. Also recommended is the **Kreuzkapelle** (chapel) overlooking town, with a unique stone relief called "Christ in the Wine Press" (open Easter–Sept; otherwise, ask for the key from the tourist office). Signs show the way from Hochstrasse.

As the Mosel loops towards the famous vineyard **Bremmer Calmont**, Europe's steepest vineyard, which looks down on the ruins of a 12th-century Augustinian convent standing in splendid isolation on the opposite shore.

St Aldegund and Alf are pretty wine and resort towns. The side valleys offer scenic excursions to the Roman spa **Bad Bertrich** (late Baroque bathhouse) and to **Burg Arras**, a 100-year-old fortress now housing a history museum, restaurant and guest rooms. The best overall view of the Mosel loop near Zell is from Marienburg, once a Roman fortress and later a medieval monastery (1129). This is a great setting for a glass of wine from the **Marienburger vineyard**.

Cross the Mosel at Zell-Kaimt. From the tourist office in Zell's town hall, it is a 15-minute walk through the vineyards to Zell's landmark and last vestige of the fortifications, the **Runder Turm** (round tower). Historic houses are on Römerstrasse (nearest St Peter's Church) and the exterior of the late Gothic Electoral Palace is notable. Wine shops and *Weinstuben* abound.

RIVERBOAT EXCURSIONS (MAY–OCT)

From Koblenz: Cochem 4 1/2 hours. **From Cochem: Beilstein** 1 hour; **Zell** 3 hours; **Traben-Trarbach** 5 hours. **From Bernkastel: Traben-Trarbach** 2 hours; **Piesport** 1 hour; **Trittenheim** 2 hours; **Trier** 4 hours.

ZELLER SCHWARZE KATZ

Perhaps the shape of the steep vineyards rising up behind Zell gave rise to the name "Black Cat" . . . or is the legend true?

Three wine merchants from Aachen could not decide which of three barrels to buy. As the grower reached to draw another sample, his black cat leaped on to the cask, arched its back and hissed. Assuming that the cat was defending the best wine, they bought that barrel and sold it as "Black Cat" wine. For years thereafter they asked for wine from the same vineyard. Schwarze Katz is celebrated at a large annual festival in late June.

The Middle Mosel

Zell to Traben-Trarbach

The first town after Zell is Briedel, and its vineyard **Herzchen** (little heart) is depicted symbolically on a sign welcoming visitors. From the B 53, turn left on Hauptstrasse, then right on Zehntstrasse to see the old part of the town. The town hall (1615), *Eulenturm* (owls' tower) and **St Martin's Church** (1772) are worth seeing. Briedel has beautiful half-timbered houses.

The village of Reil had lost its past reputation for quality, but now one grower is making excellent Rieslings from the fine **Reiler Moulay-Hofberg** vineyard and a few hundred meters away is another revived steep slate vineyard at Pünderich, where one independent grower has re-established **Pündericher Marienburg** as a unique vineyard, producing fabulous Rieslings from Spätlesen to Trockenbeerenauslesen.

Enkirch is equally charming. Turn left at **Weingasse**

(wine alley), with its unusual street sign, to visit the museum and tasting room in the Rats-Weinschenke (No. 20). The 3.5 km (2 mile) Weinbaulehrpfad through the **Steffensberg** vineyard north of the town affords good views and a look at some of the challenges facing Mosel growers.

Traben-Trarbach straddles the Mosel at its next loop. In the past this was a flourishing town with some good Riesling vineyards and which exported large quantities of other Mosel wines. Here you can see a collection of unique antique furnishings and wine-related artifacts in the **Mittelmosel Museum** located in the patrician's manor, where Goethe stayed in 1794. The **Grevenburg** fortress ruins overlooking town are a good vantage point. You can also take in the scenery from the café inside the massive gate on the Mosel bridge. Both Traben and Trarbach have historic houses, including a number of splendid Jugendstil (art nouveau) buildings, such as **Hotel Bellevue** on Traben's promenade. The ruins of **Louis XIV's Mont Royal**, once the largest fortification in Europe, are also on the Traben side.

A spectacular wall of vines above the nearby village, Wolf, includes a superb Riesling vineyard, **Wolfer Goldgrube**.

Kröv to Machern

Approaching Kröv, turn right from the B 53 and drive towards the spire of St Remigius Church, which is surrounded by many historic houses. The burial chapel of the Counts of Kesselstatt on Ehrenmalstrasse is notable, as are the **Echternacherhof** (1764) and the half-timbered **Dreigiebelhaus** (1658) on the B 53.

In the first weekend in July at the **Trachtentreffen** (folk festival), music and dance groups in traditional costume from all over Europe make for a colorful wine festival. Kröv's famous vineyard site **Nacktarsch** (bare bottom) actually derives its name from the days when hedges, rather than vines, covered Kröv's high, stony cliffs.

Erden is the first village in the series of some of the greatest Riesling vineyards in the world. **Prälat** is a minute vineyard (2.2

Harvesting in Graach. The green plastic container on the grape-picker's back is a similar shape to the heavy wooden hods of the past.

hectares/5.4 acres) and its Riesling wines are impeccable. Erdener Treppchen (little steps) has vertical rock faces in the gray slate vineyard and by the Mosel sits a small presshouse, where the grapes were trodden in Roman times. The wines are classic and magically elegant. **Erdener Busslay** vineyard is on the right bank, just behind the village on flat land, and therefore its wines are extremely dull.

The next village, Ürzig, whose finest vineyard **Ürziger Würzgarten** (spice garden), has red volcanic soil mixed with slate. The wines taste spicy and have more body. The 13th-century **Cistercian monastery** at Machern is worth visiting. It is owned by the Günter Reh Foundation, an offshoot of the vast Reh wine business, and harbors a microbrewery, a toy museum and a distillery. Many events take place there, including antique markets, and there is a spacious room for weddings and special dinners.

Zeltingen to Bernkastel

The great curve of Riesling vineyards from **Zeltinger Schlossberg**, **Wehlener Sonnenuhr** (sundial), to **Graacher Himmelreich** (Kingdom of Heaven) and **Dompropst** are the birthplace of some of the finest and most elegant Rieslings, with low alcohol (8 per cent), balanced acidity. The wines at every level can improve with ageing in bottle. The famous and tiny vineyard (3.26 hectares/8 acres) **Bernkasteler Doctor** faces due south overlooking the old town and the wines are more masculine and concentrated. For a splendid view, take the first exit at Graach, turn left at Neuer Weg and drive to Schäferei (sheep farm). Looking across the river, you can see Wehlen's stately manors on the shore, and the more commercial town, Bernkastel-Kues.

Kloster Machern is over the bridge from Zeltingen. It is a monastery dating back to 1084, and there are a number of buildings, some of which have been converted for new projects, making a sort of campus. The buildings include: a museum for antique religious icons, dolls and toys; a museum of vineyard equipment; an antique shop; a distillery producing over 100 liqueurs and bran-

A view from Bremmer Calmont, the steepest vineyard in Europe, across to the tightest loop in the Mosel river.

dies, as well as vinegars and olive oils; a microbrewery; and a "Cabinet" containing a collection of fine Mosel wines from **Weingut Reichsgraf von Kesselstatt.** All these products are for sale, and there is also a small *Weinstube*.

The owners had previously acquired a beautiful tithe house in Bernkastel-Kues, built by the Duke of Trier, Carl Casper von der Layen, in 1668. Re-named "Doctor," it has been transformed into a hotel, with an elegant restaurant and a delightful *Weinstube*. There is music and dancing in part of the great cellar.

Bernkastel-Kues

Old Bernkastel is on the right bank and it is a quaint, charming town, best explored on foot. Park at the riverfront and walk to the market square. St Michael's fountain (1606) is surrounded by half-timbered houses (16th-17th century) and the Renaissance town hall (1608). The castle, Burg Landshut, was once a favorite summer residence for Trier's Electors and Archbishops. One of these was Boemund II, who once fell ill. His doctors were unable to cure him, so they brought a flask of Bernkastel wine, which he drank and then miraculously recovered. He attributed this to the healing powers of the local wine, thereafter named "Doctor."

It is easy to walk up to the ruins of the **Burg Landshut** castle to enjoy a glass of Bernkastel wine, or one from the other villages nearby ("the Doctor" is prohibitively expensive), and look at the great curve of the steep slopes, especially in November, when the leaves of the vines are golden. To see the legendary Doctor vineyard, walk along Hinterm Graben street near the old town gate, Graacher Tor.

The **Cusanusstift**, (Cusanussstrasse 2) is in Kues across the bridge from Bernkastel. Originally the St Nikolaus Hospital, it was founded in 1458 by the theologian Nikolaus Cusanus, born here in 1401, as a retirement home for men. Today it offers a modern multimedia show of the Mosel wine world and harbors a great **Vinotheck**, where you can taste and purchase wines from over 70 growers, plus the institution's own wines.

WINERIES & MORE

ZELTINGEN

Weingut Selbach-Oster
Uferallee 23
54492 Zeltingen
Tel: 06532 2081
www.selbach-oster.de

BERNKASTEL-WEHLEN

Weingut Joh. Jos. Prüm
Ufferallee 19
54470 Bernkastel-Wehlen
Tel: 06531 3091
www.jjpruem.com

BERNKASTEL

Weingut Dr Loosen
St Johannishof
54470 Bernkastel
Tel: 06531 3426
www.drloosen.de

Bernkastel-Kues to Piesport (left bank)

The first village is Lies, and Niederberg-Helden is a wonderful vineyard, but those extending into the side valleys around Maring-Noviand and Osann-Monzel produce less interesting wines. In Siebenborn (near Maring) you can visit 800-year-old cellars at Weingut Klosterhof Siebenborn, once owned by the Himmerod monastery. There is also the 2nd-century Römerkelter (Roman press house) in Noviand.

Bernkastel to Piesport (right bank)

Mülheim is famous for its wine label "Zeppelin," once served on the airship Graf Zeppelin. The best vineyards are on the fine slate slopes, **Mülheimer Sonnenlay** and **Helenenkloster** (famous for Eisweins), and nearby **Veldenzer Elisenberg**, another brilliant Riesling vineyard.

On the next stretch of the river are the vineyards **Brauneberger Juffer** on the higher part of the steep hill and lower down the even greater Brauneberger Juffer-Sonnenuhr, which benefits from the reflection of the sun from the river. The growers have their cellars in either the Mülheim or the Brauneberg villages on the right bank. There are some vineyards around Brauneberg, but the vineyards are flat and the wines from grapes other than Riesling are of poor quality. From the pretty village of Wintrich, the Mosel makes another 180° loop towards Piesport.

WINERIES & MORE

BRAUNEBERG

Weingut Fritz Haag-Dusemonder Hof
Dusemonder Strasse 44
54472 Brauneberg
Tel: 06534 410
www.weingut-fritz-haag.de

MÜLHEIM

Weingut Max Ferd. Richter
Hauptstrasse 37/85
54486 Mülheim-Mosel
Tel: 06534 933003
www.maxferdrichter.com

Piesport to Trittenheim

Turn right on Brückenstrasse and drive towards the river for a view of the vine-covered hills curving round Piesport. In the old part of town across the river is **St Michael's Church**, with its splendid Baroque interior and ceiling frescoes. Just opposite down the alley by the river is the 4th-century Roman press house, the largest so far discovered in the Mosel region. If you wish to see it you must contact the Haart family at the Weingut Reinhold Haart almost next door.

The road from the church zigzags up though the steep vineyard of the world-famous **Piesporter Goldtröpfchen**. As is often the case, the finest Riesling comes from the steep south-facing vineyards in Mosel and the flat vineyards on the other side of the river are planted with Müller-Thurgau and other inferior grape varieties.

Neumagen, said to be Germany's oldest wine village, was the site of a Roman sculptured tombstone of a boat laden with powerful rowers and barrels of wine. There is a copy in the village and the original is in the Rheinisches Landesmuseum in Trier. Other sights include a monument to the Roman poet Ausonius, whose book Mosella (AD 371) praised the beauty of the Mosel at Piesport. He is believed to have retired to what is now Château Ausone, arguably the finest Bordeaux St Emilion estate.

Trittenheim is where the first mention of Riesling in Mosel was recorded in 1562. It is a lovely town and its finest vineyard is **Trittenheimer Apotheke** on the great curve above another of the Mosel's 180° loops.

WINE ESTATE

PIESPORT
Weingut Reinhold Haart
Ausoniusufer 18
54498 Piesport
Tel: 06507 2015
www.haart.de

The Roman Wine Road

The Roman road from Trier to Mainz followed the Mosel to Leiwen and Neumagen before crossing the Hunsrück Hills, where there are higher-altitude forests and farms. When some growers formed an association in 1986, **Römische Weinstrasse** (Roman wine road) was chosen as its name. Their logo, a Roman transporting wine on a horse-drawn cart, appears on signposts and on the label of a Riesling wine produced in this area. The 10th Roman milestone on the route from Trier to Mainz is in the original Roman village of Detzem (ad decimum lapidem). This part of the Mosel valley is rich in Roman remains, and there is an important Roman villa opposite Mehring village, where, in addition to a cellar, baths, the heating system and towers, the foundations show the existence of another 18 rooms.

Leiwen village is charming but the quality of its wines went down after the 1950s, when some of the growers foolishly planted more vineyards on flat farmland. However, the finest vineyard is **Leiwener Laurentiuslay** on a very

The Roman villa opposite Mehring is well worth a visit.

steep cliff and their great Rieslings have restored the fame of the village.

On the way to Trier, **Klüsserath** parish church has notable furnishings, and you can see or watch one of the Mosel's 14 locks in action. Longuich has fine buildings and an idyllic promenade.

WINERIES & MORE

LEIWEN

Weingut Sankt Urbans-Hof
Urbanusstrasse 16
54340 Leiwen
Tel: 06507 93770
www.urbans-hof.com

BERNKASTEL WINE SHOPS

Moselland Cooperative
Bornwiese 6
54470 Bernkastel-Kues
Tel: 049 6531 570
www.moselland.de

Moselland is one of Germany's largest wine-growing cooperatives. It has 3300 members, responsible for 2350 hectares (5807 acres) of vines, average holding 0.71 hectares (1.75 acres) per member. Most of the grapes are from Mosel, but grapes from members in Nahe, Rheinhessen and Pfalz are also brought here and the wines are marketed separately.

The Ruwer Valley

Depart from Trier to the north. At the roundabout, look for signs to the suburb of Ruwer. After two railway crossings, turn right to Eitelsbach, the first important wine town on this bubbling brook, the river Ruwer. The Romans planted vines here and a Roman aqueduct supplied Ruwer water for drinking and for the baths of Trier.

The Riesling wines of this valley tend to be more fragrant with more pronounced acidity than their softer and richer Mittel Mosel counterparts. **Eitelsbacher Karthäuserhofberg** is the name of the first large vineyard, and next to it is part of a Carthusian monastery from the Middle Ages, as well as the estate house and cellars. The estate has a most unusual curved label stuck on the neck of the bottle. During celebrations in the 19th century, the bottles were cooled in large buckets with ice and water, and orthodox labels came off, so their answer was to fix the labels on the necks of the Karthäuserhofberg bottles above the water level. Their current wine list shows more than twenty different Rieslings of the current vintage from this single vineyard, including a number of great dry wines, which is unusual in the Mosel region, and a superb collection of sweet ones.

In 966 Kaiser Otto I granted the Karthäuserhofberg site to the Benedictine Abbey St Maximin. In 1822 the von Schubert family bought the property at the Napoleonic auctions. Its famous vineyards, **Maximin Grünhäuser Bruderberg, Abtsberg** and **Herrenberg** are on the opposite side of the Ruwer, almost as if they were a continuation of Karthäuserhofberg, but the soil is quite different, as are the Riesling wines. Here too, many of the Rieslings are dry.

Weingut Reichsgraf von Kesselstatt is further upstream at Morscheid and is the only estate, apart from the church, with vineyards of 12 hectares (30 acres) in each of the regions, the finest vineyards being **Josephshöfer** in Mosel, **Scharzhofberg** in Saar and **Kaseler Nies'chen** in the Ruwer valley. These too had been sold at the Napoleonic auctions. It is always fascinating to compare the very different styles of these wines.

WINERIES & MORE

EITELSBACH

Weingut Karthäuserhof
54292 Trier-Eitelsbach
Tel: 0651 5121
www.karthaeuserhof.com

MORSCHEID

Weingut Reichsgraf von Kesselstatt
Schlossgut Marienlay
54317 Morscheid
Tel: 06500 91690
www.kesselstatt.com

Trier

In 16 BC Emperor Augustus founded Augusta Treverorum on a site that had been settled for centuries by the Celtic tribe of the Treveri. Vineyards in the Saar, Ruwer and Mosel valleys existed before the Roman city of Trier and situated at the junction of major trade routes, it quickly grew into a vital trading center. The amphitheater, the Roman bridge, the Barbara thermal

The Traben-Trarbach Bridge Gate of 1898 is a romantic pastiche of the great age of castle building.

baths and the superb Roman gate, Porta Nigra, date from this prosperous early period.

After its destruction in AD 275 by Teutonic tribes, Trier was rebuilt on an even grander scale. In the late 3rd and 4th centuries, it was the imperial residence and capital of the western part of the Roman Empire, a territory extending from Britain to southern Spain. Constantine the Great built monumental public structures (imperial baths, the palace Aula palatina) and the first bishop's church of Germany.

Evidence of Trier's Roman wine heritage abounds. Parts of the Horrea (AD 330), the largest Roman warehouse north of the Alps, are Germany's oldest cellars that are still being used to store wine. (To visit, write to: Vereinigte Hospitien, Krahnenufer 19, 54290 Trier or e-mail info@vereinigtehospiten.de.) Highly recommended is the spectacular collection of wine-related Roman artifacts in the Landesmuseum.

Ecclesiastical Trier

The pagan Franks conquered Trier in the 5th

St Peter's fountain in Trier's market square dates from 1593. St Peter is the town's patron saint.

century. Christianity, however, eventually triumphed. Under Charlemagne, the Bishop of Trier was elevated to Archbishop, and in the 12th century, to Prince Elector. The Church restored Trier to a position of power and enriched it with splendid churches as well as the Electoral Palace. The vast Palastaula (Basilica), the 4th century Roman Aula palatina, was redesigned as the Archbishop's palace. It is now a Protestant church where concerts also take place. Viticulture flourished in the hands of the Church fathers whose far-sighted regulations governing work in the vineyards and the cellars did much to improve quality. Riesling requires cool temperatures at night in order to ripen its grapes slowly in the vineyards and 24 hours a day in the cellars to develop the wine slowly in *Fuders* or ultramodern tanks. Incidentally, Prince Elector Clemens Wenzeslaus went so far as to make the planting of Riesling mandatory throughout the Mosel valley in 1789. If only that decree had been put into practice.

Other sights

The finest examples of secular medieval architecture are on Simeonstrasse, the market square and Dietrichstrasse. The **birthplace of Karl Marx, Brückenstrasse 10**, has a small museum dedicated to him. (open Apr–Oct, 10AM–6PM, Mon 1PM–6PM, Nov–Mar, 11AM–5PM, Mon 2PM–5PM).

FOR FURTHER INFORMATION

Trier

An der Porta Nigra
54290 Trier
Tel: 0651 978080
www.trier-info.de
For excellent maps and brochures and exemplary guided walking tours, or to arrange wine tastings.

WINE FESTIVAL

Zurlaubener Uferfest
on the riverbank in Trier's historic fishermen's quarter, July. For a fabulous view of Trier take the cable car from Zurlauben to Weisshaus.

TRIER WINE SHOPS

Bischöfliche Weingüter
Gervasiusstrasse 1
Tel: 0651 145760
54290 Trier
www.bwgtrier.de
Mon–Fri 8AM–6PM,
Sat 10AM–2PM.

The Saar Valley

Viticulture on the Saar flourished during Roman times, but declined thereafter. Oak forests supplanted vines, and tanners replaced winegrowers. In the 19th century, when tanning was increasingly carried out with chemicals, many forest owners replanted the slopes with vines. Some vineyards are named Kupp, referring to their rounded hilltops.

Depart from Trier to the south and drive to Konz, where the Saar flows into the Mosel. Turn left onto the road immediately before the Saar crossing. The road follows the Saar's first big loop (Hamm) and crosses the river at Kanzem.

Kanzem, Wiltingen and Oberemmel

Kanzemer Altenberg is a historic vineyard that has been revived in recent decades and the Rieslings are very concentrated and individual in character. Further south, just before Wiltingen, there is a remarkable vineyard, **Wiltinger Braune Kupp**, on a steep hill above the railway line. From Wiltingen the next stop has to be the Scharzberg hill, and **Scharzhofberg**, which is the choice part of the vineyard. This is one of the five greatest vineyards in the whole Mosel wine region. Further along the road is another village and a great vineyard on a round hill, **Oberemmeler Hütte.**

Ayl and Ockfen

Returning to the Saar river follow the sign to Ayl, whose great vineyard is Ayler Kupp, a long steep hill facing south. Crossing the river again and turning left takes you to the **Ockfener Bockstein** vineyard, which has a unique style and quality.

WINERIES & MORE

AYL

Weingut Peter Lauer
Trierstrasse 49
54441 Ayl
Tel: 06581 3031
www.saarriesling.de

KANZEN

Weingut von Othergraven
Weinstrasse 1
54441 Kanzem
Tel: 06501 150042
www.von-othegraven.de

KONZ-OBEREMMEL

Weingut von Hövel
Agritiusstrasse 5-6
54329 Konz-Oberemmel
Tel: 0650 15384
www.weingut-vonhoevel.de

WILTINGEN

Weingut Egon Müller-Scharzhof
54459 Wiltingen
Tel: 06501 17232
www.scharzhof.de

Serrig

Schloss Saarfelser Schlossberg vineyard at Serrig comes into view. It is the name of both a vineyard and an estate, as is Schloss Saarstein, where the panorama from the castle above the vineyards and the river is memorable with these west-facing vines, especially in the evening sunshine. This is the most southerly wine village in the Saar valley. Serrig's name derives from the Latin *Serviacum*, referring to the Roman Servius, who is said to have founded the settlement and planted the first vines at the Herrenberg site.

WINERIES & MORE

SAARBURG

Weingut Forstmeister Gelz-Zilliken
Heckingstrasse 20
54439 Saarburg
Tel: 06581 2456
www.zilliken-vdp.de

SERRIG

Weingut Schloss Saarstein
54455 Serrig an der Saar
Tel: 06581 2324
www.saarstein.de

Saarburg

Saarburg is a picturesque town of half-timbered and Baroque buildings, old gates and towers. A brook runs through the town's lanes, forming a steep waterfall that once powered the mills. You can visit the **Mabilon bell foundry museum**, on Staden 130. For a panoramic view, visit the fortress overlooking the town. There are two great vineyards above the town, **Saarburger Rausch** and **Kupp**.

The Klause (hermitage) at the top of the cliff at Kastel-Staadt was built from 1834-1835 as a tomb for the blind King Johann of Bohemia (1296-1346). Kastel-Staadt is on the opposite side of the Saar river from Serrig but there is no bridge, so you must take the road south from Saarburg on the west side.

"Three-country corner"

From the mouth of the Saar to Perl is one of the areas where mass-produced Mosel wines are made, and includes the border between Germany and Luxembourg as the Mosel flows peacefully past orchards, forests, farms and vineyards. The Roman villa in Nennig has the most beautiful Roman mosaic tile floors north of the Alps. From here, you can enjoy 40 km (25 miles) of idyllic landscape as the Mosel gently loops towards Trier.

A view across the Saar river to the famous Ayler Kupp vineyard.

REGIONAL WINE PROMOTION BOARD

Mosel-Saar-Ruwer Wein
Gartenfeldstrasse 12a
54295 Trier
Tel: 0651 710280
www.weinland-mosel.de

Their Weinreiseführer
(wine travel guide)
Lists events and wine estates
(in German, with pictograms).

WINERIES & MORE

LIESER

Weingut Schloss Lieser
Am Martk 1-5
54470 Lieser
Tel: 06531 6431
www.weingut-schloss-lieser.de

MERTESDORF

Weingut Maximin Grünhaus Schlosskellerei C von Schubert
Haupstrasse 1
54318 Mertesdorf
Tel: 0651 5111
Contact:
Dr. C von Schubert
www.vonschubert.de

Schloss Saarstein at Serrig, the most southerly village in the Saar Valley.

WHERE TO STAY AND EAT

Alf

Burg Arras (H/R)
56859 Alf
Tel: 06542 22275
www.arras.de
Castle hotel at the top of a hill. The view of the Mosel is magnificent. Ten rooms with a restaurant serving local food.

Bömers Mosellandhotel (H/R)
Ferdinand-Remy-Strasse 27
56859 Alf
Tel: 06542 2310
www.boemershotel.de
Thirty-five rooms.

Ayl

Restaurant & Weinhotel Ayler Kupp (H/R)
Trierstrasse 49
54441 Ayl
Tel: 06581 3031
www.lauer-ayl.de
Ten very nice rooms, restaurant, Ayler Kupp, serves regional meals and five-course gourmet dinners with selected wines from Weingut Peter Lauer or "Weingut's menu," and a four-course menu with their wines. Wine tastings. Highly recommended.

Bernkastel-Kues

Doctor Weinstuben (H/R/W)
Hebegasse 5
54470 Bernkastel-Kues
Tel: 06531 96650
www.doctor-weinstuben.de

Dreis

Waldhotel Sonnara (H/R)
Auf dem Eichelfeld 1
54518 Dreis (12 km/7 miles northeast of Piesport)
Tel: 06578 98220
www.hotel-sonnora.de
Twenty elegant rooms. Three-star Michelin restaurant, with fabulous food and superb wines.

Mertesdorf (Ruwer)

Hotel Weingut Weis (H/R)
Eitelsbacher Strasse 4
54318 Mertesdorf (Ruwer)
Tel: 0651 9 56 10
www.hotel-weis.de
Family hotel with 47 rooms. Comfortable restaurant and *Weinstube*. Situated at the foot of steep Ruwer vineyards.

Grünhäuser Mühle (R)
Hauptstrasse 4
54318 Mertesdorf (Ruwer)
Tel: 0651 52434
Restaurant with classic French cuisine and Breton dishes from the owner's home region.

Mülheim

Weinromantikhotel Richtershof (H/R)
Haupstrasse 81-83
54486 Mülheim
Tel: 06534 9480
www.weinromantikhotel.de
Forty-three attractive rooms, bistro bar with light bites and "the best breakfast in the world." Elegant gourmet restaurants including Culinarum R. Fine food and great wines.

Domizil Schiffmann (H/R)
Hauptstrasse 52
54486 Mülheim
Tel: 06534 947690
www.domizil-schiffmann.de
A modern and practical hotel with 18 rooms (most with balconies) and excellent service. Good restaurant.

Hotel Weisser Bär (H/R)
Moselstrasse 7
54486 Mülheim
Tel: 06534 947700
www.hotel-weisser-baer.de
Hotel with 33 rooms and terrace overlooking the Mosel. Good wines and traditional food.

Beyond the bridge lies the vineyard of Piesporter Goldtröpfchen.

Naurath/Wald

Landhaus St Urban (H/R)
Büdlicherbrück 1
54426 Naurath/Wald
Tel: 06509 91400
www.landhaus-st-urban.de
Fourteen rooms, idyllic setting, 8 km (5 miles) south of Trittenheim/Leiwen. Gourmet restaurant (Chef Harald Rüssel), classic French cuisine and wonderful wines.

Piesport

Schanz Hotel (H/R/W)
Bahnhofstrasse 8a
54498 Piesport
Tel: 06507 92520
www.schanz-hotel.de
Family-run hotel with 12 rooms. Good food. Good value.

Saarburg

Hotel Villa Keller (H/R)
Brückenstrasse 1
54439 Saarburg
Tel: 06581 92910
www.villa-keller.de
Elegant 1801 villa with 11 rooms. Restaurant with international and regional food. Close to Saar river.

Burg Restaurant (R)
Auf dem Burgberg 1
54439 Saarburg
Tel: 06581 2622
www.burgrestaurant-saarburg.de
Castle dating from AD 964. Restaurant at top of tower with wonderful view of Saar valley.

Trier

Becker's Weinhaus (H/R)
Olewiger Strasse 206
54295 Trier
Tel: 0651 93 8080
www.beckers-trier.de
Thirty-two rooms. Modern-style restaurant, open evenings only. Becker's *Weinstube* and restaurant (at the same address) has welcoming atmosphere and service.

Restaurant Palais Kesselstatt (R/W)
Liebfrauenstrasse 10
54290 Trier
Tel: 0651 4 02 04
www.restaurant-kesselstatt.de
Gourmet dining in the palace after 5:45PM. Wine tasting in historic cellar.

Weinstube Palais Kesselstatt (R)
Libfrauenstrasse 10
54290 Trier
Tel: 0651 41178
www.weinstube-kesselstatt.de
Rustic, friendly *Weinstube*, with tree-shaded terrace in summer (closed Feb).

Cumvino (R)
Weberbach 75
54290 Trier
Tel: 0651 979409-40
www.cumvino-trier.de
Modern wine restaurant and *vinoteque* set up in former buildings of Wilhelm Gymnasium Estate, now integrated with the Bischhöfliche Weingüter.

Trittenheim village and a great loop of the Mosel seen from the Leiwener Klostergarten vineyard.

Klosterschenke (H/R)
Klosterstrasse 10
54293 Trier (left bank bank of Mosel)
Tel: 0651 96 84 40
www.hotel-klosterschenke.de
Lovely hotel with 11 rooms in 800-year-old monastery. Restaurant with terrace on river bank. (Bicycle path *Moselfahrradweg* starts here.)

Blesius Garten (H/R)
Olewiger Strasse 135
54295 Trier
Tel: 0651 36060
www.blesius-garten.de
Close to center of town. Beautiful 18th century hotel, 62 rooms. Restaurant Wintergarten, international cuisine, and microbrewery.

Trittenheim

Wein & Tafelhaus (H/R)
Moselpromenade 4
54349 Trittenheim
Tel: 06507 70 28 03
www.wein-tafelhaus.de
Guest house with nicely decorated rooms. Fine restaurant with original and traditional menus.

Gästehaus Weingut Bernhard Eifel (H/W)
Laurentiusstrasse 17
54349 Trittenheim
Tel: 06507 59 72
www.weingut-bernhard-eifel.de
Five rooms. Delightful *Weinstube*. International food. Wines from their own vineyards.

THE NAHE

THE NAHE IS A QUIET REGION situated in the Hunsrück Hills between the Mosel and Rhine valleys. The majority of the most important vineyards are quite close to the course of the Nahe river from Kirn east to Bad Kreuznach and then north to Bingen, where it joins the Rhine. The vineyards further afield are very scattered, and most of them are on gently rolling hills. The grape varieties are of less interest to a wine lover, so you'll need a good map to find the best estates and vineyards. You can follow the *Weinwanderweg Nahe* hiking trail, with its historic towns and castle ruins, or drive along the 130-km (81-mile) circular route of the *Naheweinstrasse* (Nahe Wine Road). Simply follow the signs with a Römer wine glass symbol bearing the letter "N." The unique wine festival *Rund um die Naheweinstrasse* takes place in late August and early September, when 30 villages on the wine road simultaneously celebrate wine for three consecutive weekends.

Nahewein ein Edelstein

This, the region's traditional slogan, is displayed on signposts at the edge of every wine village. It means "Nahe wine is a jewel," and refers not only to its high quality, but also to the region's mineral wealth. The hills are full of tunnels where copper, silver and mercury were once mined. Idar-Oberstein is the center of Germany's precious stone industry, and is quite close to Nahe's western vineyards.

The Romans were probably the first to cultivate grapes here, judging by the Roman wine jugs and tools found near Bad Kreuznach. Deeds of gift to the Lorsch monastery (near the Bergstrasse) contain the first written mention of winegrowing in the region (AD 766). The Church and the aristocracy expanded the vineyard area to nearly

« House at the old Egg Market of Bad Kreuznach is now a café and bar.

Daubach
Sponheim
Bockenau
Auen
Burgsponheim
B421
Waldböckelheim
Idar-Oberstein
Martinstein
Kirn
Monzingen
Merxheim
Sobernheim
Meddersheim
Nahe
Odernheim
Glan
N
S
E
W
Meisenheim
B420

B9
Rhein (Rhine)
Bingerbrück
Bingen
Münster-Sarmsheim
Genheim
Waldlaubersheim
Burg Layen
Dorsheim
Nahe
Laubenheim
B48
Windesheim
Langenlonsheim
Guldentai
Bretzenheim
Bad Kreuznach
Traisen
Bad Münster am Stein
Ebernburg
B48
Altenbamberg
B420
Hochstätten
Niederhausen
Alsenz
Alsenz

Emrich-Schönleber
2010
Halenberg
Riesling
GG
Nahe
750 ml

JAKOB
SCHNEIDER
2010
Niederhäuser Hermannshöhle
Riesling trocken
MAGNUS

Emrich-Schönleber
2010
Monzinger Frühlingsplätzchen
Riesling Spätlese
Alc. 9,5% vol
Nahe
750 ml

DÖNNHOFF
Oberhäuser Leistenberg
Riesling Kabinett
2010
alc. 8,5 % vol.
NAHE
750 ml e

DIEL
RIESLING
GG
BURGBERG

prinzsalm
2009 RIESLING GRÜNSCHIEFER

WEINGUT IM
SCHLOSS
WALLHAUSEN

3000 hectares (7414 acres) during the Middle Ages.

Viticulture suffered a great decline from the 16th to the 18th century, when vast tracts of land were laid waste by wars. Recovery started slowly in the 19th century and was greatly enhanced at the turn of the century by the founding of a winegrowers' school in Bad Kreuznach. The State Wine Domain in Niederhausen was built in 1902 and the hills were cleared of rocks, trees and scrub by prisoners of the Prussian State. It was a model of quality wine production. Eventually it was handed over to the Rheinland-Pfalz State, which decided to privatize it, and the Maurer family bought it in 1998. It is now Gut Hermannsberg.

Although the Nahe is one of the smaller wine regions (4135 hectares/ 10,218 acres), the vineyards are intermittent and widely spread over the hills and valleys. This accounts for the large number of different *terroirs*. Racy, piquant wines with a fine fruit come from slate, quartzite, volcanic and stony soils on steep hills. The gentle slopes and flatlands with heavier clay, loam and loess soils, often mixed with sand and gravel, produce milder, ordinary wines. A layer of red sandstone runs sporadically through the region, adding another dimension to the wines of some of the villages.

Grape varieties

Riesling (26 per cent of the vineyards) is the most important variety, especially from slate, quartzite and

Bottles in a wine shop at Schlossböckelheim, near Bad Kreuznach.

volcanic soils on steep hills. Silvaner, Grauburgunder, and Weissburgunder are also very successful, while Spätburgunder is gradually being planted more widely. Mild Müller-Thurgau (13 per cent) is still planted on the soft hills and flat areas in the Liebfraumilch style. The quality of the deep red Dornfelder variety is very encouraging here.

Local wine glasses

Two wine glasses are typical of the region: the *Römer*, also called *Pokal*, and the Nahe's own *Remis'chen*, a straight-sided tumbler. Both hold 0.2 liters (c. one third of a pint).

Regional specialties

Füllselkartoffeln: minced liver, ground pork and cubed potatoes are seasoned with marjoram and cooked together. Also used to stuff:

Schwenk- or Schaukelbraten spiced steaks, usually pork, roasted by swinging (*schwenken* or *schaukeln*) the grill over a fire.

Spansau roast sucking pig.

Spiessbraten shoulder of pork sprinkled with chopped onion and spices, rolled and then roasted on a spit.

REGIONAL WINE PROMOTION BOARD

Weinland Nahe
Burgenlandstrasse 7
55543 Bad Kreuznach
Tel: 0671 834050
www.weinland-nahe.de

Bad Kreuznach

Bad Kreuznach is the center of the Nahe's 2000-year-old wine culture. Located at the junction of ancient trade routes, it has been settled since Celtic times and was part of the Roman Empire for more than 400 years.

For centuries, Bad Kreuznach has been famous for its salubrious salt-water springs and mild climate. Part of today's spa facilities date from 1743, when the first two of six graduated timber framework *Salinen* (salterns) were completed. They are still visually the most striking aspect of the spa. People sit or walk by the structures and inhale the vapors from the salt water, which evaporates as it is pumped over the framework. The springs became popular as

This family-owned winery used to belong to the State Wine Domain.

medicinal baths in the 19th century and even more so after the turn of the century, when the presence of radon gas was believed to aid the cure of rheumatoid, circulatory and respiratory ailments. The neo-Baroque **Kurhaus** (1913) is the center of the spa, idyllically set in the Kurpark on the banks of the Nahe river. From April to October, there is an inviting *Weinstube*, Elisabeth Quelle, in the park. Needless to say, German doctors tend to be passionate about spas for their patients, but some doctors elsewhere are dubious about their effectiveness.

The wines

Bad Kreuznach used to be famous equally for its wine and its waters. Many of the growers' and merchants' cellars were in Kreuznach, but now there are a handful of estates with Riesling vineyards on gently sloping sites. In the meantime some of the wine dealers disappeared and Kreuznach growers sold their sites for the expansion of the town. **Kreuznacher Brückes** and **Kahlenberg** are the best vineyards and the wines have real quality.

There is a fine view of Bad Kreuznach from the ruins of the 12th-century **Kauzenburg fortress** (now a hotel restaurant). In the grounds of the botanical park below, there is a museum of prehistory in the Schloss (palace) and in the **Römerhalle** (Romans' Hall where) you can see Roman artifacts and mosaics. A Roman villa has been reconstructed nearby. There is a precious gilded reliquary in the **St Nikolaus Church**, an early Gothic basilica, and historic half-timbered houses in the old town near the Eiermarkt (egg market).

Bridge houses

The **Faust-Haus**, next to the Wilhelms-Brücke (bridge), is today a *Weinstube* with mementoes of the infamous magician, Dr. Faust, who lived there in 1507. Cross the Nahe on the Alte Nahebrücke (bridge built in 1311) to see the unusual *Brückenhäuser* (bridge houses) built on piles in the river. In the background is the Baroque tower of **St Paulus Church**, where Karl Marx was married in 1843.

WINE ESTATE

BAD KREUZNACH

Weingut Korrell Johanneshof
Parkstrasse 4
55545 Bad Kreuznach
Tel: 0671 63630
www.korrell.com

The Alsenz and Glan Valleys

Vineyards are also scattered throughout the side valleys of the tributaries of the Nahe. The Alsenz flows into the Nahe where it bends west at Ebernburg and where the fortress ruins of Altenbamberg overlook a fine vineyard, **Altenbamberger Rotenberg**. Riesling is the main grape here and Silvaner is common further south. There is also a fine panorama from the fortress ruins of Moschellandsburg, or from the Burg Hotel near Obermoschel. Meisenheim on the Glan has retained its medieval townscape, with historic houses on Ober- and Untergasse. The late Gothic **Schlosskirche** (church) has many works of art, remarkable sculpted tombs, and an organ made by the Stumm family.

Near Odernheim, at the mouth of the Glan, the monastery ruins dominate the famous vineyard **Odernheimer Kloster Disibodenberg**. In the 7th century, on the site where Celts had once worshipped, the Irish monk St Disibod founded a monastery. It was greatly expanded in the Middle Ages under the fascinating Abbess St Hildegard of Bingen, the mystic famous for her music and her scientific and medical writings.

WINE AND FOLK FESTIVALS

Kreuznacher Jahrmarkt Fri–Tue, 3rd weekend of Aug at Pfingstwiese, north edge of town. Annually, since 1361.

Nordpfälzer Herbstfest Mid-Sep in Rockenhausen, south of Bad Kreuznach via B 48. Features Alsenz valley wines.

Medieval festival

Held on the 3rd weekend of Sep in the old town center of Ebernburg. With costumes, jousts, a parade of knights, grilled meats, fish and local wines. Historic ambience.

The Middle Nahe

The *Naheweinstrasse* (Nahe Wine Road), which takes you from Bad Kreuznach to Schlossböckelheim, includes the Nahe's most dramatic scenery and many hiking trails through the forests and hills that enable you to see rare fauna and flora.

The steep vineyards have excellent exposure to the sun and the soils are mixtures of loam with sand, slate, loess, gravel or volcanic stone over substrata of porphyry or sandstone, rich in minerals and heat-retaining properties. The Nahe river tempers the climate and acts as a sun reflector. All in all, these are ideal growing conditions, yielding top-quality wines with fruit, spicy undertones, pronounced acidity and long-lasting flavors.

Riesling is the main grape variety. The steep Riesling vineyard **Münsterer Felseneck** (cliff corner) rises up on the right as you approach the town of Bad Münster am Stein, where there is yet another spa, in an 18th-century half-timbered house situated at the foot of the precipitous Rheingrafenstein. Historic buildings include the **Zehntscheuer** (1560), the barn where the tithes were stored, and the **Fischerhaus** (1561) on the riverbank. For a fine view from the ruins of the 12th-century fortress, you should take the hand-operated **ferry across the river to ascend Rheingrafenstein** (half an hour's walk). Drive or walk (half an hour) to the fortress **Burg Ebernburg** for a

The 15th-century Brückenhäuser (bridge houses) in Bad Kreuznach were built on the even older Alte Nahebrücke (old Nahe bridge).

good view of the rustic old town, the church with an 11th-century defense tower.

The Rotenfels cliff

On the left bank of the Nahe, Rotenfels is a porphyry cliff and the highest rock face (180 m/591ft) in mainland Europe north of the Alps. **Traisener Bastei**, a terraced vineyard at the bottom of the cliff by the river, and the **Rotenfels** vineyard higher up yield wines that are among the finest of the Nahe region. To get there, drive from Traisen village to the car park and then walk to the edge of the precipice. Norheim is mentioned in a deed of gift to Lorsch monastery in AD 766, and today there are three fine vineyards, **Norheimer Dellchen, Kafels and Kirschheck**.

The village of Schlossböckelheim has two remarkable vineyards, **Schlossböckelheimer Felsenberg** and **Kupfer-**

grube (an ancient copper mine discovered when State Wine Domain prisoners were clearing the hill). This area has a considerable amount of volcanic rocks in the soil, which gives the wines a distinctive flavor and quality.

Niederhausen's 12th-century church boasts frescoes and wall paintings with grape motifs. It has a plethora of great vineyards: **Niederhausener Felsensteyer, Hermannsberg, Hermannshöhle, Kertz** and **Klamm.**

The *Weinwanderweg*, a 5-km (3-mile) marked path through the vineyards, starts at the school on the edge of town nearest Gut Hermannsberg. Cross the Nahe on Luitpoldbrücke (bridge, 1889) to Oberhausen, an old wine town with two great vineyards: **Oberhausener Brücke** and **Leistenberg.**

EXCURSION VIA FEILBINGER

For the best view of Niederhausen, drive via Feilbingert (on the other side of the river) to the Nahe's highest hill, the Lemberg (422 m/1385 ft). Nearby, you can visit Schmittenstollen, a former mercury mine, or see the ruins of Burg Monfort, once the fortress of notorious robber-knights.

WINERIES & MORE

NIEDERHAUSEN

Gut Hermannsberg
55585 Niederhausen-Nahe
Tel: 06758 92500
www.gut-hermannsberg.de

Weingut Jacob Schneider
Winzerstrasse 15
55585 Niederhausen
Tel: 06758 93533
www.schneider-wein.com

TRAISEN

Weingut Dr Crusius
Haupstrasse 2
55595 Traisen
Tel: 0671 33953
www.weingut-crusius.de

The Upper Nahe

As the *Naheweinstrasse* continues westwards, the valley broadens out, and the river flows at a more leisurely pace. There are vineyards on both sides of the Nahe, but they are not always visible from the road. The steep sites near Meddersheim or Merxheim, for

A decorative welcome to Rüdesheim (Nahe).

example, are behind the villages, situated on south-facing hillsides for optimum exposure to the sun.

After crossing the Nahe at its westernmost wine town, Martinstein, the route passes through rolling hills bordered by the Soonwald (Soon Forest), once the realm of the ribald bandit Schinderhannes (the Nahe's Robin Hood) and other folk heroes. The vineyards here are on steep or sloping hills, scattered among fields, orchards and woods. The wine villages are ancient, charming in their rustic simplicity, and most have churches worth visiting.

Bad Sobernheim

The town is yet another health resort known for mud bath cures (named after their proponent, Pastor Felke), with many interesting buildings, above all the **St Matthias Church**, with its star-vaulted choir, frescoes and Stumm organ. South of the town, the open-air **Freilichtmuseum** shows the architecture and way of life typical of country villages centuries ago.

A UNIQUE REFRESHER

Barfusspfad (barefoot path), a 3.5-km (2-mile) walk on different surfaces (eg grass, sand, stones, clay); crosses the Nahe river twice (ferry and via a ford). There are lockers for your shoes at the start of the path: Quellenpavillon Bad Sobernheim. **www.quellenpavillon.de**

Meddersheim to Monzingen

Meddersheim has a Renaissance town hall and a richly furnished Protestant church, as well as farmhouses and courtyards dating from the 16th and 17th centuries. En route to Merxheim you will pass the **Rheingrafenberg** (cooperative winery with shop), named after the town's best vineyard site. Merxheim also has its historic houses and the Neues Schloss Birkenfeld (18th-century palace) is the rectory of the Catholic church.

At Martinstein the route crosses the Nahe to Monzingen. This village is so far to the west that the wines were unknown until the 1990s. Today, the two top-quality vineyards are acknowledged to be among the finest in the Nahe: the wines from the **Monzinger Halenberg** have a pronounced mineral style from blue slate and quarzite soil, while **Frühlingsplätzchen** wines have elegance and charm from red slate and pebbles. The village has half-timbered houses said to be the prettiest in the region, particularly the **Alt'sche Haus** (1589) on Kirchstrasse 2.

Ellerbach valley

The route leaves the Nahe and winds through the forest past Auen and Daubach. On the way you can see the Willigiskapelle (chapel) built in AD 1000 and the grave of the legendary Jäger aus der Kurpfalz (Hunter of the Pfalz).

The Ellerbachtal (valley) is very hilly, with vineyards on steep slopes. St Laurentius Church in Bockenau, an old potters' village, is notable for its remarkable high altar. The best vineyard here is **Bockenauer Felseneck**. For a good view of the valley, visit the ruins of the ancestral castle of the Counts of Sponheim in Burgsponheim. The masonry of the main tower (22 m/72 ft high) is exemplary for its time. Equally impressive is the monumental Romanesque church on the hilltop of Sponheim. Next to the church, the ruins of the Benedictine monastery can also be visited.

The edge of the Soon Forest

The vineyards near Mandel, **St Katharinen** and **Braunweiler** at the edge of the Soon Forest are less steep and sadly Müller-Thurgau is the main grape. The *Naheweinstrasse* continues north and east, to wine towns in the Gräfenbach and Guldenbach valleys and along the lower stretch of the Nahe river. Notable wine towns which are not directly on the *Naheweinstrasse* include Waldböckelheim, where Silvaner wines are said to be a speciality. Roxheim has a steep Riesling vineyard, **Roxheimer Berg**, which has a very good reputation. Riesling, Silvaner and Scheurebe are planted in Hüffelsheim and Rüdesheim (not to be confused with Rüdesheim on the Rhine). The wines are simple and enjoyable.

WINERIES & MORE

MEDDERSHEIM

Weingut Hexamer
Sobernheimer Strasse 3
55566 Meddersheim
Tel: 06751 2269
www.weingut-hexamer.de

The black cat of Ebernburg

The schwarze katz (black cat) of Zell/Mosel is probably the best-known cat in German wine mythology. But the town of Ebernburg also has its schwarze katz.

In the old days, coopers who worked for a wine estate were allowed to make their own wine, for free, from the grape must left over after the first pressings. The resulting wine was, however, of lower quality.

One cooper decided to improve his situation at the expense of the estate owner. He developed the habit of tapping the kegs of the estate's better wines, and replacing the difference with his own inferior wine. The reputation of the estate's wines suffered as a result and the owner resolved to catch the thief.

He let loose a black cat in the cellars. It slept, invisible in the darkness, on the warm barrels of fermenting must. When the cooper crept in to make his customary switch, the startled cat sprang out at him from the darkness and a great commotion ensued. The cooper, caught red-handed, confessed and was locked up for a short time.

After his release he could not forego his old ways and was again caught with the help of the black cat.

This time, however, he was hanged and his head placed on spikes before the estate's cellars as a warning to others. The black cat stayed on, ever vigilant, and became a symbol of pure, unadulterated wine.

The Lower Nahe

The lower Nahe includes the wine villages north and northwest of Bad Kreuznach. The vineyards lie along the valleys of three small tributaries of the Nahe – Gräfenbach, Guldenbach and Trollbach – and include the vineyards on the left bank of the Nahe. The steeper slopes are normally reserved for Riesling, while Silvaner and Müller-Thurgau are planted on the gentler slopes and flatlands. The word *Sonne* (sun) appears frequently in vineyard names, alluding to their southern exposure.

Gräfenbach valley

Wallhausen is an old wine village at the foot of the Soon Forest. The layer of colored sandstone below the loamy soil gives the wines a pronounced fruity bouquet and character. Wallsheimer Felseneck and Johannisberg are very good sites. **Schloss Wallhausen** is the home of one of the oldest winegrowing families of Germany, whose vineyard holdings date from the 13th century. The present head of the family is Prince Michael zu Salm-Salm, who was the president of the VDP. A *Rotweinfest* (red wine festival) takes place at the castle annually in May.

The Nahe flows past the town of Bingen into the Rhine (foreground).

The Catholic church near the castle has many elaborate gravestones, and there are historic houses on the Im Schafwinkel Street. The ruins of the 13th-century **Schloss** (castle) **Gutenburg** are nearby, and you can walk up to it for a good view and to see the defense wall between the two battle-scarred towers. The market square, called the **Plagge**, is the site of a wine festival and parade, and the Gothic cellars of the fortress are open to all.

Guldenbach Valley

Guldental produces ordinary Müller-Thurgau and Silvaner wines. The village has a historic fountain (1584) and a 15th-century church with a Romanesque tower. Windesheim is renowned for fine organs made by the Oberlinger family. Its church has interesting paintings on its wooden ceiling.

At Schweppenhausen, make a slight detour from the *Naheweinstrasse* to visit the 12th-century fortress of **Stromburg**, today a hotel and gourmet restaurant. The terrace affords a good view. A famous hero of the Thirty Years' War lived here, *der deutsche Michel*, a term used today to denote a valiant person.

To the north of the confluence of the Guldenbach and the Nahe there are three very good vineyards: **Langenlonsheimer Rothenberg**, **Königsschild** and **Löhre Berg**; and further north, another three: **Laubenheimer Karthäuser**, **Krone** and **St Remigiusberg**.

Trollbach Valley

Returning to the wine road, drive through the 8th-century wine villages of Genheim and Waldlaubersheim to Burg Layen, with its picturesque castle tower (1200) on the hill overlooking one of the villages. Burg Layen is adjacent to Dorsheim, where Riesling and Weiss-, Grau- and Spätburgunder grape varieties are planted. The vineyards are **Dorsheimer Goldloch, Pittermännchen** and **Burgberg**, each with a very different terroir. Armin Diel, one of the most important wine writers in Germany, owns parts of all three. The bizarre reddish-brown cliffs are named Kamel (camel), Kaffeekanne (coffee pot) and Eierfelsen (egg cliffs).

Munster-Sarmsheim

Stony loam over slate and quartzite soils, like those of Rüdesheim just across the Rhein, give lively, robust Riesling wines from the sloping vineyards close to the mouth of the Nahe. Münster-Sarmsheim has three great vineyards: **Dautenpflänzer, Pittersberg** and **Rheinberg**.

WINERIES & MORE

BURG LAYEN

Schlossgut Diel
55452 Burg Layen
Tel: 06721 96950
www.schlossgut-diel.com

Weingut Joh. Bapt. Schäfer
Burg Layen 8
55452 Burg Layen
Tel: 06721 43552
www.jbs-wein.de

MÜNSTER-SARMSHEIM

Weingut Kruger-Rumpf
Rheinstrasse 47
55424 Münster-Sarmsheim
Tel: 06721 43859
www.kruger-rumpf.com

Weingut Göttelmann
Rheinstrasse 77
55424 Münster-Sarmsheim
Tel: 06721 43775
goetellmannwein@aol.com

WINDESHEIM

Weingut Lindenhof-Martin Reimann
55452 Windesheim
Tel: 06707 330
www.weingutlindenhof.de

WALLHAUSEN

Prinz zu Salm-Salm
Schlossstrasse 3
55595 Wallhausen

The Luitpold bridge was built over the Nahe in 1849 on the road to Oberhausen, and is named for Prince Luitpold of Bavaria.

Tel: 06706 94440
www.prinzsalm.de

LANGENLONSHEIM

Weingut Bürgermeister Willi Schweinhardt Nachfolger
Heddesheimer Strasse 1
55450 Langenlonsheim
Tel: 06704 93100
www.schweinhardt.de

OBERHAUSEN

Weingut Hermann Dönnhoff
Bahnhofstrasse 11
55585 Oberhausen
Tel: 06755 263
www.doennhoff.de

BOCKENAU

Weingut Schäfer-Fröhlich
Schulstrasse 6
55595 Bockenau
Tel: 06758 6521
www.weingut-schaefer-froehlich.de

MONZINGEN

Weingut Emrich-Schönleber
Soonwaldstrasse 10a
55569 Monzingen
Tel: 06751 2733
www.emrich-schoenleber.com

WINE AND ART

Schlossgut Diel
55452 Burg Layen
Tel: 06721 96950
www.schlossgut-diel.com
The Burg Layen castle has belonged to the Diel family since 1802 and the present owner is Armin Diel. This is a prestigious wine estate. In the 1980s, artist Johannes Helle turned everything from the cellars to the vineyards into a work of art. (Tours by appointment.)

FOR CYCLING FANS

The *Radweg Nahe* is a 60-km (37-mile) marked bicycle route from Bingen to Kirn.

WHERE TO STAY AND EAT

Bad Kreuznach

Im Kittchen (R)
Alte Poststrasse 2
55545 Bad Kreuznach
Tel: 0671 9200811
Small restaurant. Evenings only. Brilliant food.

Die Stomburg (H/R)
Schlossburg Strasse 1
55442 Stromberg
Tel: 06724 931 00,
www.johannlafer.de
In Johann Lafer's Stromburg (beautifully restored 16th-century castle). Hotel with 14 rooms. Michelin-starred restaurant Le Val d'Or. Classic and modern cuisine. Superb food and wines, plus good regional cuisine in Bistro d'Or, in a lovely setting.

Kauzenberg mit Landhotel (H/R)
Auf dem Kauzenberg 1
55545 Bad Kreuznach
Tel: 0671 3 80 00
www.kauzenberg.de
Lovely, quiet hotel, 45 rooms. Castle restaurant two minutes away.

Bad Sobernheim

BollAnt's im Park (H/R)
Felkestrasse 100
55566 Bad Sobernheim
Tel: 06751 93390
www.bollants.de
Splendid traditional regional food and 66 very comfortable rooms. Two restaurants: Hermannshof, regional and mediterranian food; and Passione Rosso (separately managed, only evening), one Michelin star, Italian and regional food. Good wines in both restaurants

Guldental

Der Kaiserhof (H/R)
Hauptstrasse 2
55452 Guldental
Tel: 06707 94440
www.kaiserhof-guldental.de
Restaurant with good regional and international cuisines. Hotel has 13 rooms.

Meddersheim

Landgasthaus Zur Traube
Sobernheimer Strasse 2
55566 Meddersheim
Tel: 06751 950382
A beautiful historic inn

with good restaurant prices and regional food.

Münster-Sarmsheim

Weingut Kruger-Rumpf (W)
Rheinstrasse 47
55424 Münster-Sarmsheim
Tel: 06721 45050
www.kruger-rumpf.com
Lovely *Weinstube* with top quality wines, light lunches and delicious regional food in the evening.

The Rotenfels is the highest rock face in Europe north of the Alps.

THE RHEINGAU

THE RHEINGAU IS A RELATIVELY SMALL wine region with 3200 hectares (7907 acres) of vines, yet it is far more famous than the largest region, Rheinhessen, on the other side of the Rhine, which has 26,334 hectares (65,072 acres). There are eight great historical Rheingau estates and some 350 private growers that compete in producing fine Riesling and Spätburgunder wines.

The heart of the region borders the Rhine on its east-west course from Wiesbaden to Rüdesheim, with a broad ribbon of vineyards lining the hills from the river up to the forested summit of the Taunus Hills. Monasteries, manor houses and palaces bear witness to the traditions of affluence associated with winegrowing here for more than 1200 years.

It's easy to become acquainted with the area and its wines, thanks to three well-marked routes (driving, hiking and cycling) which wind through the grand landscape to nearly two dozen wine villages, many of which have open-air tasting stands. To meet growers informally, without an appointment, visit when estates "open the cellar door."

Viticulture in the Rheingau can be traced to Roman times, but the legacy of quality stems from the efforts of the Church in the Middle Ages. From the 11th to the 13th centuries, peasants cleared the forested slopes of the Taunus and planted them with vines. They were rewarded with their freedom, and the Rheingau became known as the land of farmers with civil rights.

It was in the economic interests of the ecclesiastical and noble estates to strive for high quality. For several hundred years they systematically improved methods of vine cultivation and winemaking, selling a proportion of their wines, thereby setting the high standards.

‹‹ Assmannshausen is an enclave of red wine grapes surrounded by white. Its steep vineyards are famous for their excellent Pinot Noir wines. The State of Hesse Wine Domain has the largest holding.

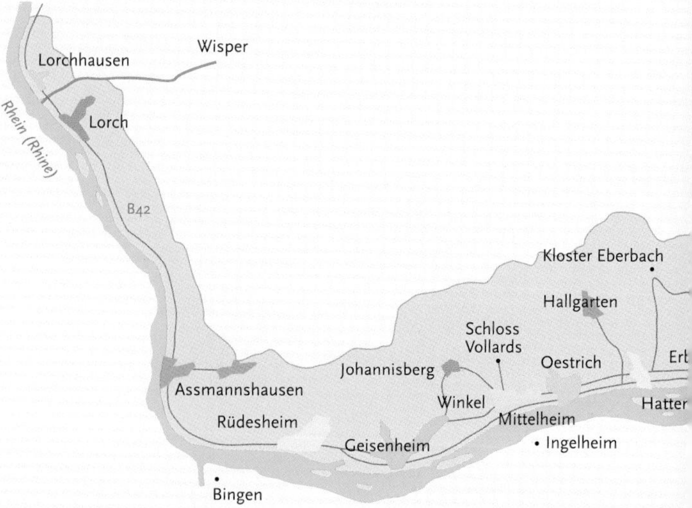
Wisper
Lorchhausen
Lorch
Rhein (Rhine)
B42
Kloster Eberbach
Hallgarten
Schloss
Vollards
Johannisberg
Oestrich
Erb
Assmannshausen
Winkel
Hatter
Rüdesheim
Mittelheim
Geisenheim
Ingelheim
Bingen

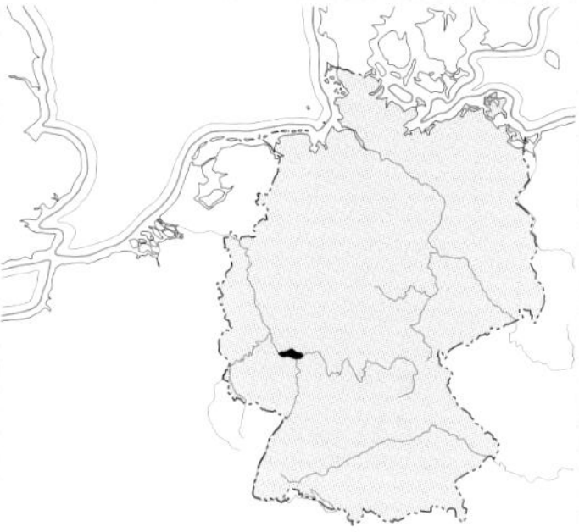

marcobrunn
SCHLOSS SCHÖNBORN
riesling
2010
ERSTES GEWÄCHS

Rheingau
Peter
Jakob Kühn
QUARZIT
2010 Riesling Trocken
alc. 12,0 % by vol.
750 ml

Fürst von Metternich
RHEINGAU
Schloss Johannisberger
2010er Riesling Kabinett Feinherb
ROTLACK

Balthasar Ress
2008
HATTENHEIM
ENGELMANNSBERG
RHEINGAU RIESLING
TROCKEN
750ML
11.5% alc. by vol.
BALTHASAR RESS

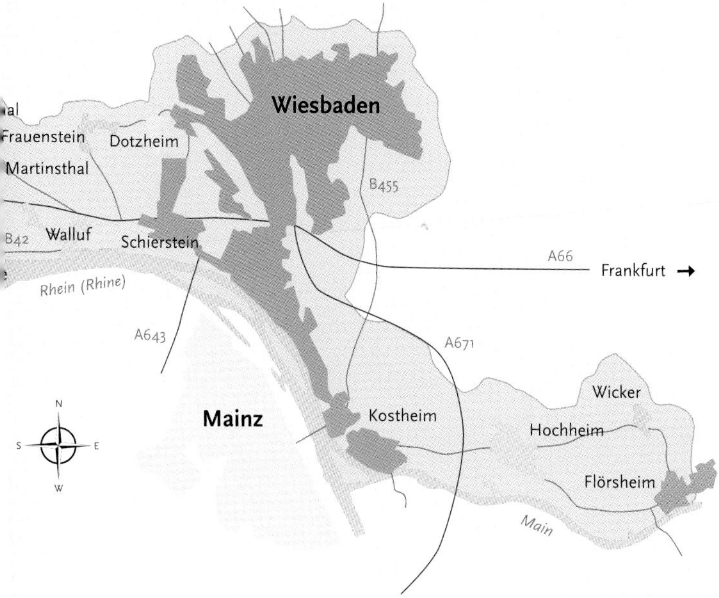
Wiesbaden
Frauenstein
Dotzheim
Martinsthal
B455
B42
Walluf
Schierstein
A66
Frankfurt →
Rhein (Rhine)
A643
A671
Wicker
Mainz
Kostheim
Hochheim
Flörsheim
Main
N
S
E
W

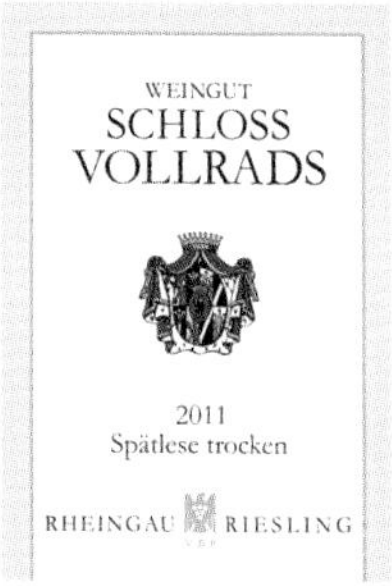
WEINGUT
SCHLOSS VOLLRADS
2011
Spätlese trocken
RHEINGAU RIESLING

Künstler
2008
HOCHHEIM
KIRCHENSTÜCK
RHEINGAU
ERSTES GEWÄCHS

WEINGUT
JOHANNISHOF
2006
Rüdesheimer
Berg Rottland
Rheingau Riesling
Auslese
alc. 10.5 % vol.
375 ml

2010er
Pfaffenberger
Gräflich Schoenborn'scher Eigenbau

KLOSTER EBERBACH
Cabinetkeller
2009er HÖLLENBERG
SPÄTBURGUNDER

Classic wine grapes

The Rheingau boasts the highest percentage of Riesling (79 per cent of vines) in all the regions of Germany, with Mosel second at 59 per cent. Before the 1930s some fine Riesling wines were matured for a longer time in barrels and were dry when they were bottled. In the late 1980s many styles of dry Rheingau Riesling were revived for drinking with food. By the end of the 20th century, these ranged from simple *Gutswein* (estate wine), to great concentrated dry *Erstes Gewächs* Riesling (an appellation unique to Rheingau), with around 13 degrees of alcohol. And of course Rheingau is still making the great traditional sweet Rieslings from Spätlese to Trockenbeerenauslese with 8 to 10 degrees of alcohol.

Spätburgunder has been important here since the 12th century, when the Cisterian monks brought the vines from Burgundy, and is now 13 per cent of vines in the Rheingau, the second highest percentage in the regions. Since global climate change became noticeable in Germany in 1989, dramatic progress has been made in quality.

Before then, Spätburgunder was a joke outside Germany. It was difficult for the grapes to reach full ripeness, so some wines were made as *Weissherbst* (admittedly a lovely pale rosé) or a rather insipid, slightly sweet red wine that was left for a short time with the skins and then kept for a while in large old oak barrels before bottling. Yields were also far too high. Today, the yields are greatly reduced, the fermentation with the skins is much longer, and the best wines are matured in oak *barriques* before developing in bottle for some years. These wines are velvety in texture and have an aroma with a hint of blackberry. Some have the subtlety of great Pinot Noir.

From east to west, the Rheingau's vineyards are increasingly steep and the soil structure changes from deep, rich soils to cliffs of quartzite and soft slate. Riesling planted on the gentle slopes from Hochheim to Hattenheim tends to show a rounder fruit and milder acidity than the firm, elegant wines

Schloss Vollrads, after 27 generations of ownership by the same family, was sold to the Nassauische Sparkasse bank in 1997.

from the steep sites or high on the hillsides some distance from the river, in particular, Rauenthal, Steinberg, Schloss Vollrads and Johannisberg.

REGIONAL WINE PROMOTION BOARD

Gesellschaft für Rheingauer Weinkultur mbH
Kloster Eberbach – Pfortenhaus
65346 Eltville am Rhein
Tel: 06723 91757
www.rheingauer-weinbauverband.de

RHEINGAU MUSIC FESTIVAL

Over 150 musical events staged in historic buildings, wine estates and riverboats (Jun–Aug). Historic buildings, wine estates and riverboats are the settings for spring and summer events.

For more information contact the regional promotion board or visit www.rheingau-music-festival.de

GLORREICHE RHEINGAU TAGE

Celebrates Rheingau wine and culture with gala culinary events and an auction (at which the wines are tasted): every Nov. www.rdp-rheingau.de/glorreiche.htm

Tag der offenen Weinkeller

This is "open house" at wine estates throughout the region. No appointment is necessary. The cellar doors are open for you to meet growers, visit cellars and sample wines. Late Apr to early May and two weekends in Sep, combined with Schlemmerwochen (gourmet food weeks), when you can try Rheingau specialties at estates and restaurants.

RHEINGAU GOURMET AND WINE FESTIVAL

(last week Feb, first week Mar)
Kronenschlösschen
Tel: 06723 640
www.kronenschloesschen.de

WINE ROUTES

Rheingauer Römer is the typical wine glass of the region and is prominent in the signs that mark the scenic driving, hiking and cycling routes.

Rheingauer Riesling Route is a 70-km (43-mile) autoroute through the entire region, from Wicker to Lorchhausen. Follow green signs with the Römer logo in white.

Rheingauer Riesling Pfad is a hiking trail (about 100 km/62 miles) from Wicker to Lorchhausen. It winds through forests and vineyards, past monuments and wine estates, with excellent panoramic views from the hilltops. Follow green signs with the Römer logo in gold.

Rheingauer Riesling Radwanderweg is a cycling route through the vineyards and along the Rhine. Signs bear the Römer and a bicycle.

Note: hiking and cycling trails also extend to Kaub.

This monument in Hochheim was dedicated to Queen Victoria in 1854. The vineyard had already been renamed Königin Victoriaberg.

The architecturally striking monks' dormitory at Kloster Eberbach, where it was bitterly cold in winter as there was no glass in the windows.

Hochheim to Wiesbaden

The most easterly wine villages of the Rheingau are just north of the Main river just before its confluence with the Rhine. The oldest reference to Riesling is an invoice dated 1435 from Klaus Kleinfisch for having delivered Riesling vines to Rüsselsheim castle, which was on the south side of the Main river opposite Hochheim.

Hochheim

Hochheim's Riesling wines rank among the finest of the Rheingau. The vineyards are on gentle slopes of deep chalky soils. Their proximity to the river and a good microclimate enable vines to ripen a week or two earlier than elsewhere in the region. The wines are stylish and full-bodied, with a balanced acidity. One of the best sites, **Hochheimer Domdechaney**, was created in the early 18th century by the Domdechanten (deans) of Mainz Cathedral, who had the swampy lowlands near Hochheim's church filled with earth and then planted with vines. The wines of **Hochheimer Kirchenstück** and **Hölle** exemplify this quality, though in different styles.

Queen Victoria and "Hock"

Queen Victoria is said to have recovered from an illness after drinking Riesling from the vineyard later named Hochheimer Königin Victoriaberg. The neo-Gothic (1854) monument dedicated to her stands in the middle of this riverside vineyard. Her enthusiasm for Hochheimer wines persuaded the English to use the word "Hock" as a short name for any wine from the Rhine, perhaps because they could not read the Gothic labels or understand German. Old Hochheim has charming half-timbered houses and cobbled alleyways. Two Baroque works of art are of interest – **the statue Madonna auf dem Plan on the market square** and the parish church overlooking the vineyards. The wine festival takes place in early July in the courtyards of the wine estates in Old Town.

Wicker, Flörsheim and Kostheim

There are three villages just to the east of Hochheim, but they are relatively unknown. Wicker is the *Tor zum Rheingau* (gateway to the Rheingau) and the start of the **Rheingauer Riesling Route**. On the western edge of town, the König-Wilhelm-Säule (monument to King Wilhelm, later Emperor) overlooks the vineyard bearing his name. In the vineyards between Wicker and Flörsheim via the Steinmühlenweg path, there is a historic (1496) watchtower in an idyllic setting.

A pruning knife found in a Roman villa unearthed near Flörsheim supports the assumption that the Romans grew grapes in the area. There is also an interesting Baroque church on the river bank. Kostheim was once an important woodworking center and the harbor for rafts laden with timber from the Franconian forests along the Main.

WINERIES & MORE

HOCHHEIM AM MAIN

Weingut Künstler
Geheimrat-Hummel-Platz 1a
65239 Hochheim am Main
Tel: 06146 83860
www.weingut-kuenstler.de

Domdechant Werner'sches Weingut
Rathausstrasse 30
65234 Hochheim am Main
Tel: 06146 835037
www.domdechantwerner.com

Wiesbaden has one tiny vineyard, Neroberg, and a park at the top of the hill above the Kurhaus. The funicular railway was built in 1888.

Wiesbaden to Rüdesheim

Wiesbaden is the capital of the State of Hesse and the largest town in the Rheingau, but is more famous for its waters than for its wine. The inscription Aquis Mattiacis above the Kurhaus refers to the Mattiaci tribe who settled here in pre-Roman times and the hot mineral springs discovered around AD 1. Charlemagne is said to have taken the waters in Wisibada, "the baths in the meadows," but today, Wiesbaden is an elegant spa, with lush parks, tree-lined boulevards and magnificent turn-of-the-century villas. Wiesbaden's only vineyard, the **Neroberg**, is near the top of a hill that can be reached by a **funicular railway**. It is overlooked by the gilded onion domes of the Russian Orthodox Chapel. **Schloss Biebrich** was built between 1700 and 1750 by the Duke of Nassau on the bank of the Rhine, and is worth a visit.

Exit from the A 66 at Frauenstein, take the B 42 (towards Rüdesheim) to Walluf, and then turn left to reach the heart of the town, on the banks of the Rhine. Viticulture in the Rheingau was first documented in a deed of gift in AD 779, when two vineyards in Walluf were presented to Kloster Lorsch.

Today, fine Riesling and Spätburgunder wines are

produced from the chalky loess soils. Walk along the old towpath next to the river (the tasting stand is located here). The two best vineyards here are **Wallufer Walkenberg** and **Berg Bildstock**, high above the village. **Weingut JB Becker** is one of the top ten estates in Rheingau and has vines in both. Becker also has a riverside wine bar, **Im Weingarten Rheinstrasse**, where you can get snacks (or bring a picnic). The wines are splendid and great value (reds, too).

Driving on the B 42 from Walluf towards Eltville, take the first right to reach Ober-Walluf and follow the signs to Martinsthal. The vine-covered hills get steeper with the approach to the village, and the Nonnenberg villa (whose vineyard is in Rauenthal) peers down from the hill on the left. This is named after the *Nonnen* (nuns), who once owned the property. Martinsthal's best-known vineyards are **Martinsthaler Langenberg**, **Rödchen** and **Wildsau**, whose name refers to the wild boar that love to eat the ripe grapes. Drive past the traffic light and turn left to reach Rauenthal, high on a hill. The tower of the 15th-century St Antonius Church is visible for a considerable distance. Inside, a late Gothic Madonna lovingly hands the Christ-child a bunch of grapes.

Rauenthal's steep Riesling vineyards, **Rauenthaler Nonnenberg**, **Baiken**, **Gehrn** and **Rothenberg** are among the finest in Rheingau. The phyllite soils, with some loess and loam, yield elegant, racy wines with great character: steely when young, they age beautifully.

Return to Martinsthal, follow the signs to Eltville, and from there take the right-hand turn to Kiedrich. Near the village, the ruins of the Scharfenstein fortress appear on the right, as well as the spires of the Gothic pilgrimage church St Valentine's (1420) with its Gothic and Renaissance altars, the Kiedricher Madonna (1330), the richly carved pews with grape motifs, and the star vaulting with original ceiling paintings. The 15th-century organ is the oldest in Germany and can be heard at Sunday mass when the male choir sings Gregorian chants. St Michael's chapel (1434-44) is next door. There is a Renaissance town hall and half-timbered manor houses on the side streets.

WINE ESTATE

WALLUF

Weingut J B Becker
Rheinstrasse 6
65396 Walluf
Tel: 06123 72523
Email: h.j.becker@justmail.de

Kloster Eberbach

Leave Kiedrich at the northern end of town and follow the signs to Kloster Eberbach (monastery) founded in 1135 by Bernhard of Clairvaux. The Cistercian monks built Kloster Eberbach into one of the largest and most successful wine enterprises of the Middle Ages. At its height, the monastery received income and produce from more than 200 towns and estates and had its own fleet of ships on the Rhine.

Despite the setbacks of wars, secularization (1803) and changes in ownership, the tradition of viticulture at Kloster Eberbach has continued uninterrupted since the 12th century. The monks and the workers of the monastery cleared the dense Taunus forest and then planted a huge vineyard in the steep, stony soil, called Steinberg, which became one of the great names in German wine. The Rieslings are powerful, with pronounced, balanced acidity and great depth of flavor.

Kloster Eberbach is now

Cistercian monks founded Kloster Eberbach in 1133.

the home of the **Hessiche Staatsweingüter Kloster Eberbach**, which has built a beautiful architectural and scientific winery in the Steinberg monastery. It has 180 hectares of vines altogether, with vineyards mainly in the best sites in Hochheim, Rauenthal, Erbach, and Rüdesheim, not forgetting the Steinberg vineyard itself, which also has a small *Weinstube*. The vineyards are planted with 91 per cent Riesling vines.

There are many facilities, including guest rooms, three restaurants, tasting rooms and a wine store. You can taste the wines in the historic **Kloster-Schänke**, or at the shop that sells wines and Sekt from the State Wine Domain, including Rieslings from the State vineyards in Hessische Bergstrasse and the great Spätburgunder wines from the domain in Assmannshausen.

Kloster Eberbach is also the cultural wine center of the Rheingau, home of the German Wine Academy, and the site for prestigious auctions, and a museum devoted to the history of the Cistercians. Wonderful concerts are held in the basilica.

The church is one of the most magnificent examples of Romanesque architecture in Germany and has many ancient tombs and a cloister garden that was reserved for the monks. The dormitory was built between 1250 and 1270 and is one of the most splendid early Gothic rooms (73 m/240 ft long) in the world. In the **Lay Brothers' Refectory** there is a collection of historic wine presses dating back to 1668, and the lovely gardens are not to be missed.

From Kloster Eberbach take the road to Hattenheim; watch for the sign on the right.

Eltville

From Kloster Eberbach, return to Kiedrich and follow the road towards the Rhine. The historic part of the town is near the river, south of the B 42. Eltville's origins date from Roman times (alta villa) but its days of glory were in the 14th and 15th centuries. A favorite residence of the Archbishops of Mainz, Eltville was the first town in the Rheingau to receive Town Rights (1332). In the tower of the Prince Elector's castle there is a memorial to Johannes Gutenberg, the inventor of movable type printing, who lived here in the 15th century. There are fine works of art and wall paintings in the late-Gothic **Church of St Peter and St Paul**. Renaissance manors line the side streets, and there is a tasting stand on the riverfront.

The best vineyards here are **Eltviller Langenstück**, **Rheinberg**, and **Sonnenberg**. These are on gentle slopes of rich loess, which yields softer and rounder wines than the steep hillside sites. Several Sekt (sparkling wine) producers have cellars in Eltville, a town immortalized by writer Thomas Mann's Felix Krull. The **Sektfest** is in July.

Erbach

Drive west on the B 42 past the last traffic light and out of town. Turn right (off the B 42) towards Erbach. On the left is 12th-century **Klosterhof Drais**, a wine estate once owned by Kloster Eberbach. The late-Gothic St Markus Kirche, a church named after the village's patron saint, is on the right. The road continues past half-timbered houses in the market square to **Schloss Reinhartshausen**, a palace and wine estate once owned by the Princes of Prussia (now a superb hotel and gourmet restaurant). The sloping vineyard from here to Hattenheim is the world-famous **Erbacher Marcobrunn**. There is a sandstone monument at St Mark's well (brunnen), from which the vineyard may take its name. Others say the name refers to the well's location at the boundary mark between Erbach and Hattenheim – both villages covet the rights to this exceptional site. The other great vineyards are **Erbacher Hohenrain** and **Steinmorgen**. There are fine Gothic crucifixes and shrines in the cemetery and vineyards. The **Erdbeerfest**, a celebration of strawberries and wine, is in June.

WINERIES & MORE

KIEDRICH
Weingut Robert Weil
Mühlberg 5
65399 Kiedrich
Tel: 06123 2308
www.weingut-robert-weil.com

ELTVILLE
Weingut Freiherrlich Langwerth von Simmern'sches Rentamt
Kirchgasse 6
65343 Eltville
Tel: 06123 92110
www.langwerth-von-simmern.de

HATTENHEIM
Weingut Balthasar Ress
Rheinallee 7-11
65347 Hattenheim
Tel: 06723 91950
www.balthasar-ress.de

Domänenweingut Schloss Schönborn
Hauptstrasse 53
65347 Hattenheim
Tel: 06723 91810
www.schoenborn.de

Hattenheim

The road continues to Hattenheim, which also has its *Brunnen* sites: **Hattenheimer Nussbrunnen** and **Wisselbrunnen**, as well as **Pfaffenberg**, each producing high-quality wines of great finesse and delicacy. The intricate designs on the houses in the market square are remarkable. Try a glass of Hattenheimer at the tasting stand on the banks of the river, in the three huge barrels opposite the Shell petrol station on the B 42, or at the *Burg* (castle) during the wine festival in August.

Hallgarten

Leave Hattenheim on the road that runs through the village (not the B 42). Near the railway crossing, watch for the right turn to Hallgarten, which is set back in the hills below the forest. As the slopes become steeper, the wines are more full-bodied and pronounced in acidity. **Hallgartener Jungfer** and **Schönhell** are the best vineyards.

In the **Maria-Himmelfahrt Kirche**, look for the Madonna with the Christchild holding a bunch of grapes (1420). For a panoramic view of the Rhine valley, visit the tasting stand at the edge of the new part of town, on the road leading into the forest.

Oestrich, Mittelheim and Winkel

Return to the B 42 and drive west to Oestrich. The 18th-century crane on the left was the start of the journey to Rotterdam for many a barrel of wine. The half-timbered façade of the Hotel Schwan is on the right. **Oestricher Lenchen** and **Doosberg** are the town's best-known sites, yielding distinguished and elegant wines.

At Mittelheim, the Rhine is at its widest (1 km/half a mile) and resembles a huge lake. The wines from this village are not well known, but **Mittellheimer Edelmann** has a good reputation. Turn off the B 42 at the first exit for Winkel. While walking along Hauptstrasse you will see 16th and 18th century houses, many of which are estates with *Weinstuben* in their courtyards that are usually open in the evenings and at weekends. The **Winkeler Jesuitengarten** vineyard is between the village and the Rhein and is highly regarded.

In 1814, Goethe found inspiration in the Rheingau's landscape and the legendary 1811 vintage during his stay with the Brentano family. You can see the rooms where Goethe worked (by appointment: **Brentanohaus**, Am Lindenplatz 2, 65375 Oestrich-Winkel. www.brentano.de). From Hauptstrasse, follow signs to Schloss Vollrads, one of the great names in German wine.

The Lay Brothers' Refectory at Kloster Eberbach today houses historic wine presses: the oldest from 1668.

Schloss Vollrads

The earliest documented sales of Vollrads wines date from 1211. In 1330, the Greiffenclau family moved from their ancestral home in the Graues Haus to the moated castle tower situated in the hills behind Winkel, at the edge of the Taunus forest. For 27 generations, members of the founding family ran the estate and lived in the 17th-century Baroque palace in the estate grounds. Erwein Count Matuscka-Greiffenclau, who tragically died young in 1996, was the last family owner and the greatest single-handed champion of Riesling worldwide. He was also the most generous host, and the **Lucullan Wine Tastings** conducted in the historic rooms of the palace were truly memorable.

Documents dating from 1728 from Schloss Vollrads and 1730 from Kloster Eberbach, show that some estates set aside exceptional wines in a special "Cabinet," a carefully locked cellar. (This is the origin of the term *Kabinett*.)

The wines of **Schloss Vollrads** are not only

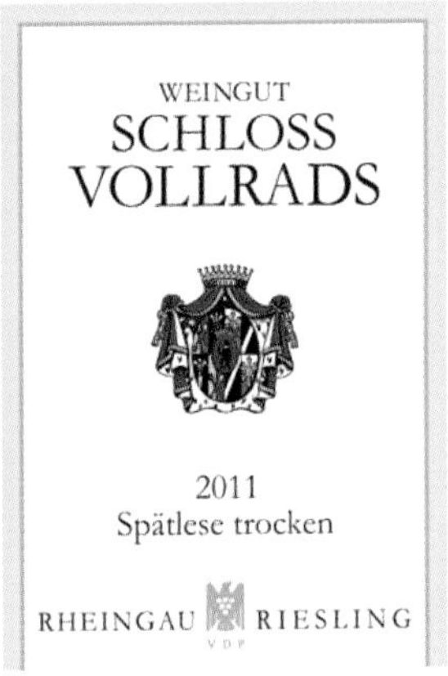

The finest vineyard of Schloss Vollrads, located above the castle tower.

beautifully balanced and elegant, but also have great longevity. You can try the wines at the **Gutsausschank** (wine shop and restaurant) in the estate grounds. The 61 hectares of 100 per cent Riesling vineyards are labelled Schloss Vollrads, except a light "Summer Wine," which is sold in their wine shop.

Schloss Johannisberg

Return to Kirchstrasse and turn right on Greiffenclaustrasse, watching for signs to Schloss Johannisberg, on the next hillside to the west. Drive through the vineyards, via Winkelerstrasse. The turning to the palace is marked, on the left.

Historically, **Schloss Johannisberg** was the greatest wine estate in Germany. It was founded by Benedictines, who established a monastery here in 1100, and the earliest cellars date from this time.

Under the ownership of the Abbey of Fulda in the 18th century, the palace and the extensive cellars were built, the planting of Riesling was made mandatory and estate bottling (a novelty at the time) began in 1750. It was during this time that the benefits of a late harvest were recognized, albeit by chance. In 1775, so the story goes, the courier sent from Johannisberg to Fulda to obtain permission to begin the harvest was delayed. Meanwhile, the grapes had started to rot ("noble rot" botrytis, not

The 1775 Spätlese Rider. His delay in bringing permission to the monks to pick the grapes resulted in a new style of sweet wine.

"gray," which is disaster), yet the monks decided to salvage what they could. To their surprise and delight, the resultant wine was superb. The modern monument to the delayed courier, the Spätlese Reiter, in the estate's courtyard is a tribute to quality-oriented growers, then and now. After the secularization by Napoleon (1802) the estate changed hands several times, until it was presented to Chancellor Metternich (1816), ancestor of the present residents.

The cellars, among the most impressive in the world, house the **Bibliotheca Subterranea** (underground library), with rarities dating from 1748. The great house and the cellars look down on the steep 35-hectare (86.5-acre) 100 per cent Riesling vineyard and a grand view of the Rhine, with a sign showing the 50th degree of latitude. The wines of Schloss Johannisberg are full and rich, with fruit, fine acidity and great longevity. Taste them at the *Gutsausschank* or in the shop, prior to purchase, both in the estate grounds.

Johannisberg and Geisenheim

Depart through the tree-lined alley, turn left and follow the road downhill and left, through the village of Johannisberg. On this road, the Grund, there are fine vineyards: **Johannisberger Hölle, Mittelhölle** and **Klaus**. Turn right into the Industriestrasse to drive to Geisenheim. Lime trees, noble manor houses, half-timbered houses and ancient fountains make a delightful setting. The late-Gothic **Rheingauer Dom** (cathedral), with its two red neo-Gothic spires, has fine altars and tombs. The **Schönborn Palace** is a beautiful building surrounded by a small vineyard. It was built in 1550, but it has not been owned by the Schönborn family since 1648, when the peace treaty ending the Thirty Years' War was drafted there. The **Domanenweingut Schönborn** owns 50 hectares (125 acres) based in Hattenheim. The wines are superb. There is another cellar in Hochheim, as well as the Weingut Graf von Schönborn Schloss Hallburg in Franken. However, the family still owns many castles and palaces in Europe.

Geisenheim's international reputation derives from its State Research Institute and School of Enology. The Institute is where many German students and potential winemakers from all over the world study wine in all its forms. The research of viticulture and winemaking is second to none in Germany, but it has been restricted by its concentration on German wine varieties, especially new German crossings, and ignoring vines from the rest of the world. It operates experimental vineyards, a modern winery and a shop where you can taste the wines. One of the best vineyards in this village is **Geisenheimer Kläuserweg** and the wines are full and round. The soils of the sloping vineyards are deep, partly stony, loamy-loess over a stratum of quartzite.

From Geisenheim, drive for two miles on the B 42 to Rüdesheim. On the hillside to the right is St Hildegard, a Benedictine nunnery in the midst of the **Rüdesheimer Klosterberg** vineyard, named after the medieval abbess Hildegard von Bingen. She founded convents and was a healer and early theologian. She was venerated in the church, wrote plays and composed music (her compositions continue to be performed and recorded today).

WINERIES & MORE

ERBACH

Schloss Reinhartshausen
Hauptstrasse 41
65346 Eltville-Erbach
am Rhein
Tel: 06123 676333
www.schloss-reinhartshausen.de
(See also Hotel Schloss Reinhartshausen Kempinski)

OESTRICH-WINKEL

Weingüter Wegeler
Friedensplatz 9-11
65375 Oestrich-Winkel
Tel: 06723 99090
www.wegeler.com

Weingut Peter Jakob Kühn
Mühlstrasse 70
65375 Oestrich-Winkel
Tel: 06723 2299
www.weingutpjkuehn.de

Weingut Querbach
Lenchenstrasse 19
65375 Oestrich
im Rheingau
Tel: 06723 3887
www.querbach.com

Weingut Joseph Spreitzer
Rheingaustrasse 86
65375 Oestrich-Winkel
Tel: 06723 2625
www.weingut-spreitzer.de

Weingut Schloss Vollrads
Vollradser Allee
65375 Oestrich-Winkel
Tel: 06723 660
www.schlossvollrads.com

GEISENHEIM-JOHANNISBERG

Domäne Schloss Johannisberg
65366 Geisenheim-Johannisberg
Tel: 06722 700990
www.schloss-johannisberg.de
Cellar visits by appointment only.

JOHANNISBERG

Weingut Johannishof
Grund 63
65366 Johannisberg
Tel: 06722 8216
www.weingut-johannishof.de

Rüdesheim

Rüdesheim is one of the best-known wine villages of Germany, not least because of its *Weinstube*-lined **Drosselgasse** (Thrush Alley) and other attractions that draw tens of thousands of tourists every year. Rüdesheim has been settled since Roman times, as evinced by pruning knives found in the vineyards, but it was during the Middle Ages that it became an impor-

tant commercial center, thanks to its location at the end of the important trade route to circumvent the unnavigable waters of Binger Loch. It is still a center of wine, *Sekt* and brandy production.

Some of the medieval townscape still exists, such as the Adlerturm (a late-Gothic defence tower, which was part of the 15th-century town wall), St Jakobus Kirche with its fine sandstone altar and tombs, **Brömserburg fortress** (now a wine museum) and patrician houses near the market square on the Steinstrasse and Oberstrasse.

There is a fine view of the Rhine from the terrace of the wine museum in Brömserburg fortress, Rheinstrasse 2. Among its exhibits is a collection of glassware dating from Roman times, and historic artifacts related to winegrowing.

There is an unusual collection of automatic musical instruments from the 18th-20th centuries at **Siegfried's Mechanical Music Cabinet** in the Brömserhof, Oberstrasse 29.

The vineyards on the weathered quartzite and slate cliffs produce some of Rheingau's finest wines, concentrated in flavor, flowery in bouquet. Riesling ripens well here, even in cool or rainy years. The best vineyards are **Rüdesheimer Berg Schlossberg, Berg Rottland, Berg Roseneck, Bischofsberg** and **Drachenstein.** You can try the wines at the tasting stand near the river, east of the Adlerturm, or at one of the dozens of *Weinstuben* on or near the Drosselgasse, if they are not too crowded. The **Breuer's Rüdesheimer Schloss** in the historic Zehnthof (tithe court) has one of the most extensive wine lists in Rheingau, including nearly 300 Rheingau wines from 1929 to the present. Older rarities are available on request.

Germania, the statue visible from miles away, is the Niederwalddenkmal (monument) built in 1883 to commemorate the re-establishment of the German Empire after the Franco-Prussian War. From the terrace the panorama comprises parts of Rheingau, Rheinhessen and Nahe. Hike, drive or ride up the hill by cable car. (Departs from Oberstrasse, Rüdesheim www.seilbahn-ruedesheim.de). An enjoyable **vineyard walk** starts at Ringmauer (near the car park north of the town center) and follows Panorama Weg to the Brömserburg.

At Rüdesheim the Rhine narrows, turns sharply and resumes its south-north course. The vineyards become increasingly steep as the ruins of Burg Ehrenfels come into view. This fortress was once a customs post and refuge for the treasures of Mainz

Rüdesheim is the tourist center of Rheingau. Just down the road is the famous Drosselgasse (Thrush Alley) where almost every building is a *Weinstube*, and which can get very crowded in summer.

Cathedral in time of war. It gives its name to a white grape variety, Ehrenfelser (a crossing of Riesling and Silvaner) developed at Geisenheim in 1929.

Assmannshausen

Assmannshausen is a town that has been synonymous with Spätburgunder for centuries. The vines ripen well on the blue-red phyllite slate, yielding velvety, fruity red wine with a fine, blackberry tone. The **Assmannshäuser Höllenberg**, largely owned by Staatsweingüter and planted with 95 per cent Spätburgunder vines, is one of the finest vineyards. For a view of the town, its vineyards and the castles on the opposite side of the Rhine, take the **chairlift up to the Niederwalddenkmal**.

Lorch and Lorchhausen

From the B 42, one would never expect to find a historic wine town hidden behind the railway embankment at Lorch. Park alongside the river and walk into the town through an underpass to discover its ancient buildings.

From its Roman and Frankish origins, Lorch developed into a powerful and prosperous town in the Middle Ages. Thanks to its situation at the mouth of the Wisper river, the start of the important overland trade route to and from Rüdesheim, Lorch was settled by clerics and aristocrats who profited from the revenues of the town's dyers, vintners, weavers, and merchants.

At the stone bridge crossing the Wisper there are remnants of the town fortifications which once extended as far as Burg Nollig (11th century, now in ruins). The **Heimatmuseum** (a local history museum with valuable art treasures) is next door to the town hall. **St Martins Kirche** is an important Gothic church overlooking the Rhine, and is famous for its richly carved high altar (1483) and choir stalls (13th century).

Walk down the ancient stone steps from the church terrace to the Rheinstrasse. The house of the Knight Hans von Hilchen (No. 48), a gem of Renaissance architecture (1546), is now a restaurant belonging to a wine estate.

Riesling hiking paths

Continue walking east, to the Bahnhof (railway station), to the start of a **Riesling Wanderweg**, a 7-km (4-mile) trail through vineyards, from Kapellenberg to Bodental-Steinberg. It's signposted with information about grape varieties and work in the vineyards, and there are fine views. At the other end of town, en route to Lorchhausen, you can walk up to the castle **Burg Nollig**, which towers over the Lorcher Schlossberg vineyard, for a view of the Rhine valley and Bacharach on the opposite shore. A path through the vineyards leads to Lorchhausen, at the border of the State of Hesse and the end of the Rheingau.

Wars, the plague and engineering on the Rhine to make the Binger Loch passable, all contributed to Lorch's decline as a commercial center. But the tradition of viticulture, dating from at least the 11th century, successfully weathered the storms.

Lorch and its suburb, Lorchhausen, have a relatively large vineyard area, planted primarily with Riesling and Spätburgunder. The quartzite and weathered slate cliffs are extremely labor-intensive, but yield fresh, lively wines with lots of fruit. Slate brings out the fruit and acidity of the Riesling grape and often imparts a slight *spritz* or natural sparkle to the wine. The Wispertal valley offers a scenic drive through beautiful forests and castle ruins, and is famous for its fresh and smoked trout. The road starts at the stone bridge in Lorch and ends in the pretty spa of Bad Schwalbach.

WINERIES & MORE

RÜDESHEIM

Weingut Georg Breuer
Grabenstrasse 8
65385 Rüdesheim am Rhein
Tel: 06722 1027
www.georg-breuer.com
(See also Breuer's Rüdesheimer Schloss hotel.)

Weingut Leitz KG
Theodor-Heuss-Starasse 5
65385 Rüdesheim am Rhein
Tel: 06722 48711
www.leitz-wein.de

ASSMANNSHAUSEN

Weingut August Kesseler
Lorcher Strasse 16
65385 Assmannshausen
Tel: 06722 2513
www.august-kesseler.de

Weingut Robert König
Landhaus Kenner 1
65385 Rüdesheim-Assmannshausen
Tel: 06722 1064
www.weingut-robert-koenig.de

Weingut Krone
Niederwaldstrasse 2
65385 Rüdesheim-Assmannshausen
Tel: 06722 2525
www.weingut-krone.de
(See also Hotel Krone.)

Hessische Staatsweingüter Assmannshausen
Höllenbergstrasse 10
65385 Assmannshausen
Tel: 06722 2273
www.weingut-kloster-eberbach.de

LORCH

Weingut Graf von Kanitz
Rheinstrasse 49
65391 Lorch im Rheingau
Tel: 06726 346
www.weingut-graf-von-kanitz.de

The town of Assmannshausen.

Assmannshausen

Hotel Krone (H/R)
Rheinuferstrasse 10
65385 Rüdesheim-Assmannshausen
Tel: 06722 4030
www.hotel-krone.com
The most famous hotel overlooking the Rhine, with an elegant restaurant and an outside terrace. Ask for a room with a river view, as the railroad is just behind the hotel.

Hotel Schön (H/R)
Rheinuferstrasse 2-4
65385 Rüdesheim-Assmannshausen
Tel: 06722 2225
www.karl-schoen.de

Eltville

Hotel Frankenbach (H)
Wilhelmstrasse 13
65343 Eltville
Tel: 06123 9040
www.hotel-frankenbach.de
Thirty-five rooms. Café but no restaurant. Good value.

Gastronomiebetriebe im Kloster Eberbach GmbH (H/R)
Kloster Eberbach
65346 Eltville
Tel: 06723 993200
www.klostereberbach.com

Parkhotel Sonnenberg (H)
Friedrichstrasse 65
65343 Eltville
Tel: 06123 6 05 50
www.parkhotel-sonnenberg.com
Quiet hotel with 30 rooms. Good value.

Erbach

Schloss Reinhartshausen Kempinski (H/R)
Hauptstrasse 41
65346 Eltville-Erbach
Tel: 06123 6760
www.kempinski.com/de
Luxurious hotel, 63 rooms, 3 restaurants: Prinzess von Erbach (fine dining), Wintergarten, Schloss Schänke (rustic regional specialties).

Geisenheim-Johannisberg

Hotel Burg Schwarzenstein (H/R)
Rosengasse 32
65366 Geisenheim-Johannisberg
Tel: 06722 99500
info@burg-schwarzenstein.de
www.burg-schwarzenstein.de
Gourmerestaurant Schwarzenstein serves fabulous food in the park. The Burgrestaurant (located in the hotel) serves regional specialties.

Hattenheim

Adler Wirschaft (R)
Hauptstrasse 31
65347 Hattenheim Tel:
06723 7982
www.franzkeller.de
Delicious food and wines.

Kronenschlösschen (H/R)
Rheinallee
65347 Eltville-Hattenheim
Tel: 06723 640
www.kronenschloesschen.de
Eighteen rooms. Bistro.
Friendly atmosphere.

Zum Krug (H/R)
Hauptstrasse 34
65347 Eltville-Hattenheim
Tel: 06723 9 96 80
www.hotel-zum-krug.de
Good regional food.
Eight comfortable rooms.
Good value.

Rüdesheim

Bistro Berg Schlossberg (R)
Grabenstrasse 8
65385 Rüdesheim
Tel: 06722 1026
Vinothek (wine shop) of
owner, Weingut Georg
Breuer, is next door.

Breuers' Rüdesheimer Schloss (H/R)
Entrance: Steingasse 10
65385 Rüdesheim
Tel: 06722 90500
www.ruedesheimer-schloss.com
Lively, but cozy indoors;
tree-shaded courtyard.
(Hotel entrance on
Steingasse, street parallel
to Drosselgasse.)

Jagdschloss (H/R)
Niederwald, 1
65385 Rüdesheim
Tel: 06722 7 10 60
www.niederwald.de
Hotel in former hunting
palace near the Nieder-
walddenkmal north of
Rüdesheim. Fine food and
wine in a forested setting.

Wiesbaden

Hotel Nassauer Hof (H/R)
Kaiser-Friedrich-Platz 3-4
65183 Wiesbaden
Tel: 0611 133666
www.nassauer-hof.de
Restaurants Ente and
Orangerie. Fine cuisine,
world-class wine list.

Käfer's Bistro (R)
Kurhausplatz 1
65189 Wiesbaden
Tel: 0611 53 62 00
www.kurhaus-gastronomie.de
Delightful bistro.

POST
Postagentur +
Teefachgeschäft
Kontor Zwingenberg

THE HESSISCHE BERGSTRASSE

THE OLD ROMAN TRADE ROUTE *strada montana* (mountain road) runs parallel to the Rhine in the foothills of the Odenwald (Oden Forest). It extends some 70 km (45 miles) from Darmstadt to Wiesloch, south of Heidelberg. The Bergstrasse is known as the spring garden of Germany, for its fruit and almond trees are among the earliest to blossom. At harvest time the slopes shimmer with the golden leaves of the vines.

It's an attractive landscape, with castle ruins on many summits and traditional vintners' huts sprinkled between the orchards and hillside vineyards. The medieval town centers are picturesque and several historic buildings house restaurants or wine pubs. You can also taste the wines at festivals from late April through September, or on May Day, when tasting stands are set up in the vineyards for the annual *Weinlagenwanderung* (vineyard walk).

Hessische Bergstrasse (436 hectares/1077 acres) is between Zwingenberg, Bensheim and Heppenheim, and there is a small vineyard at Gross-Umstadt, the northern gateway to the Oden Forest. The vineyards further south are part of the Baden region. Nearly all the vineyards are hilly parcels of land, and thus labor-intensive. The Staatsweingut (State Wine Domain) in Bensheim is the largest private estate (36 hectares/90 acres), but most growers are "hobby vintners" and belong to cooperatives.

Riesling is the premier grape variety (48 per cent), but Grauburgunder and Spätburgunder are also grown. A high proportion of the wines are dry or medium dry in style. The traditional everyday wine glass is called a *Halber* – the name refers not to a "half" liter, but rather to a quarter liter.

‹‹ Grieselstrasse (street) in Bensheim leads to the Hessische Bergstrasse State Wine Domain and St George's church.

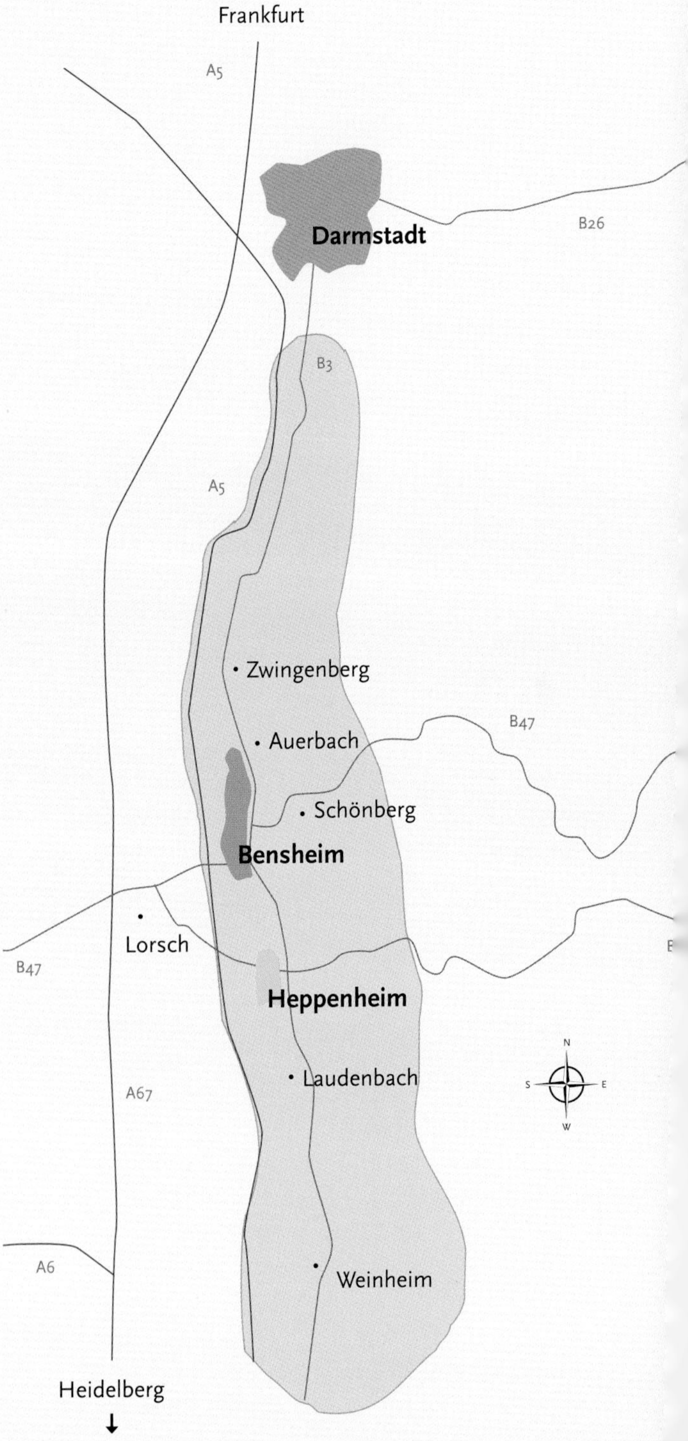
Frankfurt
A5
Darmstadt
B26
B3
A5
Zwingenberg
B47
Auerbach
Schönberg
Bensheim
Lorsch
B47
Heppenheim
N
S
E
W
Laudenbach
A67
A6
Weinheim
Heidelberg

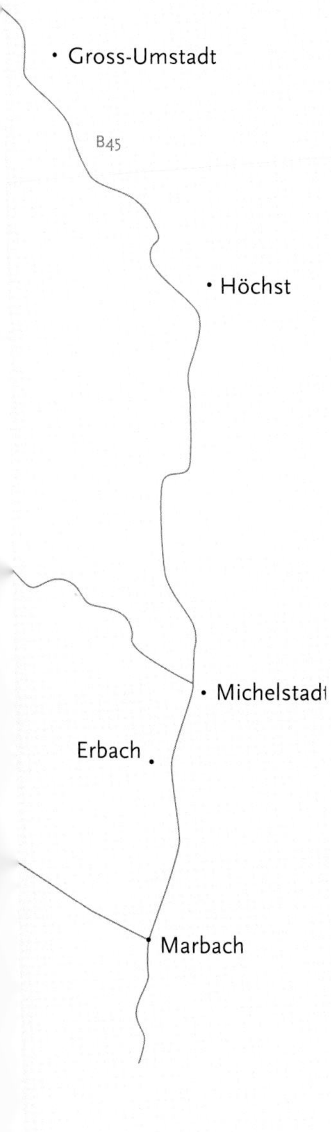
Gross-Umstadt
B45
Höchst
Michelstadt
Erbach
Marbach

A tour of the Hessische Bergstasse

From Darmstadt, drive south on the B 3 to Zwingenberg, the oldest town on the Bergstrasse. Watch for the right turn onto the historic *Scheuergasse*, a lane with old *Scheuer* or *Scheier* (barns) that were built outside the town walls due to the risk of fire. Here, and in the market square near Obertor (east of the B 3), many of the beautiful half-timbered houses are shops and pubs.

From the B 3 turn left into the Ernst-Ludwig-Promenade to visit the **Auerbacher Schloss** ruins, a good vantage-point (with a terrace café). A walk through **Auerbach's Fürstenlager park** (via Bachgasse) is recommended. It has exotic plants, Germany's tallest sequoia, a porcelain museum and a lovely café and restaurant in the Herrenhaus.

Bensheim

Between Zwingenberg and Bensheim the soils are loess-loam and weathered granite, an important building material in Roman times. East of the B 3 (towards Lautertal-Riechenbach) you can visit the geological site known as the **Felsenmeer**, testimony to the Romans' skill as stonemasons.

The Old Town of Bensheim is very picturesque. Between the Marktplatz, (the town was granted the right to hold a market in AD 956) and the Rinnentor Turm (once a town gate) on Neumarkt are many historic houses and fountains. Via the Kalkgasse near the Stadtpark there is a scenic path through the vineyards to the **Kirchberghäuschen** at Weingut der Stadt Bensheim. The terrace is perfect for a glass of wine with a view.

Heppenheim

The most splendid view of the Rhine valley is from the Starkenburg fortress ruins (1065), overlooking Heppenheim's steep vineyards (a short drive plus a ten-minute walk, or 30 minutes on foot). The fortress tower and the café-restaurant **Burgschänke** have a panoramic view. Sights include the 16th-century town hall, complete with

The Hessische Bergstrasse State Wine Domain in Bensheim.

The author (left) and a worker at a recently replanted vineyard.

a Glockenspiel; the neo-Gothic Church of St Peter, called the **Cathedral of the Bergstrasse**; and half-timbered houses on the market square.

REGIONAL WINE PROMOTION BOARD

Weinbauverband Hessische Bergstrasse
Kettelerstrasse 29
64646 Heppenheim
Tel: 06252 75654
www.bergstraesser-wein.de

WINERIES & MORE

BENSHEIM

Hessiche Staatsweingüter Domäne Bergstrasse Kloster Eberbach
65346 Eltville im Rheingau
Tel: 06251 3107
www.weingut-kloster-eberbach.de
(Restaurant Klosterschänke serves regional dishes.)

Weingut der Stadt Bensheim
Darmstädter Strasse 6
64625 Bensheim
Tel. 06251 580017
www.weingut-der-stadt-bensheim.de
(*See also* restaurant Kirchberghäuschen).

ZWINGENBERG

Weingut Simon-Bürkle
Weissenpromenade 13
64673 Zwingenberg
Tel: 06251 76446
www.simon-buerkle.de

HEPPENHEIM

Bergsträsser Winzer Cooperative
Darmstädter Strasse 56
64646 Heppenheim
Tel. 06252 79940
www.bergstraesserwinzer.de
Cooperative and wine shop.

WHERE TO STAY AND EAT

Bensheim-Auerbach

Parkhotel Herrenhaus (H/R)
Im Staatspark Fürstenlager
64625 Bensheim-Auerbach
Tel: 06251 70900
www.parkhotel-herrenhaus.de
Quiet, nine-room hotel in a park. Elegant restaurant. Historic site.

Alleehotel Europa (H/R)
Europa Allee 45
64625 Bensheim
Tel: 06251 1050
www.alleehotel.de
Business hotel with a rustic wine store and restaurant.

Hotel Restaurant Felix (H/R)
Dammstrasse 46
64625 Bensheim
Tel: 0651 80060
www.hotelfelix.de

Between May and October you can taste and buy wines at the State Wine Domain's pavilion at the top of the Centgericht vineyard.

RHEINHESSEN

RHEINHESSEN IS THE LARGEST of Germany's wine regions with 26,334 hectares (63,500 acres) of vines. It is also the origin of Liebfraumilch, which, with its innocuous sweet nonentity, harmed the reputation of German wines and virtually destroyed that of some of the best wines of Rheinhessen. This was because Liefraumilch was based on the Müller-Thurgau grape and the so-called "New" sweet white crossed varieties, such as Bacchus, Faberrebe, Huxelrebe, Kerner, Mori-Muscat and Ortega.

The cooperatives and their main customers, known as the "Big Bottlers," blended and marketed the mass-produced wines and have continued to do so. However, Reh Kendermann have marketed Kendermanns Dry Riesling Roter Hang, which is from a group of growers with vineyards in the Rhein Terrasse near Nierstein who produce really good-quality inexpensive Riesling wines. The St Ursula winery has also worked with five cooperatives for their Devil's Rock Riesling brand.

There are four areas in Rheinhessen where the special terroirs bring out the character and quality of the wines: the Rhein Terrasse south of Mainz, just before Nierstein; Bingen, east of the confluence of the Nahe river and the Rhine; Siefersheim, a village east of Bad Kreuznach in Nahe (just one brilliant estate so far); and last but most important, Wonnegau, the "Happy Land," west of Worms. A reformation started in the early 1990s in the Wonnegau region and today this has become the most progessive wine-producing area in Rheinhessen.

Rheinhessen's gentle, rolling hills lie within the large elbow formed by the Rhine river as it flows from Worms to its sweeping bend around Mainz and west to its next turn at Bingen. Much of this is spacious, fertile farmland

‹‹ Hillside vineyards near Westhofen planted on deep limestone – a special terroir for Riesling.

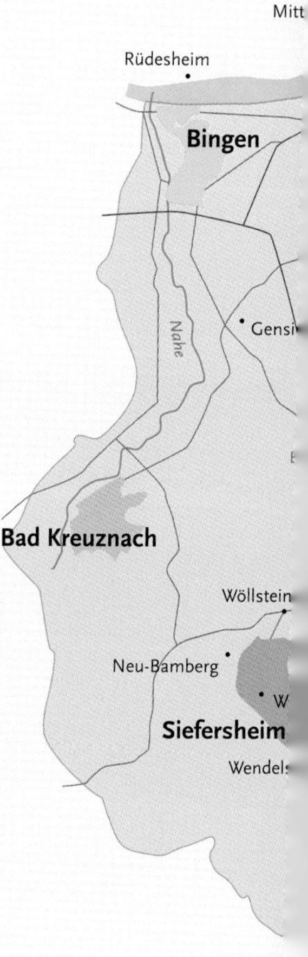
Rüdesheim
Bingen
Nahe
Bad Kreuznach
Wöllstein
Neu-Bamberg
Siefersheim

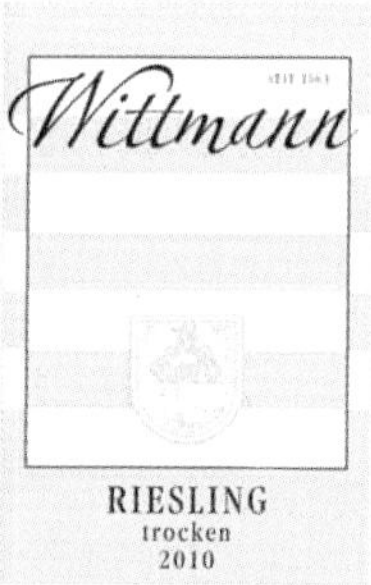
Wittmann
RIESLING
trocken
2010

GUTZLER
2007
WESTHOFENER
SPÄTBURGUNDER
IM BARRIQUE GEREIFT

WAGNER STEMPEL
2007 HEERKRETZ
SIEFERSHEIM

BATTENFELDSPANIER
Kirchenstück
2010
Riesling GG

Wiesbaden
A643
B455
Rhein (Rhine)
Mainz
A60
Ingelheim
lgesheim
B9
Bodenheim
Elsheim
Gau-Bischofsheim
Nackenheim
Stadecken
Harxheim
Rhein
Terrasse
Jugenheim
Nieder-
Olm
Lörzweiler
Partenheim
Nierstein
B40
St. Johann
Hahnheim
llingen
Wörrstadt
Oppenheim
Bickelheim
B420
Undenheim
Armsheim
A63
Selz
heim
Bechtolsheim
Guntersblum
Rheinhessen
"Switzerland"
Albig
Gau-Odernheim
Alsheim
Alzey
Mettenheim
Dittelsheim
Hessloch
Bechtheim
B9
Westhofen
Osthofen
B40
B271
Flomborn
Rheindürkheim
Wonnegau
Flörsheim
Dalsheim
Herrnsheim
Monsheim
Worms
B47
B271
N
S
E
W
A61

carpeted with fields of grain and vegetables, orchards and too many vineyards in unsuitable soils.

Mainz is an important center of the wine trade and has many historic and cultural sights. It is also worthwhile exploring certain small wine villages, rich in artistic detail, from beautifully carved courtyard portals to treasures in the parish churches. From *Hoffeste* (festivals in vintners' courtyards) to festive *Wanderungen* (hikes) through the vineyards, there are hundreds of events at which to taste Rheinhessen's lesser wines.

The region is ringed by forests and hills that protect the farms and vineyards from cold winds and excessive rainfall. The Romans settled in some areas near the Rhine and planted vineyards. During the rule of the Frankish kings, viticulture expanded to meet the increased demand for wine by the Church and the court. Charlemagne, in particular, fostered improvements in growing vines and wine making and is credited as an initiator of the *Strausswirtschaft* (the right of a grower to sell his wine in his home for a few months of the year). The Church also promoted quality winegrowing and, as owner of many vineyards, exerted considerable influence on the region's viticultural development.

Müller-Thurgau is still Rheinhessen's main variety (16 per cent), but, hopefully, Riesling (13 per cent) will overtake it very soon. Silvaner was the main grape variety here before Müller-Thurgau was developed, and is gradually making a comeback. Dornfelder (13 per cent) is the principal red variety: with very high yields it has little quality but with moderate yields it can be excellent. Spätburgunder is much more expensive, and on good sites the wine can be superb.

REGIONAL WINE PROMOTION BOARD

Rheinhessen Marketing eV
Otto-Liliental-Strasse 4
55232 Alzey
Tel: 06731 951074 50
www.rheinhessen.de

Mainz

Mainz is situated on the Rhine, opposite the mouth of the Main. From a citadel built by Roman legionaries in 38 BC, Moguntiacum developed into the most important military town of the region and was made capital of the Roman province Germania Superior in AD 297. There is a wealth of Roman artifacts (some related to wine) at the **Römisch-Germanisches Zentralmuseum** and the **Mittelrheinisches Landesmuseum**, as well as at the **Museum für Antike Schiffahrt** where you can see 4th-century Roman ships (museums all closed Mon, web.rgzm.de).

St Boniface and St Willigis

Mainz declined in importance when the Romans departed in the 5th century, but blossomed again in the 8th century, when the Pope sent Boniface to evangelize the Germans. Mainz became an archbishopric and developed into the most important center of Christianity north of the Alps. In AD 975, Willigis was named archbishop and work was started on the cathedral. As chancellors of the Holy Roman Empire and Prince-electors, the archbishops of Mainz wielded power for centuries, far beyond the borders of the city. The art treasures in the cathedral museum are testimony of their wealth and are well worth seeing.

Mainz's most famous son

By the 13th century Mainz was a prosperous, free imperial city known as *Aurea Moguntia* (Golden Mainz). Johannes Gutenberg set up his famous printing press with movable type in Mainz in about 1450. Gutenberg's revolutionary invention is demonstrated daily, on a replica press in the **Gutenberg Museum**. The university of Mainz, founded in 1477, was renamed in his honor in 1946.

Palaces and mansions

After great destruction in the 17th century (the Thirty Years' War and Louis XIV's rampage through the Rhineland), Mainz enjoyed another period of glory in the 18th century, when Prince-electors and noble families built splendid palaces and mansions. Several are located on Schillerplatz and Schillerstrasse;

Weihergarten (see the courtyard of house no. 5); and opposite the Theodor-Heuss-Brücke, along the street parallel to the Rhine.

Mainz and wine

Given its situation at the intersection of important trade routes and its location in the heart of Germany's winelands, it is not surprising that Mainz developed into a major wine center. Today, barrels of wine are no longer loaded on to boats here. Nevertheless, as the capital of Rheinland-Pfalz, which includes six of the thirteen German wine regions, Mainz is an important administrative center for wine and the site of trade fairs.

The *Weinbörse* (wine market) of the VDP (Association of German *Prädikat* Wine Estates) is held in April in the Rheingoldhalle on the bank of the Rhine in Mainz. It is the most important wine tasting in Germany, but it is only open to wine professionals. Some 150 of the top wine estates show the wines of their previous vintage and of the year before for the *Grosses Gewächs* and *Erstes Gewächs* prestige wines.

Celebrations with wine

Johannisnacht (late June) and *Weinmarkt* (late Aug) are other wine festivals in Mainz. In the carnival season, from November 11 to Ash Wednesday, wine flows freely at costume balls and parties, and during the huge parade through Mainz on Rosenmontag (the German name for the Monday before Lent. The name comes from dialect, which roughly translates as "Wild Monday").

A walk through Mainz

The market square is a good place to begin a walking tour of this 2000-year-old town. From 7AM to 2PM (Tue, Fri, Sat) the farmers' market fills the square with fresh flowers and vegetables from nearby fields. In the midst of the colorful stands is Germany's oldest (1576) Renaissance fountain and the entrance to **St Martins**, one of the three (Mainz, Worms and Speyer) spectacular Rhenish imperial cathedrals.

To see historic books with illuminated letters and the

The market by the cathedral in Mainz. The surrounding area is the center of asparagus cultivation in Germany.

Gutenberg Bible, walk in the direction of the Rhine to the **Gutenberg Museum** (except Mon) on Liebfrauenplatz. Mainz's Old Town lies along Augustiner Strasse and its side alleys behind the Dom (cathedral). The beautiful half-timbered houses are now boutiques and *Weinstuben* – very lively at night.

From the cathedral, walk along Ludwigsstrasse to Schillerplatz, ringed by Baroque palaces, to see the modern fountain devoted to Mainz's famous carnival festivities. Turn left to walk up the Gaustrasse to **St Stephan's Church**, worth visiting for its stained glass windows by Chagall.

WINE SHOP
Weincabinet am Dom
Leichhofstrasse 10
55116 Mainz
Tel: 06131 228858
Outstanding selection of German wines.

The Rhein Terrasse

This was one of Germany's classic Rhine wine areas, producing a whole range of very fine Riesling wines. Sadly, after the end of World War II, most of the owners of the fine vineyards started also to produce cheap sweet Nierstein, Oppenheim and Liebfraumilch wines. Because they were dealing in these mass-produced wines, they were unable to maintain the quality of the wines from their great vineyards. They lost the plot.

Fortunately, there are two estates on the Rhein Terrasse that have continued to make magnificent Riesling wines. They both have parcels in the best vineyard – **Nackenheimer Rothenberg**. They also both own part of **Niersteiner Pettenthal**, another fine vineyard, but one also owns parcels in **Niersteiner Oelberg** and **Oppenheimer Sackträger** for Riesling, plus **Oppenheimer Kreuz** for fine Spätburgunder. Gradually the great wines of Nierstein and Oppenheim will become famous again.

The steep slopes of *Rotliegendes* benefit from the iron sand in the soil of Rhein Terrasse that gives these vineyards their red color. The slopes face east and the heat of the sun is mirrored

The interior of Mainz Cathedral is as splendid as the exterior.

from the surface of the Rhine in the morning, but later in the day the grapes do not suffer from sunburn. The Riesling wines have an ideal balance of rich fruit and fresh acidity.

Nackenheim and Nierstein

A bust of Nackenheim's favorite son, writer Carl Zuckmayer (1896-1977) adorns the half-timbered town hall. He dubbed Rheinhessen wine "the wine of laughter . . . charming and appealing." At the edge of town, it's worth stopping to see the interior of the Baroque **St Gereon's Church.**

En route to Nierstein, you pass the other famous vineyards: **Niersteiner Brudersberg, Hipping,** and **Glöck** (possibly Germany's oldest vineyard, recorded in AD 742), which surrounds St Kilian's Church. Turn right at Breitgasse to reach the market square. Nierstein has its wine festival on the first weekend in August, with a parade in medieval dress – a great tasting opportunity.

For an outstanding view, walk or drive into the vineyards *Roter Hang* (red slope) from Karolingerstrasse. From the *Wartturm* (watchtower) turn right and continue towards the Rhine, to the lookout stand in the Brudersberg vineyard. Vintners set up wine stands along this path in mid-June – a delightful setting for a tasting.

Oppenheim

Above Oppenheim is the glorious pink sandstone Gothic church with an intricately carved exterior – the most important church between Cologne and Strasbourg. The interior is equally beautiful with magnificent 14th-century stained glass windows. Other historic buildings are grouped around the medieval town hall on the market square. Here, too, is a lovely *Weinstube*, **Gillot Haus.** The Guntersblum village is famous for its **Kellerweg,** an alley lined with some 100 cellars and press houses of the town's winegrowers since the 17th century.

Alsheim

Rheinblick means "a glance at the Rhine." This is also the name of Alsheimer's wine festival in mid-June. In September (third Sunday), wine stands are set up along a scenic marked path between Alsheim and Hangen-Wahlheim.

Mettenheim marks the end of the gentle hills of this area and it has a Baroque church and a lovely town hall. Twenty Mettenheimer vintners operate a *Weinstube* at "Sandhof." From the B 9 drive towards Eich near the Rhine. Watch for the right turn after one km (half a mile).

WINERIES & MORE

OPPENHEIM

Untergrundführungen (underground tours) of the town's ancient cellars.
Contact: Sektkellerei Gillot
Wormser Strasse 84
55276 Oppenheim
Tel: 06133 3239
www.gillot.de
Or inquire at Gillot Haus (Merianstrasse 1-3).

Deutsches Weinbaumuseum
Wormser Strasse 49
55275 Oppenheim
Tel: 06133 2544
www.weinbaumuseum.com
Fascinating history of winegrowing and production in Germany from Roman times to the present.

NACKENHEIM

Weingut Gunderloch
Carl-Gunderloch-Platz 1
55299 Nackenheim
Tel: 06135 2341
www.gunderloch.de

NIERSTEIN

Weingut Heyl zu Herrnsheim
Willhelmstrasse 4
55283 Nierstein am Rhein
Tel: 06133 509110
www.heyl-zu-herrnsheim.de

Wonnegau

This is the winegrowing area between Worms and Alzey and has been known for centuries as Wonnegau, "the Happy Land." It is a bit like the Shire in *The Lord of the Rings* and until about 1990 was a semi-legendary, almost forgotten hilly area, spreading north and west of Worms.

There were vineyards here in Roman times, but it was in Charlemagne's time that they spread to other areas. Riesling was recorded as early as 1490, which indicates that it has always thrived here. The climate is soft and sunny and the terroirs differ from one slope to another. They are composed in various proportions of limestone and clay in some places and alluvial gravels and sandstone in others, sometimes overlaid with wind-blown loess, all of which favor the production of fine wines.

As already mentioned in the introduction to this chapter, this is where the reformation of the wines of Rheinhessen began in the 1990s. In the past, the growers used to sell their wines to the merchants in Worms and elsewhere, so the merchants made their own blends and sold the wines under their labels. Most of the growers bottled enough of their wines, usually their best Rieslings, and kept them in their cellars for their families and for special occasions. They had great pride in these, but when the reputation of many Rheinhessen wines deteriorated, two of the growers decided to bottle and sell their wines themselves. Today there are many growers who have followed their example.

Message in a Bottle

In the 1990s the growers' sons and daughters, who had attended the Wine Institute at Geisenheim, or other wine colleges, were determined to use their knowledge and passion. Some of their parents, who were not ready to retire, decided to let them gradually make use of this knowledge, and then to take over the responsibility for the family vineyards. If they wanted to travel for a few months to Burgundy, Australia, the USA or elsewhere, to learn about winemaking, their parents would look after everything.

Message in a Bottle is a dynamic association of young growers in Rheinhessen, who share their love of wine, their experiences and their ambitions to make fine wines. From this, a whole new generation of young growers has developed in Wonnegau, as well as elsewhere in Germany.

Their primary goal is to return the growers' vineyards to the minimal use of chemicals and pesticides and to encourage the return of natural management of the vines. Secondly, they aim to reduce the yields to get more concentration in the grapes. Thirdly, they aspire to ferment the grapes and develop the wines with the least interference. These are core parts of the principles of every member of the VDP in order to make great wines.

A tour of the wine villages of Wonnegau

In many of the villages, even simple structures often have artistic details, such as a beautiful portal or a carved cellar door. Peep into the courtyards. Unique to the Wonnegau are the *Trulli*, **cone- or dome-shaped vintners' huts** used as tool sheds and shelters for vineyard workers. These huts are in the vineyards southeast and northwest of Alzey.

Before visiting the old wine villages, you should acquire a fairly large-scale map. Leave Worms from the northwest and drive on a round trip. At Herrnsheim, you can stop to see the castle and its English gardens, and then to Osthofen, the gateway to Wonnegau, turn left and 5 km (3 miles) west is Westhofen.

This village was first documented in AD 744 and today it has about 3300 inhabitants. There are two beautiful churches, a Baroque town hall, and in the Kellergasse (cellar lane), 12 vaulted cellars built about 1600 deep below the marketplace. One is opened during the wine festival. There are four great vineyards close to the village: **Westhofener Aulerde; Kirchspiel; Morstein** and **Brünnenhäuschen**.

Take the road northeast to Bechtheim, with its prime Rosengarten vineyard, and on to the northwest. There are several very good estates there. Then you will come to Dittelsheim and its splendid vineyard, **Leckerberg**.

Turning south you arrive again at Westhofen, from where you go southwest to Flörnsheim and its great **Frauenberg** vineyard and **Dalsheim** and its equally fine **Dalsheimer Bürgel** and **Hubacher vineyards**. These two villages are so close to each other that they have been amalgamated, though there is an unusual *Fleckenmauer*, a medieval notched stone wall, surrounding the center.

You can then head a little further south to the village of Kriegsheim and its **Rosengarten** vineyard, and the adjacent village of Monsheim, with its

The town hall of Alsheim, formerly a busy Rhine wine town.

vineyard **Silberberg**. You can also see a Stone Age monolith, the Hinkelstein, in the Schlosshof (castle courtyard). Then you could join the main road B 247 to Alzey.

Alzey

Along the side streets of Obermarkt (market square) there are many beautiful half-timbered houses. The Renaissance town hall on **Fischmarkt** and the fountains and historic buildings on **Rossmarkt** are also worth seeing, as are the 12th-century castle and remnants of the town's fortifications. The tourist office in the Rathaus (town hall) has brochures in English describing a 90-minute circular walk of Alzey. On the outskirts of the town is the grape-breeding institute where Georg Scheu bred many of the aromatic crossings of different vine varieties.

WINERIES & MORE

WESTHOFEN

Weingut Wittmann
Mainzer Strasse 19
67593 Westhofen bei Worms
Tel: 06244 905036
www.wittmannweingut.com

Weingut Seehof-Ernst Fauth
Seegasse 20
67593 Westhofen
Tel: 06244 4935
www.weingut-seehof.de

BECHTHEIM

Weingut Dreissigacker
Untere Klinggasse 4
67595 Bechtheim
Tel: 06242 2425
www.dreissigacker-wein.de

Weingut Spiess
Gaustrasse 2
67595 Bechtheim
Tel: 06242 7633
www.spiess-wein.de

Weingut Oekonomierat Johann Geil Erben
Kuhpfortenstrasse 11
67595 Bechtheim
Tel: 06242 1546
www.weingut-geil.de

Worms

Worms is one of Germany's oldest cities. It was the capital of a large Celtic settlement and an important Roman garrison town before becoming the short-lived capital of Gunther's Burgundian kingdom (AD 413). Its destruction by the Huns (AD 436) is retold in *The Song of the Nibelungs*. During its golden era, the free and imperial town of Worms was the site of more than 100 Imperial Diets (synods), including that of 1521 at which Martin Luther refused to revoke his writings. After this significant event, Worms' political importance declined as the German emperors lost their authority. Although much of the town was devastated during the Thirty Years'

Surrounding the Church of Our Lady, the Liebfrauenstift-Kirchenstück vineyard in Worms gave its name to Liebfraumilch.

War, the War of the Palatinate Succession and World War II, there are still many historic treasures.

One of Germany's three great Rhenish Imperial Cathedrals, **St Peter's**, was built in the 11th and 12th centuries on the site of the old Roman forum. The ornate exterior is worth seeing before viewing the works of art inside, including the Baroque high altar by Balthasar Neumann and the rococo choir stalls.

Europe's oldest surviving Jewish cemetery, with tombstones dating from the 11th century, is on **Andreasring**. Germany's oldest synagogue (1034) and the **Rashi House**, a museum devoted to the history of Worms' Jewish community, are located on Judengasse, once the heart of the Jewish quarter.

Liebfraumilch

In the 18th century wines from the vineyard surrounding the Gothic Liebfrauenkirche (Church of Our Lady) were called Wörmser Liebfrauenstift Kirchenstück. This vineyard produces excellent Riesling wines today.

The medieval watchtower in the Dalsheimer Hubacker vineyard in Wonnegau, part of which is owned by the Keller wine estate.

Later, the wines from larger areas began to be sold as Liebfraumilch, literally "Milk of the Blessed Mother." As demand increased, this became a mass-produced wine from any source in Germany (and elsewhere, including Austria). Its quality declined to a level described by the German insult, "Zuckerwasser" (sugar water).

"Rheinhessen's Switzerland"

This very small area a few miles southeast of Bad Kreuznach has beautiful steep hills with volcanic terroir including porphyry, a hard reddish rock with crystals of feldspar, similar to those around the famous Schloss Böckelheim in the Nahe region. The village at the center of this area is Siefersheim, and the Wagner family knew that very good wines were made there a century ago. The talented Daniel Wagner studied viti- and viniculture at Geisenheim and by 2002 he was making his first wines. Gradually he improved the vineyards and in 2009 the wines of the Weingut were one of the three finest in Rheinhessen. No doubt there will be a rush follow his example.

The family estate has large parcels in two steep vineyards, **Siefersheimer**

Heerkretz and **Höllberg**, and these are ideal for Riesling, Silvaner, Weiss- and Grauburgunder. The Wagner family also have a very attractive guesthouse and *Weinstube*.

To visit this small but enchanting area, you could start at Gau-Bickelheim and drive on a circular route through Wöllstein, Neu-Bamberg, Wonsheim, then Siefersheim, and on to Wendelsheim, Flonheim and Armsheim. From here it is an easy drive back to Bingen via the A 61. On the road from Wendelsheim to Nack, watch for the sign to the *Teufelsrutsch* (devil's slide) vantage-point for a stunning view. There are also several *Trulli*, or vintners' huts, in the vineyards between Wendelsheim and Flonheim.

Bingen and around

Bingen has the region's only quartzite-slate soil, similar to that above Rüdesheim on the north side of the river. The steep south-facing **Binger Scharlachberg** vineyard has the potential to produce great Riesling wines. The view from the top is glorious.

The strategic position of Bingen at the confluence of the Nahe and Rhine rivers was enhanced when the Roman Drusus built the first bridge, the foundations of which still support Bingen's oldest exisiting bridge (c.10th century) across the Nahe. Medieval Bingen was an important conduit for goods and armies between Mainz, Koblenz and Trier and it is still a center of the wine trade. **St Martin's Basilica**, near the Drusus bridge, is a Gothic church with an 11th-century crypt, beautiful vaulting and medieval sculptures.

Since Celtic times, Klopp hill in the center of Bingen has been the site of fortresses that were burned down, blown up and bombed through the centuries. Today, the reconstructed Klopp fortress houses the town hall and an interesting history museum. From its tower you have a sweeping view of the area. The **St Rochus Kapelle** is a hillside chapel with an impressive altar and crucifix outside. Perched at the top of the Rochusberg, it is visible for miles, especially when it is illuminated at night.

Ingelheim

Charlemagne had his summer palace here. One winter's day, it is said, he noted that the snow had already melted on the opposite side of the Rhine (today the site of Schloss Johannisberg) and ordered vines to be planted there. The remains of his palace and its Saalkirche (church) are worth a visit and also the Burgkirche. Ingelheim's chalky clay soil yields some good Spätburgunder, Dornfelder and simple Portugieser red wines, as well as Silvaner and Riesling white wines. There is a large, celebrated wine festival, *Rotweinfest*, in late September.

If you visit in May or June you can enjoy famous Ingelheimer asparagus and attend "International Days," six weeks of art exhibitions, cultural events and wine tastings. (For details, contact the sponsor: Boehringer, Internationale Tage, www.internationale-tage.de.)

From Igelheim, there is a pleasant drive south via Jugenheim, Partenheim and St Johann (all have treasures in their churches) to Sprendlingen.

WINERIES & MORE

BODENHEIM

Weingut Kühling-Gillot
Oelmühlstrasse 25
55294 Bodenheim
Tel: 06135 2333
www.kuehling-gillot.de

BIEBESHEIM AM RHEIN

Weingut K F Groebe
Bahnhofstrasse 68-70
64584 Biebesheim
Tel: 06258 6721
www.weingut-k-f-groebe.de

DITTELSHEIM-HESSLOCH

Weingut Winter
Hauptstrasse 17
67596 Dittelsheim-Hessloch.
Tel: 06244 7446
www.weingut-winter.de

GUNGHEIM

Weingut Gutzler
Rossgasse 19
67599 Gundheim
Tel: 0644 905221
www.gutzler.de

FLORSHEIM-DALSHEIM

Weingut Keller
Bahnhofstrasse 1
67592 Flörsheim-Dalsheim
Tel: 06243 456
www.keller-wein.de

HOHEN-SÜLSEN

Weingut Battenfeld-Spanier
Bahnhofstrasse 33
67591 Hohen-Sülzen
Tel: 06243 906515
www.battenfeld-spanier.de

SIEFERSHEIM

Weingut Wagner-Stempel
Wöllsteiner Strasse 10
55599 Siefersheim
Tel: 06703 960330
www.wagner-stempel.de

Possibly Germany's oldest, the vineyard of Glöck, by the church of St Kilian, Nierstein, was first recorded in AD 742.

WHERE TO STAY AND EAT

Bodenheim

Weingut Kühling-Gillot
Am Pavillon (W)
Olmühlstrasse 25
55294 Bodenheim
Tel: 06135 23 33
www.kuehling-gillot.de
Weinstube in the beautiful garden and superb wines in a very modern pavillion.

Gau-Bischofsheim

Weingut Nack (R/W)
Pfarrstrasse 13
55296 Gau-Bischofsheim
Tel: 06135 3043
www.restaurant-nack.de
Former historic vineyard, now a restaurant/*Weinstube* in a vaulted wine cellar, international food and fine wines, Wed-Fri evenings only, weekends lunch and dinner.

Mainz

Hyatt Regency (H/R)
Malakoff-Terrasse 1
55116 Mainz
Tel: 06131 731234
www.mainz.regency.hyatt.de
Bellpepper Restaurant serves high quality international cuisine.

Favorite Parkhotel (H/R)
Karl-Weiser-Strasse 1
55131 Mainz
Tel: 06131 80150
www.favorite-mainz.de
Restaurant Bierkutsche (separately managed, Michelin star), very high quality food.

Geberts Weinstuben (R/W)
Frauenlobstrasse 94
55118 Mainz
Tel: 06131 611619
www.gebertsweinstuben.de
Lovely restaurant with excellent food.

Riesling grapes ready for harvest.

Barrels in the 16th-century cellar of Weingut Wittmann, Wonnegau.

Buchholz (R)
Klosterstrasse 27
55124 Mainz-Gonsenheim
(8 km on Saarstrasse)
Tel: 06131 9712890
www.frank-buchholz.de
Michelin-starred restaurant. Expensive, but immaculate and original.

Drei Lilien (R)
Ballplatz 2
55116 Mainz
Tel: 06131 225068
Inviting and friendly.

Haus des Deutschen Weines (R)
Gutenberg-Platz 3-5
(next to the theater)
55116 Mainz
Tel: 06131 221300
www.hdw-gaststaetten.de
Large selection of German wines (also by the glass).

Siefersheim

Weingut Wagner-Stempel (H/W)
Wöllsteiner Strasse 10
55599 Siefersheim
Tel: 06703 960330
www.wagner-stempel.de
Guesthouse and *Weinstube*.

Prädikats Weine
Lingenfelder
Weingut
PROBE+
VERKAUF

PFALZ

THE PFALZ IS THE GARDEN OF EDEN of the German wine regions. Figs, lemons, sweet chestnuts, almonds, and of course grapes, thrive in this exceptionally warm and sunny climate, protected from bad weather by the Haardt Mountains. Pfälzer hospitality is as inviting as the climate, and game from the forests adds another dimension. The world's largest wine festival is held in Bad Dürkheim, and the region's typical wine glass, the *Schoppen*, holds half a liter of wine. Share a *Schoppen* in a *Weinstube* or at one of the Pfalz's many wine festivals. *Zum Wohl*. Cheers!

The Pfalz is bordered by Rheinhessen to the north and Alsace to the south. For 95 km (60 miles), a ribbon of vineyards runs parallel to the steep foothills of the forested Haardt Mountains. To become acquainted with the landscape and picturesque wine villages from Bockenheim to Schweigen, walk the marked *Wanderweg* (hiking trail), or you can drive along the *Deutsche Weinstrasse* (German Wine Road), which includes the best of the wine villages. Dating from 1935, it was the first of its kind in Germany and is a route that runs the length of the Pfalz. The last Sunday in August it is the site of a huge wine and folk festival, *Erlebnistag*, with all kinds of activities and tasting stands en route.

The word Pfalz derives from the Latin *palatium*, meaning palace. The imperial residence in Ancient Rome was on the Palatine Hill, and *Kaiserpfalz*, for example, is an Imperial Palace. The Pfalz owes its German heritage to its "wealth of wine," for when the Carolingian Empire was divided in AD 843 (Treaty of Verdun), the Pfalz was ceded to Louis the German to ensure the eastern territory's supply of Communion wine.

‹‹ The Lingenfelder wine estate in the traditional wine village of Grosskarlbach, which holds a wine festival in summer.

Weingut Haardt/Pfalz
Müller-Catoir
Breumel in den Mauern GG

SIEGRIST
SONNENBERG GG
2008

Dr. von Bassermann-Jordan
Pfalz
2010
Hohenmorgen
GG

GIES-DÜPPEL
WEISSER BURGUNDER
2010
KASTANIENBUSCH

Deidesheim
2010
Forster Jesuitengarten
Riesling Auslese
Pfalz
alc. 8,5% by vol.
375 ml

VON BUHL
RIESLING
TROCKEN
2007
WEINGUT REICHSRAT VON BUHL

KNIPSER
2007
»Kalkmergel«
Spätburgunder
13,5% vol
PFALZ
0,75 l

WEINGUT THEO MINGES
RIESLING
Gleisweiler Hölle
Spätlese
2010

Gleisweiler
Albersweiler
Birkweiler
Annweiler
Ranschbach
Leinsweiler
Eschbach
Klingenmünster
Ilbesheim
B48
Impflinger
Gleiszellen
Billigheim
B38
Bad Bergzabern
Dörrenbach
B427
Schweigen
B38

Morschheim
B40
Kirchheim-Bolanden
Alzey
B47
Zellertal
Monsheim
Worms
Pfrimm
Dreisen
Bockenheim
B271
Grünstadt
Dirmstein
Laumersheim
Grosskarlbach
A6
Neuleiningen
Kleinkarlbach
Weisenheim am Berg
Freinsheim
Leinstadt
Kallstadt
B37
Ungstein
Bad Dürkheim
A650
Wachenheim
Forst
Deidesheim
Niederkirchen
Gimmeldingen
Ruppertsberg
A65
Haardt
Mussbach
N
S
E
W
Maikammer
B39
Speyer
B272
Queich
Bellheim

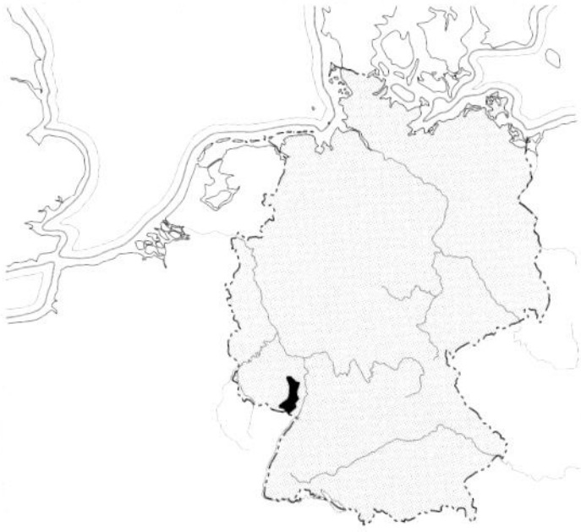

Roman origins

The great tradition of vine growing in the Pfalz dates from Roman times. Of the many Roman wine artifacts unearthed throughout the region, three finds are particularly exciting. Two Roman farms, where vines were also cultivated, were discovered in the 1980s when the vineyards east of Wachenheim and north of Ungstein were reorganized. Both sites, the **Villa rustica** and the **Römerkelter**, are worth visiting. The third find was a glass amphora dated about AD 300, sealed airtight under a layer of resin and oil, which enabled the wine to survive for more than 17 centuries. It was found near Speyer and you can see the glass amphora in the fascinating Speyer wine museum.

Pfalz is Germany's second largest wine region with 23,389 hectares (57,780 acres). Most of the best vineyards are on the slopes at the foot of the Haardt Mountains. There are many soil types in a region this large. Loam soil predominates, in a variety of mixtures with colored sandstone, chalk, loess, clay, sand and volcanic rock.

Riesling is the most important white grape variety (22 per cent), from powerful dry Grosses Gewächs to the glorious rich Auslese wines. The amount of Müller-Thurgau (10 per cent) has dropped by more than half in two decades. It is mainly planted in lower, flat mass-production areas to the east of the *Deutsche Weinstrasse*. The increasingly successful varieties near the Weinstrasse are Riesling, Weissburgunder, Grauburgunder, Silvaner, Scheurebe, delicate traditional Muscateller and Gewürztraminer (sometimes labelled Traminer, because it is lighter than the Alsace style and has more of a fragrant bouquet of roses). In other regions, Chardonnay and Sauvignon Blanc are not very good, but here they can be delicious.

Of the red varieties, Dornfelder wines are often excellent and it is widely planted (14 per cent) in the Pfalz. It is mainly marketed in Germany, because there is a wide difference in quality between a wine from an estate and that sold in a supermarket. Spätburgunder is always very choosy in its terroir and the way it is

Rainer Lingenfelder shows the development of his grapes.

made. Nevertheless, more and more is being planted in suitable sites. Other red varieties, Merlot, Cabernet Sauvignon and Syrah are also proving their merits, and many estates produce really good *Sekt*.

Cobbled streets full of flower boxes and vine-clad houses, delicious wine and food and friendly, outgoing people make the Pfalz especially inviting. The best time to enjoy this ambience is between March, when the almond trees blossom, and the end of the harvest in mid-November.

Bockenheim to Bad Dürkheim

The *Deutsche Weinstrasse* (German Wine Road) begins in Bockenheim and ends some 80 km (50 miles) south at Schweigen on the French border. It corresponds mainly to the B 271. The *Wanderweg* (German hiking trail) also begins in Bockenheim, to the right of Leininger Ring and opposite St Martin's Church. St Lambert's Church, further south on the right, has a notable Madonna and Christ-child with a cluster of grapes. You can always walk a section and return to your car by bus or train. Signposts feature a green cluster of grapes on a white background.

Leiningerland

From 1100 to the French Revolution, the Counts of Leiningen ruled the area surrounding Grünstadt, where they built their residence after their fortresses in Neuleiningen and Altleiningen were destroyed. All three places are worth a visit, particularly the romantic medieval town of Neuleiningen. Remains of the fortress crown tiers of winding alleys lined with half-timbered houses, all of which are encircled by the ancient town walls. There are wonderful views from all levels.

From here, follow the road parallel to the Eckbach (stream) from Kleinkarlbach to Grosskarlbach, a traditional wine village with Renaissance manors built around spacious courtyards. Explore the town on foot to see the beautifully carved portals, old mills and art treasures in both churches. Historic **Kändelgasse**, a picturesque lane along the stream, is the site of a typical wine festival in late July or early August.

The best vineyard here is **Grosskarlbacher Burgweg.**

The little chapel of St Michael is surrounded by the tiny vineyard of Dürkheimer Michelsberg at the very edge of the town of Dürkheim.

From there, head north about three miles to Laumersheim and its best site, **Laumersheimer Mandelberg**. The next village, Dirmstein also has a fine vineyard, **Dirmsteiner Mandelpfad**, and noble mansions (Marktstrasse, Obertor and Metzgergasse) as well as a church designed by the great architect, Balthasar Neumann.

Then return to Grosskarlbach and on to Freinsheim, another medieval gem, surrounded by town walls, which are punctuated at intervals by watchtowers and gateways. The best walking tour is along the winding alley next to the old walls, starting from the Baroque town hall and Gothic church at the heart of town. The walls are also the unique setting for the *Stadtmauerfest* (wine festival) in mid-July.

Kallstadt is on the *Deutsche Weinstrasse*, further south and west, and is renowned for great Riesling and Spätburgunder wines. **Kallstadter Saumagen** (sow's stomach), is the name both of its best vineyard and of a rather alarming Pfälzer specialty made of minced pork, potatoes and spices cooked in a casing (sow's stomach). You can also enjoy this at the wine festival in early September.

A Roman wine estate

This was discovered in **Ungsteiner Weilberg**, when the vineyard was uprooted in 1981 as part of the vineyard reorganization program. The owners of this great vineyard generously agreed to forfeit part of it to enable archeologists to continue excavation and restoration work. While it is interesting to view Roman artifacts in a museum, it is even better to see the origins of German viticulture on site, a reminder that even 2000 years ago these sunny hillsides were favored locations for growing grapes.

Bad Dürkheim

This busy town is a dormitory for those who work in the cities of Ludwigshafen and Mannheim and also the link between the northern traditional wine villages and the greatest concentration of the glorious historical wine villages as far as Neustadt. The town has two great vineyards, **Dürkheimer Michelsberg** and **Spiegelberg**.

The harvest at the Pfefflingen estate in Bad Dürkheim.

The *Wurstmarkt* is the world's largest wine and sausage festival dating from the 14th century. It takes place in mid-September near the **Dürkheimer Riesenfass**, the 1,700,000-liter (449,092-gallon) cask near the entrance to the town. You can taste the local wines and regional specialties in the restaurant inside the cask. Try a *Leberknödel* (liver dumpling) or *Pfälzer Rumpsteak* (roast beef with onions), and after that you can recover at the neoclassical Kurhaus, which has a casino and the huge Philippshall Saline (salt works). The last-named, although hideous, is a listed cultural monument. Opposite the giant cask, **Weingut Fitz-Ritter** has a unique gift shop with wine-related objects, as well as the estate's still and sparkling wines.

WINERIES & MORE

LAUMERSHEIM

Weingut Knipser
Hauptstrasse 47
67229 Laumersheim
Tel: 06238 742
www.weingut-knipser.de

Weingut Philipp Kuhn
Grosskarlbacher Strasse 20
67229 Laumersheim
Tel: 06238 656
www.weingut-philipp-kuhn.de

KALLSTADT

Weingut Koehler-Ruprecht
Weinstrasse 84
67169 Kallstadt
Tel: 06322 1829
www.koehler-ruprecht.de

BAD DÜRKHEIM

Weingut Pfeffingen-Fuhrmann-Eymael
Deutsche Weinstrasse
67098 Bad Dürkheim

Tel: 06322 8607
www.pfeffingen.de

Weingut Fitz-Ritter
Weinstrasse Nord 51
67098 Bad Dürkheim
Tel: 06322 5389
www.fitz-ritter.de

Bad Dürkheim to Neustadt

This section of the German Wine Road includes some of Germany's most famous wine villages. The classic vineyards on the hillsides yield big, ripe, dry, and sweet Riesling wines, full of character. Here, as throughout the Pfalz, there are traditional family estates, large and small. The area's fame, however, is derived from its Rieslings and from the "three B's of the Pfalz": Dr. von Bassermann-Jordan, Dr. Bürklin-Wolf and Reichsrat von Buhl – far-sighted estate owners who were staunch supporters of high-quality wines. Today, most of their wines are brilliant, but so are those of other other top quality estates.

The picturesque forests of the Haardt Mountains are as popular today as they were in Roman times. The surrounding woods are not only beautiful, but they are also rich in historic sites. **The Heidenmauer**, a Celtic bulwark, a Roman quarry, and the ruins of both the Gothic **Limburg Abbey** and the mighty **Hardenburg** fortress are all worth a visit.

Wachenheim, Forst, Deidesheim and Ruppertsberg

Panoplies of vines – green in summer and brilliant golden red in autumn – adorn aristocratic manors along the narrow streets of these wine villages. Wachenheim's hillside landmark, the **Wachtenburg**, has a good view and a chance to sample the local wines listed. **Wachenheimer Gerümpel** is the most famous vineyard. To see the *Villa Rustica* (Roman farm, AD 20) drive towards Friedelsheim (east of the B 271).

The drive from Wachenheim to Forst is scarcely half a mile, but to see the beautiful Renaissance houses and historic wine estates of Forst, you must bear to the right at the fork in the road just before the town or you will miss "old" Forst completely. The Baroque statue of the Madonna in the vineyards overlooking the town is the namesake of the Mariengarten site. Forst has a plethora of great vineyards – **Forster Ungeheuer, Jesuitengarten, Freundstück, Kirchenstück** and **Pechstein.** *Pechstein* means the black volcanic basalt that gives these vineyards their unique character.

The market square in Deidesheim, with the 16th-century town hall and Gothic church of **St Ulrich**, is among the most memorable in the Pfalz. This is the site of the annual *Geisbockversteigerung* (goat auction) on Pentecost Tuesday, a custom dating from the Middle Ages, when neighboring Lambrecht paid tribute to Deidesheim for grazing rights.

A stroll along romantic Feigengasse, Deichelgasse or Heumarktstrasse is a bonus. Anyway, enjoy a glass of wine in **Schloss Deidesheim** or in its idyllic garden. The great vineyards here are **Deidesheimer Grainhüber, Kalkofen, Hohenmorgen** and **Langenmorgen.**

In Ruppertsberg, which is attached to Deidesheim, the great vineyards are **Ruppertsberger Gaisberg, Reiterpfad** and **Spiess.**

Deidesheim's Winzerverein was the first cooperative in the Pfalz in 1898. You can taste the wines prior to purchase, and they have a restaurant.

Königsbach and Mussbach

The next wine village is Königsbach and it has a wonderful vineyard, **Königsbacher Idig**, whose wines are equally perfect as a great dry Riesling Grosses Gewächs, and as a superlative sweet Riesling Trockenbeerenauslese. From the vineyard, there is a panorama of the Rhine valley. Gimmelldingen is another beautiful wine village high up on the mountain, whose great vineyard is **Gimmelldinger Mandelgarten** (almond garden), and the penultimate village is Haardt and its two famous vineyards, **Burgarten** and **Herrenletten.**

The important viticultural teaching and research institute of Mussbach owns the Pfalz's oldest (8th century) wine estate, **Johannitergut.** Within its stone walls there is a beautiful courtyard and a medieval garden (always open) and

This friendly Ungeheuer (monster) greets you at the entrance to Forst. Ungeheuer is also the name of the village's finest vineyard.

a wine museum in the Herrenhof (by appointment only, www.herrenhof-mussbach.de). Eselshaut (donkey's hide) is the name of Mussbach's best-known vineyard.

Neustadt

The wine suburbs of Neustadt have large areas of flat vineyards and the wines are not memorable, as they were largely used for Liebfraumilch. Nevertheless, in late September, Neustadt hosts a major wine event, the *Deutsche Weinlesefest* (German wine harvest festival). The ten-day celebration includes a colorful parade and the coronation of the German Wine Queen. The market square, the center of the Old Town, is dominated by the Baroque town hall and the Gothic **Liebfrauenkirche** church, which has a decor rich in sculptural details.

Historic houses of interest are in the streets near the market square, such as Metzgergasse, Rathausstrasse and Hauptstrasse. From May to Oct you can travel on the *Kuckucksbähnel* (historic train) from Neustadt to Elmstein, for a scenic ride through the beautiful Pfälzer forest.

REGIONAL WINE PROMOTION BOARD

Pfalzwein e.V.
Martin-Luther-Strasse 69
67433 Neustadt
Tel: 06321 912328
www.zum-wohl-die-pfalz.de

WINERIES & MORE

WACHENHEIM

Weingut Dr Bürklin-Wolf
Weinstrasse 65
67157 Wachenheim
Tel: 06322 95330
www.buerklin-wolf.de

DEIDESHEIM

Weingut Reichsrat von Buhl
Weinstrasse 16
67146 Deidesheim
Tel: 06326 96500
www.reichsrat-von-buhl.de

Weingut Geheimer Rat Dr von Bassermann-Jordan
Kirchgasse 10
67146 Deidesheim
Tel: 06326 6006
www.bassermann-jordan.de

Weingut Dr Deinhard
Weinstrasse 10
67146 Deidesheim
Tel: 06326 221
www.dr-deinhard.de

Museum für Weinkultur
Marktplatz
67146 Deidesheim
Tel: 06326 981561
www.weinkultur-deidesheim.de
Wine articles of cultural-historical significance, in the historic town hall. Wed–Sun 3PM–6PM. Closed Jan-Feb.

FORST

Weingut Georg Mosbacher
Weinstrasse 27
67147 Forst
Tel: 06326 329
www.georg-mosbacher.de

HAARDT

Weingut Müller-Catoir
Mandelring 25
67433 Haardt
Tel: 06321 2815
www.mueller-catoir.de

NEUSTADT-HAARDT

Weingut Weegmüller
Mandelring 23
67433 Neustadt-Haardt
Tel: 06321 837 72
www.weegmueller-weine.de

Haus des Weines
Rathausstrasse 6
67433 Neustadt
Tel: 06321 355871
www.haus-des-weines.com
Showcase for Neustadt wines and grape-based products, with 30 wines to taste by the glass. In a Gothic house (1276). Tues–Fri 10AM–6PM, Sat 10AM–3PM, Closed Sun.

Speyer

Speyer is situated on the Rhine some 25 km (15 miles) east of Neustadt. Its origins date from settlements during the Stone, Bronze and Iron Ages. In Roman times, it was an important military and commercial center of the upper Rhine, and in the 11th century Speyer was named capital of the German Empire.

The magnificent Kaiserdom (imperial cathedral) testifies to Speyer's importance as a center of temporal and ecclesiastical power during the Middle Ages. **The Historisches Museum der Pfalz** has excellent displays recounting Speyer's 5000 years of history, and it houses the Domschatz, the original art and historic treasures of the cathedral. (www.museum.speyer.de). Speyer was a bishopric as early as the 4th century. The bishops were the heads of Church and State until 1294, when they renounced their secular authority and Speyer was declared a free imperial city. Henceforth, the "border" between the spiritual and worldly realms was symbolized in front of the cathedral by the *Domnapf* (basin), which was traditionally filled with wine for the populace whenever a new bishop was consecrated.

The Bishops of Speyer owned many of the most important vineyards in the Pfalz from 1100, until Napoleon secularized church properties in 1803. The wine museum in the Historisches Museum der Pfalz chronicles 2000 years of viticulture with historic and cultural objects related to wine, including the world's oldest bottle of wine.

Birkweiler's vineyards have limestone soils rich in marine fossils.

Historic sights

Not far from the cathedral, on the Judengasse, is the former center of Jewish culture in Speyer. The 11th-century synagogue is gone, but you can visit the women's baths, which are underground – the oldest and largest of their kind in present-day Germany.

Town fortifications were built during the 13th century. Two of the original 68 towers are intact: **Altpörtal**, the impressive western gate on Maximilianstrasse, and **Heidentürmchen**, a two-story defence tower in the garden behind the cathedral. Baroque enthusiasts will enjoy the rich decor of the **Dreifaltigkeitskirche** (Church of the Holy Trinity) and the archive and chambers of the town hall. The neo-Gothic **Gedächtniskirche** (Memorial Church) commemorates those who protested at the edict of the Diet of Speyer in 1529, which rejected Luther's theses (hence the name Protestants).

The cathedral

In 1027, Konrad II was crowned Emperor by the Pope. Three years later, he laid the cornerstone of Germany's supreme work of Romanesque architecture. The cathedral is remarkable for its innovative vaulted bays, probably the earliest use of extensive groined vaulting in Europe. During the second period of construction (1082-1125), the flat wooden ceiling of the nave was replaced with vaulting. The beautiful crypt is the burial place of four emperors, three empresses, four kings and five bishops. (www.speyer.de)

An apricot tree stands next to an old grape press near Edenkoben.

The Southern Wine Road

The large winegrowing area from Neustadt to the French border at Schweigen is known as the *Südliche Weinstrasse* (Southern Wine Road). This takes you into a series of lovely villages where many of the best wines are to be found.

Since 1990 the Southern Pfalz has completely changed. Historic buildings have been lovingly restored and richly adorned with flowers. Individual houses and entire villages compete to be named the "prettiest." The quality and value of good wines has soared, encouraged by the success wines of five dynamic growers known as *Fünf Freunde aus der Südpfalz* (Five Friends of the Southern Pfalz).

Hambach, Maikammer and St Martin

The **Hambacher Schloss**, where 30,000 people demonstrated for freedom and unity in 1832, merits a visit (www.hambacherschloss.eu). The **Kalmit**, highest summit (673 m/2208 ft) of the Pfälzer woods, is the backdrop of the wine villages Maikammer and Alsterweiler. To the east, a veritable sea of ordinary vineyards stretches from the edge to the center of the Rhine plain.

Maikammer has cheerful half-timbered houses and in the Alsterweiler Kapelle (chapel) there is a remarkable Gothic triptych. Just to the east there are two highly-regarded vineyards, **Kirrweiler Mandelberg** and **Duttweiler Kalkberg**. The scenery along the road to St Martin via the Kalmit is worth the slight detour from the wine road. St Martin, a romantic little wine village, is considered by many to be the prettiest in the Pfalz. The town's patron saint and namesake is honored with a parade and festival on November 11. You can enjoy a good view over a glass of wine at the **Kropsburg fortress** above the town.

Edenkoben to Rhodt

Edenkoben is a charming wine town. A *Weinlehrpfad* (educational wine trail) through the vineyards leads to **Schloss Ludwigshöhe**, a palace built in the 1850s in the style of a Pompeian villa by King Ludwig I of Bavaria. The period rooms and art gallery with works of the leading German impressionist, Max Slevogt (1868-1932), are worth a visit (www.landesmuseum-mainz.de/enid/836).

From here, take the **Rietburgbahn** (chairlift, **www.rietburgbahn-edenkoben.de**) further uphill to the Rietburg fortress ruins for a spectacular panorama extending to Heidelberg, Worms and Speyer on a clear day. In Rhodt, you can see Germany's oldest productive vines, a plot of Traminer more than 350 years old, in the Rosengarten site opposite the Co-operative. Theresienstrasse is the premier attraction of Rhodt. Vines and fig trees embellish the façades of growers' houses on this lane. Historic sights include St Georgskirche, Baroque houses, a town hall dating from 1606, the 18th-century Schlössl (little palace) and the best vineyard, **Rhodter Schlossberg**, at the northern edge of town.

The names of a number of villages end with *weiler*, the German word for hamlet. Much of their appeal lies in the natural beauty of their surroundings. In Burrweiler there is an unusually ornate sandstone portal carved with animal symbols (near the corner of Hauptstrasse and Weinstrasse). **Burrweiler Schäwer** is a fine vineyard. Gleisweiler is a health resort with a subtropical park near the Kurhaus (clinic). On Bergstrasse you can see works of the local artist Herbert Lorenz in a sculpture garden in front of his home. This village too has a fine vineyard, **Gleisweiler Hölle**.

Annweiler and Burg Trifels

To visit one of Germany's most impressive fortresses, **Burg Trifels**, drive west from Siebeldingen via Albersweiler to Annweiler, a quaint little resort. On Wassergasse, Quodgasse and Schipkapass, you can see the historic houses and a paddle-wheel picturesquely situated along the stream running through the town.

Burg Trifels, a former imperial residence, is built into a rocky cliff in the Pfälzer woods. The crown jewels were stored in the chapel during the 12th and 13th centuries (copies are on display here; the originals are in Vienna). King

The Deidesheimer Hof is one of the most famous hotels in the Pfalz, with two restaurants serving very good regional food.

Richard I of England (the Lionheart) was imprisoned here from 1193 to 1194. Burg Trifels was never captured, but was damaged by lightning in 1662. It has been rebuilt in neo-Romanesque style over the past 50 years.

Siebeldingen and Birkweiler

This area is the geological heart of the Southern Wine Road. There are volcanic faults in the Vosges Mountains in Alsace, France, the best known of which is around Ribeauvillé. These volcanic faults created the complexity of soils and *terroirs* for producing great wines. The Haardt Mountains are a continuation of the Vosges Mountains and the same applies to vineyards here. This is where the five dynamic growers known as the *Fünf Freunde aus der Südpfalz* inherited their vineyards, and discovered how to maximize the quality of their great wines from Siebeldinger Sonnenberg, Birkweiler Kastianienbusch and Mandelberg.

Landau and suburbs

Landau, the wine capital of the southern Pfalz, was under French rule from 1648 until the early 19th century. After a devastating fire in 1689, Louis XIV sent his military engineer Vauban to rebuild Landau into the "mightiest fortified town of

Christendom." The French Gate and the German Gate are well preserved. The rest of the extensive ramparts and moats have been turned into beautiful gardens.

The *Purzelmarkt*, one of Germany's oldest folk festivals, dating from 1450, is held in Billigheim in mid-September. There is a parade featuring historical costumes, followed by an afternoon of horse races and medieval games, including a *Purzel* (somersault) race. Wine stands are set up in growers' courtyards and on the market square.

You can return to the wine road via Ilbesheim, which has a notable Gothic town hall and half-timbered houses.

Leinsweiler

The town is situated at the foot of the Slevogthof, Slevogt's hillside summer home, which he decorated with remarkable frescoes depicting scenes from operas by Mozart and Wagner (www.slevogthof-neukastel.de). The finest vineyard here is **Leinsweiler Sonnenberg.**

Eschbach to Bad Bergzabern

Viewed from Eschbach, the ruins of the 11th-century Madenburg fortress look like a miniature city on top of the hill. It affords a good view and has interesting details, such as Renaissance portals and tower staircases. Klingenmünster and Gleiszellen (on Winzergasse) have pretty, half-timbered houses.

Bad Bergzabern is a spa with notable buildings on its market square. On Königstrasse 45, you can dine in the most magnificent Renaissance house of the Pfalz, the **Gasthaus Zum Engel** (except Wed). Down the street, have a look inside the courtyard of the 16th-century ducal palace.

Dörrenbach to Schweigen

Idyllically set in a side valley is the wine village of Dörrenbach. An awe-inspiring fortified church is an interesting counterpoint to the half-timbered houses it overlooks. Vineyards and orchards line both sides of the wine road as it winds past steep hills

Leinsweiler is but one village whose wines benefit from the complex soils resulting from the volcanic fault in the Haardt Mountains.

toward Schweigen. Weingut Friedrich Becker consistantly produces fabulous Spätburgunder wines from three vineyards, the finest of these being **Schweigener Sonnenberg**. These vineyards are so close to the border with Alsace that some of the vines are actually in France!

From the platform of the monumental **Deutsches Weintor** (German Wine Gate), you have a good view of the vineyards, German to the north and French to the south. Near the gate there are arrows to the *Weinlehrpfad* – Germany's first educational wine path – a pleasant walk through the vineyards and lined with historic objects and sculptures. The Weintor marks the end of the wine road.

WINERIES & MORE

GIMMELDINGEN

Weingut Christmann
Peter Koch Strasse 43
67435 Gimmeldingen
Tel: 06321 66039
www.weingut-christmann.de

MAIKAMMER

Weingut Faubel
Marktstrasse 86
67487 Maikammer
Tel: 06321 5048
www.weingut-faubel.de

FLEMLINGEN

Weingut Theo Minges
Bachstrase 11
76835 Flemlingen
Tel: 06323 93350
www.weingut-minges.com

SIEBELDINGEN

Weingut Ökonomierat Rebholz
Weinstrasse 54
76833 Siebeldingen
Tel: 06345 3439
www.oekonomierat-rebholz.de

BIRKWEILER

Weingut Dr Wehrheim
Weinstrasse 8
76831 Birkweiler
Tel: 06345 3542
www.weingut-wehrheim.de

Weingut Gies-Düppel
Am Rosenberg 5
76831 Birkweiler
Tel: 06345 919156
www.gies-dueppel.de

Weingut Siener
Weinstrasse 31
76831 Birkweiler
Tel: 06345 3539
www.weingutsiener.de

LIENSWEILER

Weingut Siegrist
Am Hasensprung 4
76829 Liensweiler
Tel: 06345 1309
www.weingut-siegrist.de

SCHWEIGEN

Weingut Friedrich Becker
Hauptstrasse 29
76889 Schweigen
Tel: 06342 290
www.friedrichbecker.de

WHERE TO STAY AND EAT

Bad Dürkheim

Hotel Annaberg (H/R)
Annabergstrasse 1
67098 Bad Dürkheim
Tel: 06322 94000
www.hotel-annaberg.com
Once a famous *Weingut* but now the four buildings have been converted to a hotel with 32 rooms. Restaurant with international food. In the heart of Annaberg vineyard overlooking Dürkheim and the Rhine Valley.

Philips Brasserie (R)
Römerplatz 3
67098 Bad Dürkheim
Tel: 06322 68808
www.philips-brasserie.de
Attractive restaurant with Mediterranean-style food and reasonable prices.

Birkweiler

Keschdebusch (W)
Hauptstrasse 1
76831 Birkweiler
Tel: 06345 949988
www.keschdebusch-weinstube.de
Delightful *Weinstube*, with delicious traditional food and good wines.

Deidesheim

Deidesheimer Hof (H/R)
Am Marktplatz 1
67146 Deidesheim
Tel: 06326 96870
www.deidesheimerhof.de
Great hotel with 28 rooms. Michelin-starred restaurant Schwarzer Hahn serves classic and original dishes, evenings only. Also St Urban restaurant with regional dishes and fine wines.

Gasthaus zur Kanne (H/R)
Weistrasse 31
67146 Deidesheim
Tel: 06326 96600
www.gasthauszurkanne.de
Pfalz guesthouse from 1160 owned by Weingut Bürklin-Wolf, with their impressive wines and typical fresh regional dishes.

Ketschauer Hof (H/R)
Ketschauerhofstrasse 1
67146 Deidesheim
Tel: 06326 70000
www.ketschauer-hof.com
Another great hotel with 18 rooms. Very elegant Michelin-starred restaurant Freundstück serves creative dishes and seasonal food, plus the splendid

wines from Weingut Bassermann-Jordan among others. Also Weinbistro Bassermännschen, a more modern and lighter style with regional dishes.

Freinsheim

Freinsheimer Hof (H/R)
Breite Strasse 7
67251 Freinsheim
Tel: 06353 5080410
www.restaurant-freinsheimer-hof.de
Very attractive 18th-century winegrower's house with a courtyard open in summer. Restaurant has seasonal food in a lovely atmosphere. Four rooms.

Luther (H/R)
Hauptstrasse 29
67251 Freinsheim
Tel: 06353 93480
www.luther-freinsheim.de
Hotel (closed January) with 20 rooms. Michelin-starred restaurant, great menus and wines (closed Sunday).

Grosskarlbach

Gebrüder Meurer (H/R)
Karlbacher Hauptstrasse 67
67229 Grosskarlbach
Tel: 06238 678
www.restaurant-meurer.de
Restaurant with an idyllic Tuscan flavor and international menu, plus a dream of a garden. Fifteen rooms.

Kallstadt

Weinkastell Zum Weissen Ross (H/R)
Weinstrasse 80-82
67169 Kallstadt
Tel: 06322 5033
www.weinkastell-kohnke.de
Fine regional fare and superb Koehler-Ruprecht wines. Closed mid-Jan to mid-Feb. Beautiful half-timbered inn from 1488 and vaulted wine cellar from 1556.

Leinsweiler

Hotel Leinsweiler Hof (H/R)
Weinstrasse 1
(on the road to Eschbach)
76829 Liensweiler
Tel: 06345 4090
www.leinsweilerhof.de
Restaurant with international food. Beautiful terrace with panorama. Sixty-five rooms.

Pleisweiler-Oberhof Weingut and Landhaus Wilker (H/W)
Hauptstrasse 30-31
76889 Pleisweiler-Oberhofen
Tel: 06343 700700
www.wilker.de

Family hotel with 22 rooms. Regional food and their own wines.

Rhodt

Wohlfühlhotel Alte Rebschule (H/R)
Theresienstrasse 200
76835 Rhodt unter Rietburg
Tel: 06323 70440
www.alte-rebschule.de
Thirty rooms, modern restaurant. Views of the vineyards.

St Martin

Consulat des Weins (H/R)
Maikammerer Strasse 44
67487 St Martin
Tel: 06323 8040
www.schneider-pfalz.de
Very attractive hotel with a wine store.

Wiedemann's Weinhotel (H/R)
Einlaubstrasse 64-66
67487 St Martin
Tel: 06323 94430
www.wiedemann-wein.de
Modern guesthouse with 20 rooms. Restaurant with rustic food.

Winzerhof (H/R)
Maikammerer Strasse 22
67487 St Martin
Tel: 06323 4440
www.wein-und-sekt-becker.de

Wachenheim

Hotel Goldbächel (H/R)
Walstrasse 99
67157 Wachenheim/Weinstrasse
Tel: 06322 94050
www.goldbaechel.de
Hotel with 16 rooms. Restaurant with typical local dishes and wines.

Mobile advertising outside Deidesheim's friendly wine cooperative.

FRANKEN

FRANKEN, the hill region east of Frankfurt, lies between the Spessart Hills and the Steiger Forest. Most of the vineyards follow the zigzag of the Main river through a countryside rich in art treasures, from simple wayside shrines and chapels to churches and palaces within the towered gates of medieval wine villages. Würzburg is both the wine and cultural center of Franken.

Franken is best known for dry, powerful, wines bottled in a distinctive round flagon called a *Bocksbeutel*. You can enjoy the wines with local specialties (fish, sausages, sauerkraut, potato dumplings) in an atmospheric country inn or at a colorful wine festival. Wine tastings take place in the historic Marienberg fortress in Würzburg. You can also taste wines at cooperative wineries or Würzburg's three major estates, and family estates throughout the region. The vineyards are very scattered, but most of the best ones are not far from the Main river. There are excellent cycle paths throughout Franken and many places to rent bicycles.

The region was settled by and named after a Germanic tribe, the Franks. Christianity came with the Irish missionaries in the 7th century. St Kilian, the most famous of these, became patron saint of the region's winegrowers. By the 8th century, the monasteries were spreading viticulture throughout the land.

Würzburg's charitable hospitals

Franken was Germany's largest winegrowing area (40,000 hectares/98,800 acres) in the Middle Ages, but this figure almost certainly included other nearby wine regions such as Austria and Hungary, when the vineyards and the wine trade were principally in the hands of the monasteries

‹‹ The Rödelseer Tor is one of Iphofen's three 15th-century town gates.

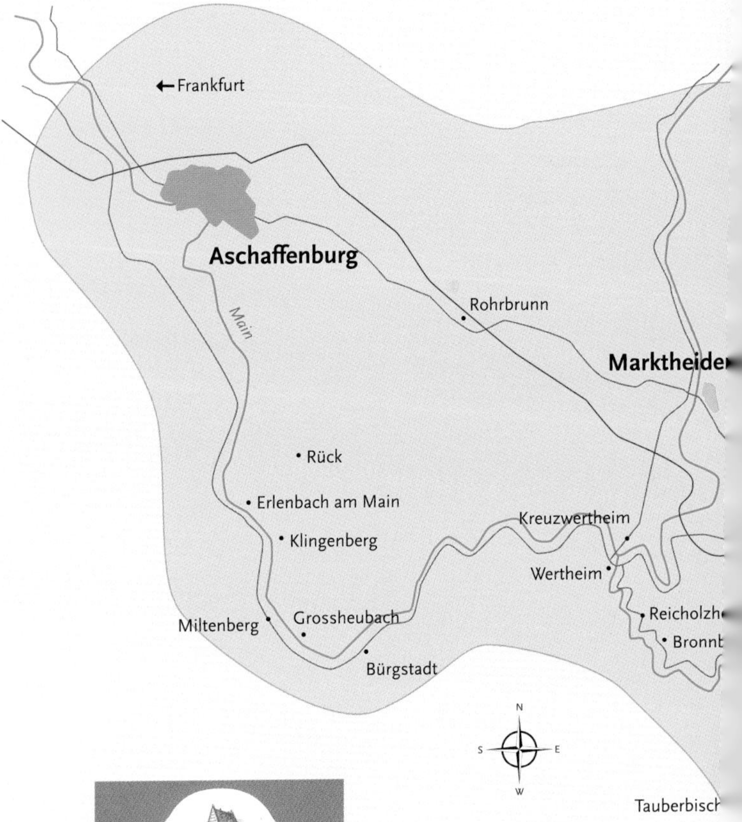
Frankfurt
Aschaffenburg
Main
Rohrbrunn
Marktheide
Rück
Erlenbach am Main
Klingenberg
Kreuzwertheim
Wertheim
Reicholzh
Bronnb
Miltenberg
Grossheubach
Bürgstadt
N
S
E
W
Tauberbisch

Weingut Schloss Sommerhausen
Silvaner GG 1
Lage verpflichtet
Sommerhäuser Steinbach

STIFTUNG SEIT 1316
BÜRGERSPITAL
WÜRZBURG
2010
SILVANER
Würzburger Pfaffenberg
Kabinett trocken
FRANKEN

1576
Juliusspital
WEISSER BURGUNDER GG
VOLKACHER KARTHÄUSER 1 trocken

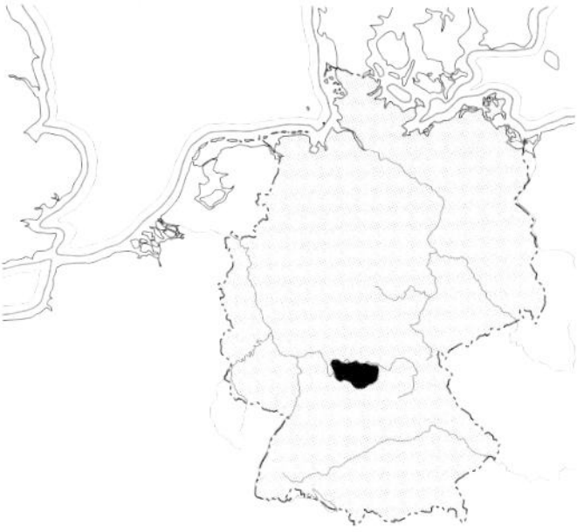

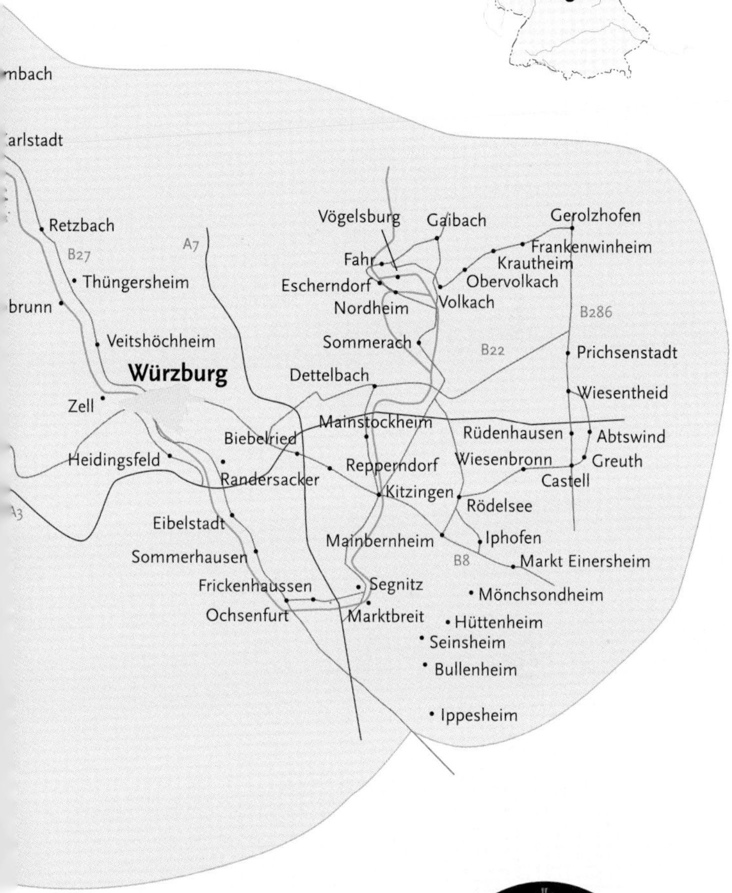
mbach
Karlstadt
Retzbach
B27
A7
Thüngersheim
brunn
Veitshöchheim
Würzburg
Zell
Heidingsfeld
A3
Biebelried
Randersacker
Eibelstadt
Sommerhausen
Frickenhausen
Ochsenfurt
Vögelsburg
Gaibach
Gerolzhofen
Frankenwinheim
Krautheim
Fahr
Escherndorf
Obervolkach
Nordheim
Volkach
B286
Sommerach
B22
Prichsenstadt
Dettelbach
Wiesentheid
Mainstockheim
Rüdenhausen
Abtswind
Repperndorf
Wiesenbronn
Greuth
Castell
Kitzingen
Rödelsee
Mainbernheim
Iphofen
B8
Markt Einersheim
Segnitz
Mönchsondheim
Marktbreit
Hüttenheim
Seinsheim
Bullenheim
Ippesheim

CASTELL
SCHLOSSBERG
SILVANER
GG

1576
Juliusspital
WÜRZBURGER STEIN
SILVANER GG

and the aristocracy. The Church and the nobility, however, were not the only ones to benefit from wine. For centuries, revenues from two of Franken's renowned wine estates in Würzburg have funded charitable foundations for the sick, the poor and the elderly: Bürgerspital (1319) and Juliusspital (1576). From the 16th to the 19th century, viticulture declined as a result of wars and secularization, and also as coffee and tea became available.

Grape varieties

Franken's 6081 hectares (15,020 acres) of vineyards are planted mostly with Müller-Thurgau (31 per cent), Silvaner (21 per cent) and Bacchus (12 per cent) and a small amount of succulent Rieslaner (a local Auslese speciality). Riesling is grown only in very warm sites, which are quite rare. A small amount of Spätburgunder is produced, mainly in the west, especially at Bürgstadt and Miltenberg. During the 20th century the vineyards were reorganized, but the supply of Franken wine is still limited, because of the cold continental climate, compared with the milder Mosel and Rhine regions. The cold climate gives more character and good acidity to Müller-Thurgau and Bacchus, and they both ripen sooner than Silvaner and Riesling, so they are the less expensive stable quality wines of the region.

Soil types

The soils north of Aschaffenburg are a mixture of primitive rock and mica schist. Elsewhere in the western part of Franken, the superb Bürgstadter Centgräfenberg vineyard has weathered colored sandstone that favors Riesling, Silvaner, Weissburgunder, and Spätburgunder. In the heart of the region, including Würzburg, the shell limestone soils are dry, stony and heat-retaining. The vines skirting the Steiger Forest in the east flourish in deep, fertile keuper and red marly soils.

Würzburg

Würzburg is a classic wine city on the Main river. From a Celtic fort on the hilltop site of today's

Juliusspital is a charitable hospital founded by the prince bishop Julius Echter in 1576.

Marienberg and a small village of fishermen and raftsmen, the town developed into a center of European culture under the rule of bishops and prince bishops (1030-1802). They left a legacy of Gothic and Baroque masterpieces and world-famous wine estates.

Famous historic estates

The charitable institutions have always been for the poor, the sick and the old. Bürgerspital and Juliusspital are among the greatest historic wine estates of Germany, founded in 1319 and 1576 respectively. Both have beautiful vaulted cellars with richly carved wooden casks. Both own vines in Würzburg's finest wine sites, and in other areas of Franken.

The **Bürgerspital Weinstube** and wine store are open much of the time. Weingut Bürgerspital owns 110 hectares (279 acres), mostly of prime vineyards, and wine festivals are held in the courtyard of the Bürgerspital in June.

Weingut Juliusspital has 170 hectares (420 acres) of mostly prime vineyards that were donated from its foundation by Prinz Julius Echter in 1576 and many others over the centuries.

Juliusspital hosts concerts during "Culture Days" in May.

Staatlicher Hofkeller was founded in 1128. It has 110 hectares (279 acres) of vines in some prime vineyards: **Würzburger Stein** and **Innere Leiste**, as well as **Randersacker Pfülben**, and others. Sadly, their wines have been poor in quality for a long time, possibly because of bureaucratic management. Perhaps one day they will catch up?

The former prince bishops' palace (now called **The Residenz**), was built between 1720 and 1744 from plans by Balthasar Neumann, and ranks as one of the finest Baroque structures in Europe. Frescoes by Tiepolo decorate the Imperial Hall and the cupola above the magnificent staircase. Don't miss the richly adorned court church, the palace gardens and the rococo wrought-iron gates (www.residenz-wuerzburg.de). There are wine festivals in the gardens of the Residenz (early July).

The vineyards

Baroque sandstone statues of rulers and saints line the 15th-century Alte Mainbrücke (stone bridge). From here there is a fine view of Würzburg's landmark, the **Marienberg fortress**, majestically overlooking the Schlossberg vineyard. The great south-facing Riesling site, Würzburger Innere Leiste is on the steep slope below the fortress, which faces due south.

The Stein vineyard

The famous vineyard **Stein** also faces due south and has some 85 hectares (210 acres) of Riesling and Silvaner vines covering the chalky hills north of the city. The Silvaners are rich in bouquet, full-bodied and dry. The Rieslings have finesse, fruit and fine acidity, with full, long-lasting flavors.

Walk along the *Stein-Weinpfad*, an educational path through the vineyards, with ancient and modern open-air sculptures. Allow 2.5 hours for the entire route, and half that for a shorter walk from near the railway station to the castle hotel **Schloss Steinburg** (restaurant open daily) overlooking the vineyards and the city.

Marienberg fortress

The fortress complex dates from 1201 and served as the residence of the prince bishops from 1253 to 1719. Today, the Baroque armory houses the **Mainfränkisches Museum** with a wine museum, Franconian folk art and works by the Gothic sculptor Tilman Riemenschneider. A gala culinary wine tasting is held in the Kelterhalle (hall with wine presses) in autumn. You can also visit the Marienkirche (originally a rotunda) and the palace gardens.

Treasures of art history

The prince bishops (such as Julius Echter and members of the Schönborn family) were great patrons of the arts. The town has many historic fountains, monuments, churches and buildings in styles ranging from Romanesque to rococo. **The Cathedral of St Kilian, Neumünster** and **Marienkapelle** are highly recommended. Try to see the town hall and the old university as well as the beautiful rococo façade of the Haus Zum Falken (near the market square), where guided tours begin.

REGIONAL WINE PROMOTION BOARD

Gebietsweinwerbung Frankenwein-Frankenland GmbH
Hertzstrasse 12
97076 Würzburg
Tel: 0931 390110
www.frankenwein-aktuell.de
There is also a wine store.

One of many pleasure boats moored on the river Main in Würzburg.

CRUISE THE MAIN

By boat from Würzburg dock Alter Kranen (old crane) to Veitshöchheim (45 min) to visit the 17th to 18th century castle and its superb rococo gardens. Open Apr-Oct 9AM–6PM (except Mon). Gardens open daily, all year, until dusk.

MUSIC AND WINE

The Baroque Festival (May) and Mozart Festival (Jun) feature great orchestras and top wines of Franken in the magnificent Würzburg Residenz.

WINERIES & MORE

WÜRZBURG

Weingut Bürgerspital Zum Heiligen Geist
Theaterstrasse 19
97070 Würzburg
Tel: 0931 35030
www.buergerspital.de

Staadtlicher Hofkeller Würzburg
Residenzplatz 3
97070 Würzburg
Tel: 0931 3050923
www.hofkeller.de

Western Franken

The westernmost vineyards of Franken are less than half an hour's drive east of Frankfurt, just north of Aschaffenburg. The primitive rock and mica schist soils yield hearty, pithy wines. Aschaffenburg is notable for its Romanesque cloisters and works of art by Cranach and Grünewald in the Stiftskirche St Peter and St Alexander (Collegiate Church) and Schloss Johannisburg, a Renaissance palace.

Miltenberg and Bürgstadt

Upstream, a deep ribbon of colored sandstone provides excellent conditions for producing velvety, Spätburgunder and Portugieser wines near Rück, Erlenbach, Klingenberg and Grossheubach. Further south and east is picturesque Miltenberg, which has beautiful half-timbered houses on the market square and along the Hauptstrasse. Walk up to the **Mildenburg fortress** for a good view of the town and the Main valley. The next town is Bürgstadt, where

The attractive market square in the ancient wine town of Iphofen.

the great steep **Centgrafenberg** vineyard yields amazing wines, Spätburgunder (40 per cent) Riesling (18 per cent), plus Weissburgunder and Silvaner, especially those from Weingut Rudolf Fürst.

From here, drive to Kreuzwertheim and then south on the B 469 to visit the former **Benedictine monastery in Amorbach** with its richly furnished library, banqueting hall and church (Stumm organ recitals May–Oct). Then return to the road along the Main to Wertheim.

Wertheim

The oldest parts of the town date back to the 12th century. For the best view, take the steps up to the **Burg Wertheim** ruins, where you can also enjoy a glass of wine at the restaurant terrace (Easter–Oct).

Historic houses line Maingasse, Münzgasse and the market square. Opposite the Renaissance well at the center of the square, are the Gothic Stiftskirche, **St Kilian's Chapel** and an interesting history museum (closed Mon) in a group of buildings linked by an unusual double winding staircase. Its collection of costumes (1800–1950), coins, silhouettes and paintings is worth seeing. Nearby, on Mühlenstrasse 24, the Glasmuseum chronicles glass-making from Egyptian times to present (closed Mon; Nov and Jan–Mar).

Reicholzheim and Bronnbach

Germany's largest collection of red sandstone crucifixes, wayside shrines and a Baroque church are worth seeing in Reicholzheim. In 1151, Cistercian monks founded **Bronnbach monastery**. The cloisters, Baroque Josephssaal and church (rococo choir stalls) are the settings for concerts and can be visited during tours (www.kloster-bronnbach.de).

The Bocksbeutel Route

This route follows the Main river through several important wine villages south of Würzburg. Depart on the B 13 and return on the B 8.

The wine routes in Franken are not actually signposted. If Bavaria ever grants permission to mark them, the signs will doubtless depict Franken's wine logo, the Bocksbeutel.

Most of the wine villages have a medieval townscape, with all or part of a town wall, gateways and defence towers. Gabled Renaissance town halls, often with carved balustrades, are typical of the area. Elaborate statues of the Virgin Mary are frequent, as are statuettes adorning façades or corner niches of houses.

Nearly all the vineyards are on steep or sloping south-facing hills of shell-limestone soils. Silvaner and Müller-Thurgau are the main grape varieties. The wines are aromatic and hearty with a powerful fruity flavor. They are usually very dry.

Randersacker to Ochsenfurt

The finest Riesling and Silvaner vineyards immediately to the south of Würzberg are **Randersacker Pfülben** and **Sonnenstuhl**, which are on a par with Würzberger Stein. Look for the late Romanesque tower of St Stephen's Church as a starting point for a walk through the Old Town. Within the town walls of Eibelstadt are the Baroque town hall and ornate statue (1660) of the Virgin Mary on the market square.

The ancient towers of Sommerhausen, the next wine village, have become home to an artists' colony and a well-known theater in the Würzburger Tor (tower gate). Among the historic buildings on the main street are the 16th-century town hall with

The vineyard below the Marienberg fortress is called Innere Leiste.

pinnacled gables and a Renaissance castle. The most famous vineyard here is **Sommerhäuser Steinbach.**

Cross the Main on a 550-year-old stone bridge to Ochsenfurt, a town with lovely half-timbered houses and picturesque wrought-iron signs. The "new" town hall (c.1500) has a Glockenspiel (1560) with symbolic figures, including two oxen (Ochsenfurt means "oxen ford") and the figure of Death turning an hour glass, alluding to the thousands killed during the Peasants' Revolt (1525).

Also of note are the painted Renaissance ceilings of the Ratssaal (council chambers) inside the town hall. A Riemenschneider statue and lavish tracery in the **St Andreas Church** are worth seeing.

Around a loop of the Main

Frickenhausen is a restored medieval town. The Valentiuskapelle is a Baroque chapel overlooking the Kapellenberg vineyard, the town and the Main valley. At the other end of the loop, the towers, historic buildings and old crane of Marktbreit form a romantic silhouette. The town hall, built into the old town wall, is part of an interesting ensemble of Renaissance buildings. Sulzfeld also has medieval towers, gates and half-timbered houses.

Kitzingen and Repperndorf

Kitzingen, which had a bridge across the Main by the 13th century, was an important medieval trading center. There are many old buildings near the market square, including a splendid three-storey town hall with patterned gables; St Johannis Church, with 15th-century choir stalls and wall paintings; and the parish church in Italian Baroque style. To see carnival masks and costumes, visit the **museum in the Falterturm** (www.kitzingen.de). Also worth seeing is **Balthasar Neumann's Heilig Kreuz Church** in the suburb of Etwashausen. From here, continue on the B 8. Repperndorf is the region's large, modern cooperative, and it has a wine shop and museum. In Biebelried, the **Riemenschneider sculpture** in the parish church merits a visit.

WINERIES & MORE

RANDERSACKER

Weingut Schmitt's Kinder
Am Sonnenstuhl 45
97236 Randersacker
Tel: 0931 7059197
www.schmitts-kinder.de

SOMMERHAUSEN

Weingut Schloss Sommerhausen
Ochsenfurter Strasse 17–19
97286 Sommerhausen
Tel: 09333 260
www.sommerhausen.com

OCHSENFURT

Tourist Office
Hauptstrasse 39
Tel: 09331 5855
www.en.ochsenfurt.de
Guided tour of Old Town, including the Trachten Museum with ornate traditional costumes. Easter-Oct, Sat-Sun 2PM. The *Bratwurstfest* (sausage festival) takes place on Whit Mon, when the colorful costumes of Ochsenfurt are worn.

Sulzfeld

Sulzfeld is famous for *Meterbratwurst*, sausage sold by the meter! Also try *Blaue Zipferl*, boiled or roasted sausage served in a tasty onion-and-wine marinade.

Steigerwald

This route includes Franken's easternmost wine towns on the foothills of the Steiger Forest. Leave Würzburg on the A 3; exit at Schweinfurt Süd/ Wiesentheid and drive south to Rüdenhausen. Return to Würzburg from Gollhofen on the A 7 or B 13 (the *Bocksbeutel* Route via Ochsenfurt).

The wines

In this rural countryside, vineyards are scattered on sloping hillsides capped by protective forests. Mineral-rich, heavy gypsum keuper soils give the wines great substance. Here Müller-Thurgau wines can be refreshing and pleasing in summer, in contrast with those from the Rhine regions, while the Silvaners are full-bodied, mouth-filling wines with a distinctive bouquet and flavors.

Castell

From the Autobahn exit drive via Rüdenhausen to reach the village of Castell, where the Castell family have had vineyards since at least the 11th century. The Casteller Schlossberg vineyard was first documented in 1258. The Silvaner vines were the first to be imported in Germany from Austria on April 5, 1659, by the Castell family and today the **Casteller Schlossberg** vineyard is the best vineyard for Riesling, Silvaner, and Rieslaner Auslese in the area. The present head of the family, Ferdinand Graf zu Castell-Castell, is responsible for the high quality of their wines.

For centuries, the Castell family have been very successful bankers, and have also set very high standards of quality in farming and wine production. The cellars, a wine shop and a *Weinstube* are in the grounds of the family's late 17th-century mansion in the village. The classical interior of the Schlosskirche is decorated with local alabaster and comes as a surprise after its Baroque exterior. From **Wiesenbronn** there is a good view of Castell and its vineyards.

The Schwanberg

"Swan Hill" is covered with a vast expanse of superb vineyards near the town Rödelsee. Walk (half an hour) or drive (five minutes) to **Schloss Schwanberg** at the top of the hill to enjoy the views over a glass of wine from the great vineyard **Rödelseer Küchenmeister**.

Drive via Mainbernheim, ringed with a massive 15th-century stone wall and 18 towers, to Iphofen, an ancient wine town, seemingly untouched by time. Its medieval townscape is authentic, with intact walls, towers and one of Germany's most picturesque town gates, the **Rödelseer Tor**. A walk through the winding streets takes you past half-timbered houses, which contrast with the Baroque town hall. In the Gothic **St Veit's Church** look for the sculpture of St John by Riemenschneider.

The greatest vineyard in this area is **Iphöfer Julius-Echter-Berg**, which is a continuation of the long slope of Rödelsee. It has been famous for centuries for Riesling and Silvaner wines.

From Iphofen, drive east on the B 8 to Markt Einersheim, where the town hall and church are part of the fortifications. Then turn south to Mönch-

The famous Lump vineyard at the entrance to Escherndorf village.

sondheim and follow the country roads to the wine towns of Hüttenheim, Seinsheim, Bullenheim and Ippesheim. The medieval town of Uffenheim, no longer part of today's wine country, is nevertheless worth a visit.

Ancient walls and town gates

The southern part of this route winds through forests and ancient wine towns unknown outside their borders. Fortified churches are an interesting feature of this area. They often provided the only refuge for peasants during the centuries of war that plagued the region.

WINERIES & MORE

CASTELL

Fürstlich Castell'sches Domänenamt
Schlossplatz 5
97355 Castell
Tel: 09325 60160
www.castell.de

IPHOFEN

Weingut Johann Ruck
Marktplatz 19
97346 Iphofen
Tel: 09323 800880
www.ruckwein.de

Weingut Hans Wirsching
Ludwigstrasse 16
97346 Iphofen
Tel: 09323 87330
www.wirsching.de

Knauf Museum
Am Marktplatz
97343 Iphofen
Tel: 09323 31528
www.knauf-museum.de
Unusual display of plaster copies of major works of antiquity.

RÖDELSEE

Winzergenossenschaft
Schloss Strasse 2
97348 Rödelsee
Tel: 09323 3416
www.schloss-crailsheim.de
In Schloss Crailsheim (1696). Lovely setting for co-op's wine shop.

The Mainschleife

Schleife means "loop." This route includes the wine towns on the Main river, northeast of Würzburg. Drive east on the A 3; exit at Schweinfurt Süd/Wiesentheid. Return to Würzburg on the B 22 via Dettelbach.

To Volkach via the medieval towns

From the Autobahn exit, drive north on the B 286 to Prichsenstadt, a picturesque wine town ringed by a moated stone wall. Enter at the gateway tower to view the half-timbered houses and town hall on the Hauptstrasse. You can see historic buildings on Gerolzhofen's market square, which is also the site of a huge wine festival in mid-July. From here drive to Volkach, in the heart of the Mainschleife.

Volkacher Ratsherr

In Volkach, Ratsherr (councillor) is not only the name of the town's large vineyard (150 hectares/370 acres), but also the town's "ambassador of wine" who dresses in medieval costume for festivals and tastings. See the Renaissance town hall (1544) and beautiful fountain in the market square. The finest vineyard here is **Volkacher Karthäuser.**

In the midst of the vineyards northwest of the town is one of Riemenschneider's most famous Madonnas, in the Gothic pilgrimage church, **Maria im Weingarten.**

Vogelsburg to Escherndorf

The best panoramic view of the Main loop and its wine towns is from the top of the Vogelsburg (birds' fortress) west of Volkach. The monastery at Vogelsburg near the top of the Eschendorfer Lump vineyard is run by Augustinian nuns and supported by the Juliusspital in Würzburg since 2011. There is a 2-hectare (5-acre) ecological vineyard, and a *Weinstube* with rooms. You can stay there, see the many birds and enjoy the view of the "loop" of the Main river below.

There is also a small church dedicated to St Kilian, the Celtic Bishop of Würzburg and the patron saint of Franken. Kilian was reputedly murdered in 689 AD by Geliana, who hoped to marry Gosbert, the Duke of Würzburg, but who had been instead married to his brother.

On the path through the vineyards from Vogelsburg to Escherndorf there is a beautifully carved stone statue of Christ bearing the Cross. At Weinherbst, where wine festivals take place every weekend (September to November), you can taste the wines from the famous vineyard **Eschendorfer Lump**.

Nordheim and Sommerach

From Escherndorf, cross the Main to Nordheim, where viticulture has been documented from AD 892. Its sites of Vögelein and Kreuzberg cover some 400 hectares (1000 acres).

The Madonna fountain, decorated for Easter, in front of Volkach's Renaissance town hall.

Two Renaissance buildings are of particular interest: the **St Laurentius Church**, with its beautiful sculptures, and the **Zehnthof** (tithe court), now a restaurant that serves the local Cooperative's wines. Divino Norheim is one of the half-dozen best Winzergenosssschafts in Germany.

Drive towards Volkach and have a meal in the romantic garden at **Schloss Hallburg**, which is owned by Graf von Schönborn and where you can enjoy their fine wines.

Sommerach, the other wine town on the "island" between the Main river and Rhein-Main-Donau canal, has retained its medieval look and has many half-timbered houses and Baroque mansions. Franken's oldest Cooperative (1901) produces most of the town's wine, from the Katzenkopf and Rosenberg sites. From late April to June 24, try the Mainschleife's other delicious specialty, asparagus.

Dettelbach via Schwarzach

See the intricately carved wayside shrine **Graue Marter** (1511, Riemenschneider school) en route to Dettelbach, the last medieval wine village on the route and well worth a visit. Also try to see the rococo interior of the pilgrimage church Maria im Sand east of the town. Return to Würzburg on the B 22.

CRUISE THE MAIN

By boat on a Mainschleifen-Rundfahrt (round trip) in 1.5 hours from Volkach.

WINERIES & MORE

BÜRGSTADT AM MAIN

Weingut Rudolf Fürst
Hohenlindenweg 46
63927 Bürgstadt
Tel: 09371 8642
www.weingut-rudolf-fuerst.de

KLEINHEUBACH

Weingut Fürst Löwenstein
Schlosspark 5
63924 Kleinheubach
Tel: 93 71 9486600
www.loewenstein.de

FRICKENHAUSEN AM MAIN

Weingut Bickel-Stumpf
Kirchgasse 5
97252 Frickenhausen
Tel: 09331 2847
www.bickel-stumpf.de

The wall of the medieval wine town of Dettelbach by the river Main.

ESCHERNDORF

Weingut Horst Sauer
Bocksbeutelstrasse 14
97332 Escherndorf
Tel: 09381 4364
www.weingut-horst-sauer.de

VOLKACH

Weingut Graf von Schönborn – Schloss Hallburg
Hauptverwaltung
Schlossplatz 1
97353 Wiesentheid
Tel: 09383 97 530
www.schoenborn.de

NORDHEIM AM MAIN

Divino Nordheim Winzergenossenschaft
Langgasse 33
97334 Nordheim
Tel: 09381 80990
www.divino-nordheim.de

WHERE TO STAY AND EAT

Castell

Weinstall Castell (R)
Schlossplatz 3
97335 Castell
Tel: 09325 90 25 61
www.weinstall-castell.de
Fine regional cuisine. Wines from the Castell estate. Pleasant terrace.

Gasthaus Zum Schwan (H/R)
Birklinger Strasse 2
97355 Castell
Tel: 09325 9 01 33
www.schwan-castell.de
Traditional family guest-house with nine rooms. Delicious food and their own wines. Very good value.

Fürstlich Castell'sches Domänenamt (R)
Schlossplatz 5
97355 Castell
Tel: 09325 0160
www.castell.de
Fine regional cuisine.

Iphofen

Zehntkeller (H/R)
Bahnhofstrasse 12
97346 Iphofen
Tel: 09323 84 40
www.zehntkeller.de
Fifty-nine rooms in historic house first documented in 1436. Restaurant in tithe cellars. Regional and international food.

Klingenberg

Zum Alten Rentamt (R)
Hauptstrasse 25a
63911 Klingenberg
Tel: 09372 2650
www.altes-rentamt.de
Michelin starred.

Der Schafhof Amorbach (H/R)
Schafhof 1
63916 Amorbach
Tel: 09373 973 30
www.schafhof.de
Wonderful monks' cellars and building from 1524 with 24 rooms. Gourmet fare in Michelin-starred Abtstube. Simpler fare at Benediktinerstube.

Randersacker

Gasthof Bären (H/R)
Würzburger Strasse 6
97236 Randersacker
Tel: 0931 70510
www.baeren-randersacker.de
Lovely family guesthouse with 36 rooms. Rustic restaurant.

Sommerhausen

Restaurant Philipp (H/R)
Hauptstrasse 12

97286 Sommerhausen
Tel: 09333 14 06
www.restaurant-philipp.de
Three guest rooms.
Michelin-starred restaurant.

Schwarzach

Schwab's Landgasthof (H/R)
Bamberger Strasse 4
97359 Schwarzach
Tel: 09324 1251
www.landgasthof-schwab.de
Eleven rooms. Wonderful Swabian dishes with Franken wines.

Volkach

Zur Schwane (H/R)
Hauptstrasse 12
97332 Volkach
Tel: 09381 80660
www.schwane.de
Historic guesthouse (1404) with 36 rooms in the center of the town. Charming. Good food and wine.

Schloss Hallburg (R)
Schloss Hallburg 5
97332 Volkach
Tel: 09381 2340
www.weinrestaurant-schlosshallburg.de

Würzburg

Best Western Hotel Rebstock Würzburg (H/R)
Neubaustrasse 7
97070 Würzburg
Tel: 0931 30930
www.rebstock.com
Hotel with beautiful rococo facade (1737), 70 rooms, exceptional restaurant. Seasonal and Mediterranean food.

Weingut Juliusspital (W)
Klinikstrasse 1
97070 Würzburg
Tel: 0931 393 1400
www.weingut-juliusspital.de
Weinstube and wine shop.

Gambero Rosso (R)
Lehmgrubenweg 13
97084 Würzburg
Tel: 0931 6 52 09
www.gambero-rosso.eu
Italian cuisine.

Hotel Walfisch (H/R)
Am Pleidenturm 5
97070 Würzburg
Tel: 0931 35200
www.hotel-walfisch.com
Family-owned hotel with 40 rooms. Restaurant with quality regional food. Terrace and Main river view.

Reisers Restaurant (R)
Mittlerer Steinbergweg 5
97080 Würzburg
Tel: 0931 286901
www.der-reiser.de
Splendid restaurant (closed Sun).

WÜRTTEMBERG

WÜRTTEMBERG IS A RURAL AREA of considerable natural beauty lying between the foothills of the Swabian Jura and the Tauber river valley. Stuttgart and Heilbronn are the region's major cities; both are rich in history and culture. But it is in the countryside and villages which line the valleys of the Neckar river and its tributaries that the character of Württemberg really comes alive. The *Schwäbische Weinstrasse* (Swabian Wine Road) and the signposted *Radweg* (bicycle trail) show the way as they wind across the region from Weikersheim to Metzingen.

The Swabians are known for their hospitality, hearty country cooking and delicious red and white wines served in the *Viertele* – a round, quarter-liter glass with a handle, difficult to tip over. *Besenwirtschaften* (wine taverns sometimes in vintners' homes) serve the local wines. Look for a birch-broom or wreath over the doorway.

Viticulture in Württemberg dates back at least to the 8th century. It was probably introduced by monks from Burgundy when they established monasteries in the region. Today, most of the 16,500 winegrowers are part-time vintners with less than half a hectare (one acre) of vines, so the majority of "Neckar wines" are produced and marketed by well-equipped local cooperatives.

Württemberg is the fifth largest winegrowing region of Germany (11,526 hectares/28,480 acres). It is planted with slightly more red than white grape varieties. The countryside is a patchwork of fields and forests with vineyards and orchards scattered throughout – but not at random: they are planted only on warm, south-facing slopes, usually along river valleys.

Most of the vineyards were originally terraced with stone walls by the growers to prevent erosion, retain and reflect heat and serve as property boundaries.

‹‹ Riesling grows well in the vineyard of Stettener Pulvermacher.

Neckarzimmern
Neckar
Gundelsheim
B27
Bad Rappenau
Bad Wimpfen
B293
Heilbronn
Stetten
Schwaigern
Eppingen
Neipperg
Sulzfeld
Haberschlacht
Nordheim
Flein
Stockheim
Brackenheim
Lauffen
Talheim
Güglingen
Cleebronn
Neckar
Bretten
B27
Freudental
Knittlingen
Hohenhaslach
Besigheim
Mundelsheim
B35
Maulbronn
Horrheim
Hessigheim
Bietigheim-Bissingen
Pleidelsheim
Illingen
Mühl
Vaihingen
Enz
B10
Asperg
Markgröningen
Möglingen
B10
N
S
E
W
Stuttgart
B27
Tübingen

Öhringen
A6
B39
Winnenden
Buoch
B29
Remshalden
Schorndorf
Schnait
Winterbach
Plochingen

WEINGUT
Jürgen Ellwanger
LEMBERGER
Hebsacker Lichtenberg
trocken
2009
Württemberg

Weingut J.Ellwanger
Nikodemus
2007
trocken
DIGRAREX + HEINRICVS
10 46
enthält Sulfite Württemberg
14% Vol. · 0,75 l · Qualitätswein · AP-Nr. 270 059 09
Gutsabfüllung Jürgen Ellwanger · D-73650 Winterbach

During the past 40 years, the vineyards have been "modernized" and most of the walls removed to improve efficiency. To prevent erosion, grass and other plants have been sown between the rows of vines. Nevertheless, a few sites still retain their original character, notably those near the Felsengärten (cliff gardens) above the bends of the Neckar river between Mundelsheim, Hessigheim and Besigheim, where modernization is impossible.

Regional specialties

The ruby-red Trollinger wine (23 per cent) is the regional favorite and is seldom found outside Württemberg. It is generally blended with Lemberger, which on its own yields deep red, racy and powerful wines, with a lingering aftertaste. Elegant, aromatic red wines are also produced from Spätburgunder and Schwarzriesling (Pinot Meunier), as well as Clevner and Samtrot, which are clones of Pinot Meunier.

Riesling (18 per cent) is the most important white grape variety, but Silvaner is also to be found in some vineyards. The Kerner vine, which is a crossing of Trollinger and Riesling was developed in Württemberg and named after the physician and poet Justinus Kerner.

REGIONAL WINE PROMOTION BOARD

Werbegemeinschaft Württembergischer Weingärtnergenossenschaften eG
Raiffeisenstrasse 6
71696 Möglingen
Tel: 07141 24460
www.wwg.de

Stuttgart

Stuttgart, the capital of Baden-Württemberg, is situated in a wooded basin on the Neckar river. Full of gardens and parks, it also has about 40 hectares (100 acres) of vineyards within the city limits, while Greater Stuttgart's vineyard area is larger than that of Sachsen. The annual wine festival *Stuttgarter Weindorf* (wine village) in late August and early September attracts up to 100,000 people daily.

Stuttgart is the home of Porsche (museum in Zuffenhausen, open Tues–Sun 9AM–6PM) and Daimler-Benz, whose

Vineyards surround the village of Stettin near Stuttgart.

famous Mercedes first appeared in 1901. You can visit the Daimler-Benz Museum in the factory grounds (Mercedesstrasse 100, open Tue–Sun 10AM–6PM).
An important publishing center, Stuttgart is also well known for the production of optical, photographic and electrical equipment. Its ballet, theater, concerts and museums are as famous as its historic and contemporary buildings.

Stuttgart's wine suburbs

Bad Cannstatt, just across the Neckar river, is a town of wine and water. Its mineral springs, dating from Roman times, are the most productive in Europe. (The combination of wine and water is not to be recommended, but a good map of Stuttgart is essential.)

Red and white grape varieties are planted on the steep shell-limestone slopes surrounding the town. A scenic trail through the vineyards starts near the street Roter Stich in Burgholzhof. The next wine town along the Neckar is Untertürkheim, and the best vineyards are **Untertürkheimer Gips, Mönchberg** and **Herzogenberg.**

There is also a new small cooperative, called

Weinmanufaktur Untertürkheim at Strümpfelbacher Strasse 47. Despite its off-putting name, it competes with the equally small Mayschoss Cooperative in the Ahr Valley, the oldest cooperative in Germany (1868), for the crown as the best cooperative in the Germany. On the hillside above is the village of Rotenberg, where there is a mausoleum containing the graves of Queen Katharina and King Wilhelm I built on the site of the House of Württemberg's ancestral castle. The town's vineyard is named **Untertürkheimer Schlossberg**. From here to Uhlbach there is a marked vineyard path. The region's largest wine museum is on Uhlbacher Platz 4, in a restored press house (open Apr–Oct, Sat-Sun 2PM–6PM). Then drive to Obertürkheim and follow the Neckar river road to Esslingen.

Esslingen

Esslingen is an important wine center and is where the great trade route from Flanders to Venice crossed the Neckar. The former free imperial town can look back on 1200 years of viticulture. It is also the home of Kessler *Sekt*, the oldest sparkling wine producer of Germany (1826).

The market square is a good starting place for a walking tour. Visit the **Church of St Denis**, a Gothic basilica with exquisite stained glass windows and two Romanesque

Weingut Haidle in Stettin specializes in Riesling and red wines.

towers that are linked by a footbridge. Just opposite the rococo-style Neues Rathaus (new town hall) is the Renaissance façade of the former town hall, with a two-storeyed belfry and a Glockenspiel.

There are many splendid half-timbered houses near the Innere Brücke, one of the oldest post-Roman bridges of Europe. If you walk up to the Burg (fortress), you can enjoy the views and the historic tower. From here, continue to Plochingen, which has 17th-century half-timbered houses on the market square and a Gothic fortified church. Cross the Neckar and travel south on the B 313.

The Upper Neckar valley

The southernmost vineyards of the region are scattered along the Neckar river at the edge of the Swabian Jura. The Swabian Wine Road begins at Metzingen, remarkable for its seven ancient presses (**Kelterplatz**) and **wine museum** in the Herrschafts-kelter (Open Fri 5–8PM, Sat 11AM–8PM, Sun 11AM–6PM). Follow signs to Neuffen to see the ruins of Hohenneuffen fortress (1100) that rise above the town's medieval center. Continue on the scenic road to Nürtingen and then back to Esslingen and Stuttgart.

Cruise the neckar

Float by scenic vineyard country, departing from Wilhelma dock in Bad Cannstatt. Daily round trips, Mar-Oct, to Ludwigsburg, Marbach, Felsengärten and Lauffen.

Panoramic view

For a view extending all the way to the hills of the Swabian Jura, ascend the Fernsehturm (television tower) in the suburb of Degerloch. Total height: 217 m (712 ft). Observation platforms at 150 m (492 ft).

The "onions" of Esslingen

The town's nine-day wine festival in August is called the *Zwiebelfest* (Onion Festival). Why the people of Esslingen are nicknamed "onions" is open to debate. Is it due to the large quantities grown nearby – or the huge number used to make *Zwiebelkuchen* (onion quiche), a favorite food served in fall with the new wine?

Legend has it that the devil once gleefully walked through the town unrecognized by its proud citizens. At the market, he tried to beguile a vendor into giving him an apple: she obliged with an onion. Enraged, the devil ran from town, crying that henceforth its "sharp" citizens should be called "onions."

A walk through Stuttgart

From the main railway station, walk along the elegant Königsstrasse. To the left is the beautiful **Oberer Schlossgarten** (palace garden) with the **Staatstheater and Staatsgalerie** (art museum; famous Picasso collection). The **Neues Schloss** on Schlossplatz is modelled on Versailles. The Altes Schloss (old castle) on Schillerplatz was built in 1320 as a moated castle and "modernized" in the 16th century in Renaissance style. In the summer concerts are held in the courtyard with its three-storeyed arcade. Today, it is the Württemberg Landesmuseum with historical exhibits and art treasures (www.landesmuseum-stuttgart.de).

Also on Schillerplatz, see the **Stiftskirche** (Collegiate Church), a late Gothic hall church with impressive 16th-century sculpted tombs of the Counts of Württemberg. Nearby are the Markthalle (market hall) and Marktplatz (market square).

Stuttgart is also known for its elegant shops, from Klett Passage (arcade) near the main station and along Königsstrasse and its side streets, including Calwerstrasse and the famous Calwer Passage.

East of the Neckar

From Ludwigsburg drive north on the B 27 to the fortified town of Besigheim. The market square is ringed with 15th-century houses, and the parish church contains a late Gothic altar carved by the Master of Urach. The best vineyards here are **Besigheimer Wurmberg**, and, eight miles to the north, **Bönningheimer Sonnenberg**.

The half-timbered Guesthouse Rose in Grossbottwar, north of Ludwigsburg, is owned by a local brewery.

From Besigheim, the road to Hessigheim, Mundelsheim and Pleidelsheim follows the course of the Neckar as it cuts through steep shell-limestone hills to form a series of spectacular loops. The terraced vineyards rising from the banks of the river are **Mundelsheimer Käsberg**, and **Besigheimer Wurmberg**. Trollinger and Riesling are the primary grape varieties. The local Cooperative in Hessigheim, the **Felsengartenkellerei** and its share of the Felsengarten vineyard (cliff gardens – as they really are), is a good vantage point. It's also a good place to taste and purchase wine. In Marbach, you can visit Schiller's birthplace in the Old Town and the museum named after him in a palace just outside the village. (**Schiller National Museum** is open Tues–Sun 10AM–6PM; exhibits on Schiller, Kerner, Rilke and other German writers.)

The Bottwar Valley

Further north along the Swabian Wine Road, there is a series of small villages with vineyards scattered throughout the hillsides. Here, too, Trollinger and Riesling are the main grape varieties. Steinheim made headlines in 1933, when the skull of a primitive man (250,000 years old) was discovered. You can see it and other historic exhibits in the **Urmensch Museum** just off the market square and left of the fountain (www.stadt-steinheim.de).

Half-timbered houses and the Romanesque **St Georgskirche**, with its 9th-century frescoes are worth seeing in Kleinbottwar. The hillside mansion above the town, Schloss Schaubeck, is the beautiful home of Michael Graf Adelmann, one of the region's noble families, which has a renowned wine estate.

Here the greatest vineyard is **Kleinbottwarer Oberer Berg**, where Muscateller and Samtrot grape varieties thrive.

Grossbottwar has a beautiful half-timbered town hall (1526) with a clock where a stork strikes the hour. The Schiefes Haus is a curiously slanting vintner's home from the 16th century.

Ruins with a view

Travel along the scenic road to Oberstenfeld and watch for the turning to the 13th-century **Burg Lichtenberg** (fortress) for a view of the entire Bottwar valley. The ruins of Burg Hohenbeilstein ("Langhans" fortress) overlook the village of Beilstein, and there is a falconry. The **Hohenbeilsteiner Schlosswengert** is another fine vineyard. From Löwenstein and Willsbach follow the road to Staatsweingut Weinsberg, Germany's oldest enological school (1868). **Weinsberger Schemelsberg** is its great vineyard, and the Justinus Kerner House is now a museum celebrating both the poet and the grape variety named for him. Nearby, you can walk the extensive wine trail on the Schemelsberg and visit the ruins of the Weibertreu fortress (273m/896ft high). **Verenberger Verenberg** is a very fine vineyard that is a little out of the way to the east of Heilbronn.

Women and wine

Weibertreu refers to the town's "faithful wives" who outwitted the Hohenstaufen Emperor Conrad III in 1140, when he besieged the town. He offered them safe conduct out of town and permission to take their dearest possessions with them.

They went through the town gate carrying their husbands on their backs!

Heilbronn was immortalized in Heinrich von Kleist's play *Käthchen von Heilbronn* (1808). Kathy is a symbol of female beauty, virtue and devotion and is still a key figure in the town's activities. The town hall's astronomical clock and **Kilianskirche** (St Kilian's Church) with its Gothic high altar and ornate Renaissance tower are worth seeing. The annual **Weindorf** (huge wine festival, mid-September) is among the region's most popular. Try the red wines, particularly the Lemberger. Ascend the Wartberg for a view of the medieval town and surroundings. **Heilbronner Stiftsberg** is the best vineyard here.

WINERIES & MORE

HEILBRONN

Weingut Drautz-Able
Faisstrasse 23
74076 Heilbronn
Tel: 07131 177908
www.drautz-able.de

WEINSBERG

Staatsweingut Weinsberg
Traubenplatz 5
74189 Weinsberg
Tel: 07134 504167
www.sw-weinsberg.de

West of the Neckar

From Ludwigsburg, follow the signs to Möglingen, home of Württemberg's Zentralgenossenschaft (central cellars), the umbrella organization of the entire region's local cooperatives. Their shop offers a vast selection of wines (in the Gewerbegebiet, industrial park, Mon–Fri 8AM–5PM), so beware of tasting them all!

Stop at the former free imperial town of Markgröningen, with its fine market square. Rich in historic buildings from the 15th century to the 17th, it has one of the most skilfully crafted half-timbered town halls in Germany. The **Schäferlauf** (Shepherds' Festival) takes place in late August.

Stromberg and Heuchelberg

The vineyards and wine towns are scattered throughout the countryside and to follow the Swabian Wine Road means some backtracking. Castles dot many of the summits and the oldest sections of the villages (usually the market squares) have retained their medieval character.

Here is a fairly direct route, which gives you a flavor of the area. Travel from Vaihingen, notable for its steep terraced vineyards on the slopes beneath Schloss Kaltenstein, to Horrheim. The town's old press house, now a wine museum, has a massive old press made from a 10.5m/34.5ft tree trunk (open May 1 and at festivals). At Hohenhaslach follow the signs to Freudental, Cleebronn and Brackenheim. Turn west and drive to Stockheim and Haberschlacht, a very attractive stretch. **Schloss Stocksberg** towers above and provides the best view of the countryside.

Continue north to Neipperg, a village in the shadow of the double-towered Romanesque castle of the noble family of the same name. The rococo **Neipperg Schloss** is the heart of a group of historic buildings, including the **Neipperg wine estate**, a restaurant, the town hall, and the 12th-century Stadtkirche with its elaborate altars and furnishings. Their great vineyards, which are to the west of the town, are **Neipperger Schlossberg** and in the next village **Schwaigerner Ruthe**.

This is the viticultural heart of the area, where the slopes of the wide valleys are thick with vineyards. One third of production consists of strong, dry white wines, but the area is especially known for its powerful, full-bodied reds, where Lemberger, Trollinger, Schwarzriesling and Spätburgunder thrive on the keuper and marl soils. They are excellent with fresh game from the forests and fields nearby.

Lauffen

From Schwaigern, travel the country road via Nordheim to Lauffen, situated on a loop of the Neckar, and there are many classic terraced vines. Lauffen is one of the most important winegrowing centers of the region. Schwarzriesling is the main grape variety, but Trollinger and a small amount of white varieties are also produced. The

The busy wine town Besigheim, where the Enz river joins the Neckar. Each summer the town holds a medieval market.

town traces its origins to the 3rd century and excavations have unearthed a Roman farm. It is a typical medieval townscape and the poet Friedrich Hölderlin was born here. To the east of Lauffen, there are two remarkable vineyards: **Schozacher Roter Berg**, and **Maulbrunner Eilfingerberg-Klosterstück**, once belonging to a monastery.

Bietigheim-Bissingen

Travel south on the B 27 to Bietigheim-Bissingen, where the Enz and Metter rivers join. The 1200-year-old town of Bietigheim has many beautiful buildings, notably the **Hornmoldhaus** (next to the town hall), remarkable for the 16th-century Renaissance paintings that decorate the walls and ceilings of the interior. Most of the town's wine is produced at the cooperative Felsengartenkellerei (www.felsengartenkellerie.de). Return to Ludwigsburg to complete the circular tour.

Excursions west of Vaihingen

Visit the former Cistercian monastery **Kloster Maulbronn** with its well-preserved Romanesque and Gothic buildings (**www. maulbronn.de**). Its best vineyard is **Maulbronner Eilfingerberg-Klosterstück**. In Knittlingen, you can visit the museum devoted to the alchemist and magician Dr Faust (closed Mon). **Pforzheim's Schmuckmuseum** has splendid jewelry from 5000 years ago to the present (www.schmuckmuseum-pforzheim.de).

WINE ESTATE

BÖNNIGHEIM
Weingut Dautel
Lauerweg 55
74357 Bönnigheim
Tel: 07143 870326
www.weingut-dautel.de

The Rems Valley

This part of Württemberg is especially beautiful in spring, when the cherry trees blossom, and in autumn, when the vineyards turn golden and the aroma of new wine and *Zwiebelkuchen* (onion quiche) is in the air. The vineyards lie in the side valleys of the Rems river. There are dozens of tiny inns with evocative signs hanging over their doors, bearing names like Ochsen (oxen), Lamm (lamb), and Hirsch (deer) or Post (referring to the old post road stations), where you can sample the local wine and dishes. Most of the wines are produced by the local cooperatives, but a few of the inns offer their own (*Eigenbauweine*). Trollinger and Riesling are the main varieties. Compared to their counterparts from the Middle and Lower Neckar valley, the Rems wines are generally lighter and livelier thanks to their fruity acidity.

South of the Rems

Three side valleys south of the Rems river, with the wine villages of Kernen-Stetten, Strümpfelbach and Schnait, whose best vineyards are **Altenberg** and **Burghalde** are easily reached from Stuttgart via Bad Cannstatt and Fellbach (roads B 14 and B 29).

The marked hiking trail through the vineyards, of which **Fellbacher Lämmler** is a very fine example, begins near the cooperative and leads up to the **Kappelberg**, offering a good view of the valley. Follow signs from the suburb of Rommelshausen to Kernen-Stetten, an old winegrowing town with a 14th-century castle and a hiking path around the ruins of the Yburg fortress. The finest vineyard for

One of Weingut Dautel's cellars, with new oak barrels for the red wines: Zweigelt, Spätburgunder, Lemberger and Merlot.

Riesling is **Stettener Pulvermächer**, and **Schnaiter Burghalde** for red wines. Rather than returning to the B 29, follow the winding country road south (towards Esslingen). As the road ascends into the forest, look back at the Yburg ruins amid the steep vineyards lining the cone-shaped hills.

Watch for signs to Aichschiess and Schanbach – this route brings you into the next valley, to Strümpfelbach, an idyllic village full of half-timbered houses. Now return to the B 29 to reach Beutelsbach, the heart of viticulture in the Rems valley. At the **Remstalkellerei** (regional cooperative) you can sample and purchase wines from all of the villages on this route. Follow the signs to Schnait, where you can see the altar in the **Church of St Wendelin** and the Silcher Museum (in 1837 Silcher wrote the music to Heine's *Song of Loreley*). Return to the B 29 and cross the Rems at Winterbach, whose best vineyard is **Winterbacher Hungerberg**.

North of the Rems

Remshalden is a pretty town with colorful half-timbered houses and an old watchtower. The scenery from nearby Grunbach, north to Buoch and Winnenden is very attractive. There is a wonderful view of the old-style vineyards with their stone walls and terraces just as the forest clears and you descend into the valley at Winnenden.

From Winnenden, drive south to Korb and Waiblingen, with its pretty market square and two churches of interest, the **Nonnenkirche** (1496) and **St Michael's** (1480). To complete our loop through the Rems valley, return to the B 29 at Fellbach.

SCHILLERWEIN

This is a 300-year-old Württemberg specialty made by pressing and fermenting red and white grapes together and named after the play in colors (*schillern*) from red to pink to white of this fruity wine as it shimmers in a glass.

WINERIES & MORE

WINTERBACH

Weingut Ellwanger
Bachstrasse 27
73650 Winterbach
Tel: 07181 44525
www.weingut-ellwanger.de

KLEINBOTTWAR

Weingut Graf Adelmann
Burg Schaubeck
71711 Steinheim-Kleinbottwar
Tel: 07148 921220
www.graf-adelmann.com

ÖHRINGEN-VERRENBERG

Weingut Fürst Hohenlohe Öhringen
Weisenkelter
74613 Öhringen-Verrenberg
Tel: 07941 94910
www.verrenberg.de

SCHWAIGERN

Weingut Graf Neipperg
Schlossstrasse 12
74193 Schwaigern
Tel: 07138 941400
www.graf-neipperg.de

KORB

Weingut Albrecht Schwegler
Steinstrasse 35
71404 Korb
Tel: 0715134895
www.albrecht-schwegler.de

KERNEN-STETTEN IM REMSTAL

Weingut Karl Haidle
Hindenburgstrasse 21
71394 Kernen-Stetten im Remstal
Tel: 07151 949110
www.weingut-karl-haidle.de

Schloss Schaubach was built on the site of a Roman castle in 1272.

FELLBACH

Weingut Gerhard Aldinger
Schmerstrasse 25
70734 Fellbach
Tel: 0711 581417
www.weingut-aldinger.de

Weingut Rainer Schnaitmann
Untertürkheimer Strasse 4
70734 Fellbach
Tel: 0711 574616
www.weingut-schnaitmann.de

STUTTGART-UNTERTÜRKHEIM

Weingut Wörhrwag
Grunbacher Strasse 5
70327 Stuttgart-Untertürkheim
Tel: 0711 331662
www.woehrwag.de

Weinmanufaktur Untertürkheim
Strümpfelbacher Strasse 47
70327 Stuttgart
Tel: 0711 3363810
www.weinmanufaktur.de

Food specialties

Hearty Swabian cooking

Hausgemacht or *handgeschabt* refer to homemade or handmade food.

Maultaschen a spicy mixture of meat, spinach, onions in pasta squares; served in clear broth or *geschmälzt*, with melted butter and fried onions on top.

Saure Kutteln pickled tripe.

Saure Nieren pickled kidneys.

Schupfnudeln potato dough noodles.

Schwäbischer Rostbraten Swabian roast beef topped with fried onions.

Spätzle handmade noodles. Mixed with cheese, they're *Kässpätzle*.

Stuttgart

Restaurant Délice (R)
Hauptstätter Strasse 61
70178 Stuttgart
Tel: 0711 6403222
www.restaurant-delice.de
Mon–Fri evenings only. French Mediterranean cuisine, top quality wines. Michelin star.

Hotel Am Schlossgarten (H/R)
Schillerstrasse 23
70173 Stuttgart
Tel: 0711 20260
www.hotelschlossgarten.com
Michelin-starred restaurant Zirbelstube (separately managed) Tel: 0711 202 6828. Restaurant Schlossgarten Tel: 0711 202 6830, regional cuisine; wine store; Mediterranean cuisine; and Café am Schlossgarten.

Restaurant Top Air (R)
(Terminal 1, 4th floor, Airport)
70629 Stuttgart
Tel: 0711 948 2137
www.restaurant-top-air.de
Imaginative menus. Book a window table.

Stuttgart-Degerloch

Restaurant Wielandshöhe
Alte Weinsteige 71
70597 Stuttgart-Degerloch
Tel: 0711 640 8848
www.wielandshoehe.de
Closed Sun–Mon. Michelin star. Classic and regional cuisine. Fantastic view.

Fässle (R)
Löwenstrasse 51
70597 Stuttgart-Degerloch
Tel: 0711 760100
www.faessle.de
Lovely restaurant. Good quality and value. East of the Neckar river.

Metzingen

Hotel-Restaurant Schwanen (H/R)
Bei der Martinskirche 10
(next to St Martin's Church)
72555 Metzingen
Tel: 07123 9460
www.schwanen-metzingen.de
Hotel with 62 rooms. Restaurant: Swabian dishes, regional and modern. Good value.

The castle of Hohenbeilstein (1080) dominates the town of Beilstein.

Oberstenfeld

Hotel Zum Ochsen (H/R)
Grossbottwarer Strasse 31
71720 Oberstenfeld
Tel: 07062 9390
www.hotel-gasthof-zum-ochsen.de
Guesthouse (1689) with 30 modernized rooms. Restaurant with excellent regional dishes.

Plochingen

Stumpenhof (R)
Stumpenhof 1
73207 Plochingen
Tel: 07153 22425
www.stumpenhof.de
Long-established family restaurant. Rustic regional cooking. Good value.

Zweflingen-Friederichsruhe

Wald und Schlosshotel Friederichsruhe (H/R)
Kärcherstrasse
74639 Zweiflingen-Friedrichsruhe
Tel: 07941 60870
www.schlosshotel-friedrichsruhe.de
Elegant mansion hotel with 66 rooms, located 1 km (half a mile) south of Zweiflingen, in a forest. Restaurant with classic gourmet fare. Separate rustic Hunter's Stube. Golf and spa.

Lauffen

Hotel Elefanten (H/R)
Bahnhofstrasse 12
74348 Lauffen am Neckar
Tel: 07133 95080
www.hotel-elefanten.de
Family-owned hotel, 13 rooms. Restaurant with international and local dishes. Excellent value.

BADEN

BADEN, the southernmost of Germany's wine regions, stretches some 400 km (240 miles) along the Rhine from the Bodensee (Lake Constance) to the *Hessische Bergstrasse*.

The Tauber valley and its scattered vineyards were divided between Baden, Franken and Württemberg. Franken retained the last stretch before the Tauber river joins the Main river, but most of the area to the south was ceded to the Grand Duchy of Baden in 1803: the rest belongs to Württemberg. The result is that none of the three wine regions have been very interested in promoting the Tauber wines.

The *Badische Weinstrasse* (Baden Wine Road), often corresponding to the B 3, runs through Heidelberg, Baden-Baden, Freiburg and many picturesque Black Forest wine villages. Onion-domed churches and half-timbered chalets dot the landscape of vineyards, orchards and forests. The beautiful play of colors is best seen in spring or autumn.

Baden has the highest concentration of top German restaurants, a distinction that has focused attention on the best wine estates. Simple country inns also offer delicious food and wine as well as fruit brandies, a regional specialty. You can also taste wines at festivals, cooperatives and traditional wine estates.

A Gothic tribe, the Alemanni, expanded viticulture started by the Romans, but the Church provided the real impetus for the extensive development of vine-growing in Baden. In the Middle Ages, landowners often bequeathed vineyards to quite distant monasteries. To encourage quality-consciousness among its tenant growers, the Church promulgated some of the first regulations governing work in the vineyards and cellars.

After the widespread destruction of the Thirty Years'

‹‹ The village of Oberbergen, in the heart of the Kaiserstuhl (Emperor's Throne) wine-growing area, seen across recently terraced vineyards.

WEINGUT BERCHER · BURKHEIM
SEIT 1457
Grauer Burgunder
SPÄTLESE · TROCKEN
Burkheimer Feuerberg 1ᴳ Kaiserstuhl

GLEICHENSTEIN
Baron Philipp
BADEN

DR. HEGER
BADEN
ACHKARRER
SCHLOSSBERG 1ᴳ
SPÄTBURGUNDER GG
2007

GLEICHENSTEIN
2008
SPÄTBURGUNDER ROTWEIN
OBERROTWEILER EICHBERG
BARRIQUE · TROCKEN
BADEN
14,0%vol. 750ml

GUTSABFÜLLUNG
H. SCHLUMBERGER
PRIVAT-WEINGUT
2008
GUTEDEL
KABINETT TROCKEN
PRÄDIKATSWEIN
A.P.Nr. 200409 enthält Sulfite
75cl 11%vol GUTSABFÜLLUNG WEINGUT H. SCHLUMBERGER D-79295 LAUFEN BADEN

SALWEY
GG
KIRCHBERG
SPÄTBURGUNDER 2009

Riegel
Vogtsburg
Breisach
Ihringen
Merdingen
A5
Bad Krozingen
Staufen
Müllheim
Sulzburg
Auggen
Badenweiler
Schliengen
Bad Bellingen
Kandern
B3
Weil
Lörrach
Basel
Inzlingen
B316

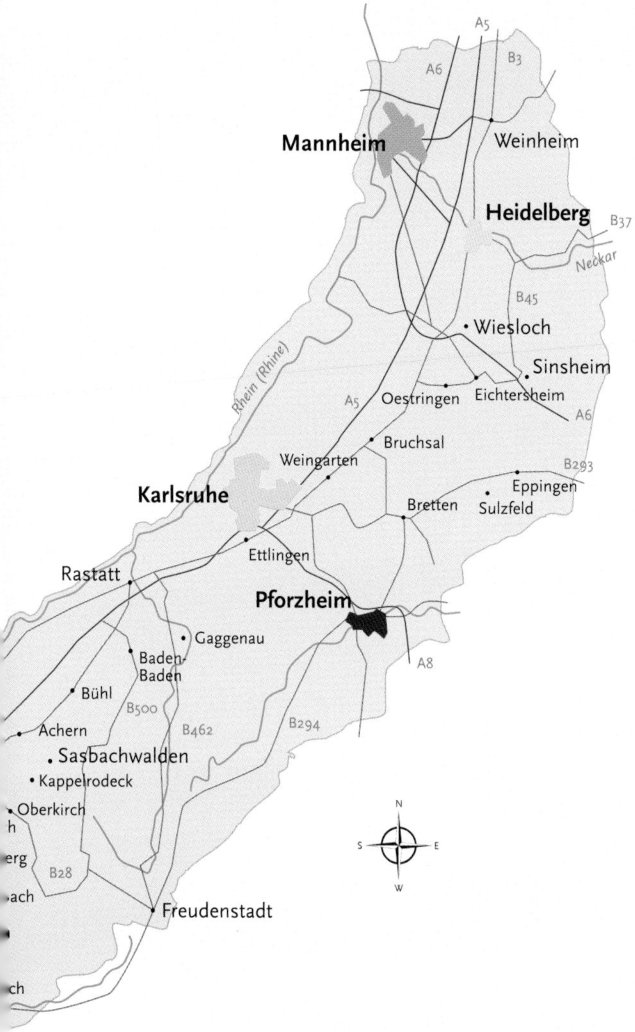
A5
B3
A6
Mannheim
Weinheim
Heidelberg
B37
Neckar
B45
Wiesloch
Rhein (Rhine)
Sinsheim
A5
Oestringen
Eichtersheim
A6
Bruchsal
Weingarten
B293
Karlsruhe
Eppingen
Bretten
Sulzfeld
Ettlingen
Rastatt
Pforzheim
Gaggenau
A8
Baden-Baden
Bühl
B500
B462
B294
Achern
Sasbachwalden
Kappelrodeck
Oberkirch
B28
Freudenstadt
N
S
E
W

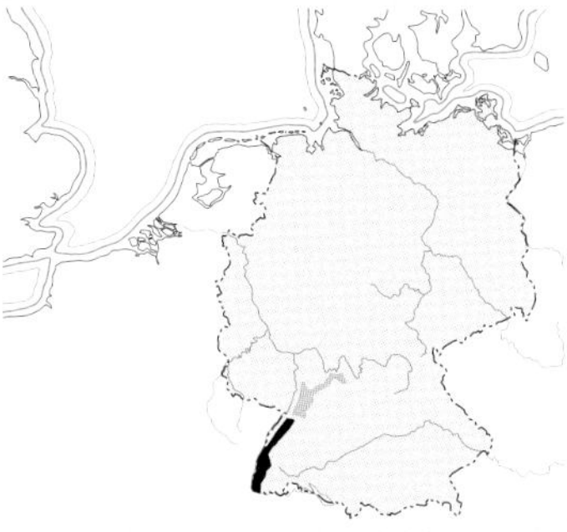

War and the War of the Palatinate Succession in the 17th century, viticulture enjoyed a period of revival, only to be plagued by a series of natural, economic and political calamities in the late 19th and 20th centuries. By 1949, Baden's vineyard area had shrunk to an all-time low of 5862 hectares (14,485 acres).

Baden today

Baden has recovered during the past six decades and is now third in size after Rheinhessen and the Pfalz, with 15,892 hectares (39,253 acres). Many vineyards had been replanted and reorganized to improve efficiency by the 1980s. Most of the region's growers are members of cooperatives, but because each grower owns, on average, just a few rows of vines, it is impossible for them to set up on their own. The cooperatives have good quality standards and modern cellar technology, but they tend to make too many different wines, which makes it very difficult to market them, especially abroad.

Today, there are some fifty wine estates, whose fine wines are in great demand, both at home and abroad. Many highly qualified young growers have the ambition to produce their own wines, and thus the numbers who take their grapes to the cooperative in Baden are dropping.

Tradition of wine and food

One of the warmest wine regions of Germany, Baden is a popular holiday resort, not least because of its great tradition of wine and food, shared with nearby Alsace and Switzerland. Each region produces different wines from some of the same grape varieties and the knowledge and importance of terroir is helping the growers to improve their soils and their vines.

The climate is more Mediterranean than in other regions, and Spätburgunder covers 37 per cent of the area of the vineyards, Müller-Thurgau 18 per cent (almost all for cooperatives) and Grauburgunder 10 per cent.

This means 35 per cent is other grape varieties. Of these, the classic white varieties include Riesling, which is remarkably successful in the right terroirs,

Weingut Schloss Neuweier, with its hotel and restaurant, is one of Baden's top Riesling estates. Mauerberg is its best site.

Weissburgunder, Gewürztraminer, Scheurebe and Muskateller, dating from Roman times and popular for family gatherings. More recently planted are Chardonnay and Sauvignon Blanc, as well as the dark red Dornfelder.

REGIONAL WINE PROMOTION BOARD

Badischer Wein GmbH
Basler Landstrasse 28 b
79111 Freiburg
Tel: 0761 89784784
www.badischerwein.de

BADEN WINE-GROWERS' ASSOCIATION

Badischer Weinbauverband e.V.
Merzhauser Strasse 115
79100 Freiburg im Breisgau
Tel: 0761 459100
www.badischer-weinbauverband.de

Heidelberg and the Neckar Valley

Heidelberg lies at the foothills of the Oden Forest on the Neckar river, not far from its confluence with the Rhine. Its natural beauty and striking townscape, crowned by majestic castle ruins, made Heidelberg a favorite among writers and artists of the Romantic period.

There are excellent views of the town and the castle from the **Heiligenberg** (mountain of saints) on the opposite side of the Neckar, site of a Celtic settlement and later a monastery, whose 9th century ruins can still be visited. Today, the Heiligenberg region has many nearby vineyards. The best is **Heidelberger Herrenberg**.

The castle and the university

The Kurfürsten (Prince Electors) of the Pfalz (Palatinate) made Heidelberg their residence for 500 years. The castle is a complex of buildings, towers and gardens built by the Electors as their residence from the 14th to the 17th centuries. The Renaissance structures are among the finest in Germany. Despite the heavy damage in 1689 and 1693, during the War of the Palatinate Succession, there is still much to see (guided tours daily, www.heidelberg.de) and from the **Great Terrace** there is a fine view of Old Heidelberg.

Germany's oldest university, founded in 1386 by Kurfürst Ruprecht, remains one of Europe's most respected educational institutions. Its library houses a splendid collection of rare medieval manuscripts (displayed during exhibitions).

ART AND HISTORY

Kurpfälzisches Museum (in Baroque Palais Moras). The 500,000-year-old jaw of Heidelberg man is on view. Garden restaurant.

Heidelberg's wine tradition

To appreciate Heidelberg's wine tradition, see the *Grosses Fass* (Great Cask) in the castle, said to be the world's largest (nearly 300,000 bottles of wine). It was built in 1751 to hold the Elector's tithe (tenth) of the Palatinate wine harvest. You can still enjoy a glass of wine at the castle, in the *Weinstube* in the grounds (from 6PM, except Wed; Sun from 12PM).

The Neckar valley

The Neckar valley is the first scenic part of the Burgenstrasse (Castle Road). This is a route through several historic wine towns near ancient castles (many now restaurants and hotels), and it leads from Mannheim via Heidelberg, Heilbronn and Rothenburg to Nürnberg (Nuremberg), through some of Germany's most picturesque landscapes. There are many places for tasting excellent wines and enjoying the cuisine of Baden, Franken and Württemberg. Leave Heidelberg from the Karlstor (gateway to eastern edge of Old Town) via the B 37 and follow the Neckar

The winegrower's cooperative in Königschaffhausen, Kaiserstuhl.

to Neckarsulm, from where you can easily return to Heidelberg via the A 6 or join the Baden Wine Road on the Bergstrasse near Wiesloch on the B 3.

Most of the villages along the Neckar have interesting historic houses, churches and castles. **Bad Wimpfen am Berg**, one of the best-preserved walled towns of Germany, is highly recommended. The tourist office in the market square has maps for a one-hour walking tour.

While the Neckar is primarily associated with the Württemberg wine region, Heidelberg and its environs were ceded to the Grand Duchy of Baden in 1803. Hence, some of the vineyards are part of Baden, yet often border on Württemberg sites. You are likely to find wines from both regions in this area's shops and restaurants.

The chalky, shell-limestone soils yield fruity Riesling and Silvaner and elegant Pinot Blanc, Gris and Noir (we are close to Alsace). For something special, try a delicately spicy Muskateller or rose petal Traminer.

The Kraichgau

The large vineyard area near Wiesloch marks the southern edge of the Bergstrasse and the beginning of the hilly region between the Oden and Black Forests known as the Kraichgau. It's a peaceful area, ideal for walking, cycling, riding and fishing.

Route B 3, on the western edge of the winegrowing

Around Durbach the houses back on to superb vineyard slopes.

area, runs through Bruchsal and Karlsruhe, each with a splendid Baroque palace. The route suggested below enables you to see both. Don't miss the little wine villages set among lush forests and meadows in the valleys lining many small streams (hence the frequency of *bach*, or stream, in many town names).

Not only do grapes and other fruits thrive in the warm Kraichgau climate, but also tobacco and saffron, which carpet the fields in pink, white and purple flowers in the spring. The heavy keuper soils yield robust, full-bodied Riesling wines with less acidity than their Rheingau counterparts. Chalky loess is the other main soil type, well-suited to the Burgundy (Pinot) family. Müller-Thurgau is still the most planted white variety, (18 per cent of the total vines), followed by Grauburgunder (10 per cent), Weissburgunder and Auxerrois (an Alsace variety). Spätburgunder is by far the most planted red grape variety (37 per cent), followed by some Schwarzriesling.

Wiesloch to Bruchsal

From Wiesloch, travel south on the B 39 to Eichtersheim, where Friedrich Hecker, the Baden revolutionary involved in attempts to form a German republic (1848) was born in the town's 16th-century moated castle. At nearby **Schloss Michelfeld**, you can taste top-quality Kraichgau wines. The best vineyard is Michelfelder Himmelberg. Turn west on the B 292 to visit St Cecelia, "Cathedral of Kraichgau" in Östringen, then follow the signs to Odenheim. The late Baroque **St Michael's Church**, town hall and Siegfried's Fountain (the site where the Nibelung hero is said to have been killed) are worth a visit.

South of Odenheim, turn left to Tiefenbach, a good place to take the *Weinlehrpfad* (educational wine trail) through the vineyards, or to enjoy the quiet beauty of Kreuzbergsee, a nearby lake. The route from Eichelberg and Elsenz to Eppingen is also most attractive. Many historic buildings and 14th-century frescoes in the **Altstädter Kirche** merit a stop in Eppingen, before you drive west to **Burg Ravensburg**, overlooking the steep **Sulzfeld** vineyards, for a wonderful view and a chance to taste the owner's wines. Among the best vineyards in Kraichgau are **Burg Ravensburger Löchle** and **Husarenkappe**.

The idyllic wine village of Gochsheim is worth a small detour (via Flehingen). Among the half-timbered houses lining Bretten's market square is the Melanchthon House, a museum for the Reformation humanist and colleague of Luther. From here, it is a brief drive to Bruchsal on the B 35. Balthasar Neumann created Bruchsal's two Baroque masterpieces: **St Peter's Church** and the magnificent staircase in the palace built for a Schönborn Prince Bishop.

Karlsruhe

Legend says that Markraf (Margrave) Karl Wilhelm built his residence here after a dream in which he saw a fan-shaped town "grow" out of a fan lost by his wife. The town that developed along the roads radiating south of the palace (rebuilt by Margrave Karl Friedrich) became the capital of the Grand Duchy of Baden (1806-1918). The **art and history museums in the palace** grounds are first-rate.

Near Durlach (site of the original residence) there is a good view from the

Durbach is a major wine village in Baden. Its pretty center has a stream running through it and flowers everywhere.

Turmberg, also the name of the 1200-year-old hillside vineyard.

Baden-Baden and Ortenau

The Ortenau district of Baden is situated in the western foothills of the Black Forest between Baden-Baden and Offenburg. The Baden Wine Road twists through the hillsides on country roads (rather than the B 3), passing ancient castles and wine villages. The vineyards stretch up to the forests at the tops of the hillsides and nearly always face south. Weathered primitive rock (granite, gneiss) is the main soil type, yielding some of the finest Rieslings in south Germany, with fine, flowery bouquets and racy acidity. Almost all Baden's finest Rieslings are from vineyards near Baden-Baden, Bühl and Durbach. Near Durlach (site of the original residence) there is a good view from the Turmberg, which is also the name of the 1200-year-old hillside vineyard. Traminer, with a delicate spiciness, and the Burgundy family are also at home here.

Baden-Baden

One of Germany's most luxurious resorts, Baden-Baden attracts the international set, reminiscent of the Belle Epoque at the end of the 19th century, when Baden-Baden was a favorite spa and rendezvous of Europe's aristocracy. King Edward VII of Great Britain loved this place and its lifestyle.

The Romans discovered the healing powers of the thermal springs. You can visit the restored ruins of a Roman bath beneath the Römerplatz, site of the modern thermal baths. Today, the hub of social life is the Kurhaus, with its casino, pump room and restaurants in the grounds of the **Kurpark** (spa park). The park along the Lichtentaler Allee, converted into an English garden in 1850, and the **Neues Schloss**, with its bird's-eye view of town, are also well worth seeing.

Many fine vineyards surround Baden-Baden in the suburbs of Varnhalt and Neuweier, Umweg and Steinbach. Together with the Baden wine towns of the Tauber valley, they are permitted to bottle their wines (Riesling) in the *Bocksbeutel*, otherwise reserved for Franconian wines. The best vineyards are **Neuweier Schlossberg** and **Mauerberg**.

Bühl to Waldulm

South of Baden-Baden, Riesling and Spätburgunder become increasingly important. Bühl is the home of the **Affentaler Cooperative**, which produces good quality Spätburgunder wines. From Bühl, drive to the Altwindeck fortress ruins for a good view, and follow the Baden Wine Road to Lauf (via Hub), Obersasbach and Sasbachwalden, a picturesque wine village. Continue through the steep hills to Kappelrodeck, once famous for its Hex vom Dasenstein red wines. For a look at **Schloss Rodeck**, drive up the narrow road to St Albinus Church (with a pretty interior) on the hill in Waldulm.

Oberkirch to Offenburg

Renchtäler is the name of the large 310-hectare (766-acre) vineyard on the hills near Oberkirch, the gateway to the Renchtal

(Rench valley). Hans Jacob von Grimmelshausen (c.1621-1676) wrote *Simplicissimus*, his satirical chronicle of the Thirty Years' War, here in 1669. The many art treasures in **Lautenbach's Maria Krönung Church** merit a visit. Backtrack on the B 28 to Gaisbach, to turn left on to the road to Durbach.

Durbach is the most important wine village of Ortenau area, and has two great vineyards, **Durbacher Plauerein** and **Schlossberg**, predominantly planted with Riesling vines (here called Klingelberger – Traminer is also known locally as Clevner). The **Durbacher Cooperative** is considered to be the best in Baden and, surprisingly, half the vines are Spätburgunder and a quarter are Riesling. Unlike some cooperatives, it doesn't overdo its grape varieties.

The ancient **Schloss Staufenberg** overlooks its own vineyards as well as those of many other growers. Enjoy a bottle of Durbacher Riesling with pretzels on the terrace. From the Schloss, there is a vast panorama of Durbach village, and, in the distance, the spire of the Strasbourg Cathedral.

Historic buildings and modern sculptures blend well on Offenburg's market square, site of a wine festival (late September or early October) featuring wines from all of the Ortenau. The rococo altars of gilded red and blue marble in the **Heilig-Kreuz Church** are superb. Travel the country road through the Kinzig valley from Offenburg to Ortenberg. The peaceful valley view from the castle above town belies a grim past – in the 16th and 17th centuries it was a center of witch-hunts. Today it is a youth hostel. **Ortenburger Schlossberg** is the best vineyard of Offenburg. There are two villages close to Offenburg that have very fine vineyards owned by Weingut Freiherr von und zu Franckenstein. They are Zell-Weierbacher Abtsberg and Neugesetz, and then a little further south, Berghauptener Schützenberg.

WINERIES & MORE

BRUCHSAL

Weingut Klumpp
Heidelberger Strasse 100
76646 Bruchsal
Tel: 07251 16719
www.weingut-klumpp.com

BADEN-BADEN

Weingut Schloss Neuweier
Mauerbergstrasse 21
76534 Baden-Baden/ Neuweier
Tel: 07223 96670
www.weingut-schloss-neuweier.de
(*See also* Hotel Schloss Neuweier.)

BÜHL-KAPPELWINDECK

Weingut Duijn
Hohbaumweg 16
77815 Bühl
Tel: 07223 21497
www.weingut-duijn.com

DURBACH

Weingut Andreas Laible
Am Buhl 6
77770 Durbach
Tel: 0781 41238
www.weingut-laible.de

Weingut Markgraf von Baden
Schloss Staufenberg
Staufenberg 1
77770 Durbach
Tel: 0781 42778
www.markgraf-von-baden.de

Durbacher Winzergenossenschaft eG
Nachtweide 2
77770 Durbach
Tel: 0781 93660
www.durbacher.de

Freiburg and Breisgau

If you travel on the B 3 south of Offenburg, you barely notice leaving the Ortenau and entering the Breisgau, for there is no break in the ribbon-like strip of vineyards and orchards on the foothills of the Black Forest. However, the hills are a little rounder and many of the Breisgau's vineyards are terraced with old stone walls. Loess soils predominate, sometimes mixed with loam and limestone. Pinot Blanc, Pinot Gris and Pinot Noir (the Burgunders) and spicy Gewürztraminer are the specialties here.

There is a delightful scenic route to the Breisgau, starting with the frescoes in the vineyard chapel Bühlwegkapelle in Käfersberg, before driving to Gengenbach, a splendid medieval town with walls and gates, half-timbered houses and an impressive town hall on Rathausplatz. At Biberach you can turn west on the B 415 to Lahr (start of the Breisgau). Here is the first great vineyard in Breisgau, **Lahrer Kronenbühl** and further south is another, **Malterdinger Bienenberg**. Or you could continue on the B 33 to Haslach, to see ornate Black Forest costumes in the Schwarzwälder-Trachtenmuseum in the Kapuziner (Capuchin) monastery (closed Sun & Mon). Nearby, between Hausach and Gutach, is a Freilichtmuseum (open-air museum) with 16th to 18th-century farmhouses (vogtsbauernhof.org).

Lahr to Freiburg

The Baden Wine Road (B 3) runs through the historic wine towns with interesting features in their old town centers: Mahlberg, Herbolzheim, Kenzingen and Hecklingen, where the best vineyard is **Hecklinger Schlossberg**. There is a panoramic view from the fortress ruins of **Burg Lichteneck** over many of Breisgau's vineyards. Enter Emmendingen through its 17th-century town gate, near the house where Goethe's sister, Cornelia Schlosser, lived. The main sights are between the Renaissance Margraves' palace and market square, with old patrician houses (see nos. 4, 5, 8 and 10) and the Baroque town hall.

Before traveling to Freiburg, you can enjoy typically rural Black Forest villages and beautiful scenery by driving in a loop via Waldkirch, Kandel mountain and St Peter (where it is worth visiting the church, the library and the Princes' Hall of a former Benedictine monastery). Then return to Denzlingen through the pretty Glottertal, a sheltered valley where Weissburgunder and Spätburgunder vines thrive on slopes of weathered gneiss.

Baden specialties

Badisch Rotgold

Made only in Baden, this is said to have its origins in the Glottertal. It combines the elegance of the (red) Spätburgunder with the full body and rich bouquet of the (white) Grauburgunder.

Langasthof Schwanen in Bad Bellingen, Markgräfenland, is a very attractive hotel within a kilometer (half a mile) of the Rhine.

Weissherbst
A rosé wine produced in Germany from only one (red) grape variety. In Baden, it is usually Spätburgunder. Should be served chilled.

Freiburg

The Dukes of Zähringen founded the town in 1120. Except for several periods of French occupation, Freiburg was under Austrian rule from 1368 until its cession to the Grand Duchy of Baden in 1805. The Münster (cathedral), built between 1200 and 1513, is the focal point of this old university town's many historical and cultural attractions. The *Official Freiburg Guide* (in English) has excellent information on local sights and customs. (Contact the Freiburg Tourist Office, www.fwtm.freiburg.de)

The Haus der badischen Weine in the historic Alte Wache (1733) offers an extraordinary selection of wines, sparkling wines and spirits from this area. For locals and visitors alike, the *Freiburger Weintage* (wine festival) in early July is an attraction, when the Münsterplatz becomes a showcase for wines from several Baden districts. Alternatively, plan your visit in January or February for the *Fastnet* (carnival) festivities, rooted in Alemannic tradition. The costumes are legendary (visit the Fastnet-museum, www.breisgauer-narrenzunft.de). On one popular mask, a bunch of grapes and grape leaves form a beard, symbolic of the desire to ward off evil from the vines.

WINE ESTATE

LAHR
Weingut Stadt Lahr – Familie Wöhrle
Weinbergstrasse 3
77933 Lahr
Tel: 07821 25332
www.weingut-stadt-lahr.de

The Kaiserstuhl

The massif of Kaiserstuhl (literally the Emperor's chair), an extinct volcano, is visible from all directions. Viticulture here dates from the 8th century, but vines were not planted on the volcanic soils in the west until a thousand years later.

The Vosges Mountains ward off rain and help to dissipate clouds, making this one of Germany's warmest and sunniest districts. The favorable climate, together with heat-retaining (volcanic tufa) and mineral-rich soils, provides ideal growing conditions for grapes. Unfortunately, the climate in summer can change dramatically. It can be unbearably hot, which causes the grapes to shrivel up and become over-concentrated, with too much sugar and therefore too much alcohol and too little acidity in the wines. Then, there is quite often a thunderstorm, which circles around the peak and drops patches of heavy hail, which can badly damage the grapes and the vines, followed by heavy rainstorms that cause serious erosion in the powdery loess soils of the vineyards. However, if all turns out well, the villages celebrate at the huge wine festival in Breisach in late August.

That said, Kaiserstuhl is Baden's largest and most concentrated winegrowing area with well over 5000 hectares (12,400 acres) of vines, and with the highest number of full-time growers. The Kaiserstuhl is renowned for powerful, full-bodied wines. Only the Ortenau area can compete in quality. The Pinot family, Spätburgunder, Weissburgunder and Grauburgunder is well represented everywhere in Kaiserstuhl. Riesling is particularly successful around Achkarren. Spicy Gewürztraminer, Silvaner and Muskateller are also grown in small quantities.

Since 1950, the vast number of narrow terraces has been consolidated into

Before 1950 the Kaiserstuhl's steep vineyards were difficult to work. These terraces were built by winegrowers.

broad, layered rows of terraces. The new arrangement is more efficient, but the landscape is almost surreal in appearance, especially in the blue-violet shades of dawn or dusk.

From Wasenweiler at the southwest corner of the extinct volcano it is only minutes to Ihringen, where the finest vineyard is **Ihringer Winklerberg**. The next village is Blankenhornsberg and its fine vineyard **Doctorgarten**, from which you can see the spires of Breisach's cathedral as you drive towards the Rhine. Among its art treasures are a Gothic altar, the Martin Schongauer frescoes and an ornate reliquary. Further north is Achkarren, where the soil is more based on limestone and the majority of vines are Riesling. Silvaner, Weissburgunder, Grauburgunder and Spätburgunder compete to be planted in this great terroir. Visit the wine museum in Achkarren.

We now come to the villages at the heart of the Kaiserstuhl. Vogtsburg is not perhaps well known as Bischoffingen, with its vineyard, **Rosenkranz**. Oberrotweil has its splendid vineyards, **Kirchberg** and **Eichberg** (the richly carved Gothic altar in **St Michaelis Church** in Niederrotweil will interest art lovers). Bürkheim is a little further north and was once a port on the bank of the Rhine: it has two great vineyards, **Schlossgarten** and **Feuerberg**, ancient houses and old town gates. Jechtingheim has its famous **Eichert** vineyard, and Sasbach has its fine vineyard **Limburg**.

The town of Endingen is close to the northwest corner of the volcano, and its great vineyard is **Engelsberg**. It also has ancient houses and old town gates, and a market square, where you will find a range of architectural styles: the old town hall (1527) has vaulted gables; the Kornhaus, or granary (1617), boasts high, stepped gables; and the new town hall is an elegant 18th-century manor house.

The country road from Riegel to Wasenweiler passes through the wine towns of Bahlingen and Bötzingen on the eastern edge of the Kaiserstuhl and completes the circuit.

If time permits, the historic train "**Rebenbummler**" is a relaxing way to enjoy the landscape between Riegel and Breisach (round trips, May-Oct).

This winegrower in Oberbergen looks pleased with his crop.

Hiking trails

Hikers can enjoy the exotic fauna and flora, including 33 different types of orchids in bloom (May and June), on the Badberg near Oberbergen. The signposted vineyard path in Achkarren also explains much about the region's geology. It begins opposite the cooperative. Allow one hour for this walk. At the Rhine crossing near Sasbach there is a fascinating trail through the Limburg nature reserve that highlights the area's natural resources and history. Allow two hours.

The Tuniberg

This is an ancient chalky hill, famous for wine and asparagus. From Freiburg, drive west on the B 31 to Tiengen and Munzingen. Apart from loess, the terroir of the vineyards is very different from that of Kaiserstuhl. It is parallel to and east of the road from Oberrimsingen to Merdingen, whose attractions include the pretty houses on the Langgasse and the **St Remigius Church**, a jewel of Baroque architecture.

Close to the bridge to France at Breisach is the **Badischer Winzerkeller** (Central Cellars of Baden Cooperatives) at Zum Kaisertuhl 6. This produces wines on behalf of its own members, as well as wines on behalf of about 90 other cooperatives. The result is a vast selection, but in general rather ordinary wines.

Growers' cooperative

Winzergenossenschaft (abbreviated WG) is a place to taste and buy wine.
Offene Winzerkeller (open house) Some cooperatives maintain a restaurant, where you can enjoy the wines with regional food (Ihringen, Bickensohl, Bischoffingen, and Oberrotweil).

WINERIES & MORE

BISCHOFFINGEN

Weingut Karl H Johner
Gartenstrasse 20
79235 Vogtsburg-Bischoffingen
Tel: 07662 6041
www.johner.de

ENDINGEN AM KAISERSTUHL

Weingut Reinhold und Cornelia Schneider
Königschaffhauser Strasse 2

79346 Endingen
am Kaiserstuhl
Tel: 07642 5278
www.weingutschneider.com

IHRINGEN

Weingut Dr Heger
Bachenstrasse 19/21
79241 Ihringen
Tel: 07668 205
www.heger-weine.de

OBERROTWEIL

Weingut Freiherr von Gleichenstein
Bahnhofstrasse 12
79235 Oberrotweil
Tel: 07662 288
www.gleichenstein.de

Weingut Salwey
Hauptstrasse 2
79235 Oberrotweil
Tel: 07662 384
www.salwey.de

VOGTSBURG-BURKHEIM

Weingut Bercher
Mittelstadt 13
79235 Vogtsburg-Burkheim
Tel: 07662 212
www.weingutbercher.de

VOGTSBURG-OBERBERGEN

Weingut Franz Keller Schwarzer Adler
Badbergstrasse 23
79235 Vogtsburg-Oberbergen
Tel: 07662 93300
www.franz-keller.de
(*See also* Hotel Schwarzer Adler.)

Markgräflerland

The broad hills of the Markgräflerland stretch from Freiburg to Basel, with vineyards, orchards and fields nestling between the Black Forest and the Rhine. It has been a route for both soldiers and merchants from Roman times. The area suffered greatly during the medieval political and religious conflicts. However, in the early 16th century when the *Markgräfler* (Margraves or Marquises) came to power, some stability was established and from then on, it became known as the Markgräflerland.

Vineyards and grape varieties

A nearly uninterrupted band of vineyards parallels the B 3 from Freiburg to Bad Bellingen, but some of the best wines come from further south. Vines thrive in the chalky loess-loam soils (heavy clay in some sites) and the mild, humid climate.

A signpost in Neuweier points to just about everywhere you could wish to find. It's even crowned with a *Bocksbeutel* flagon.

The Markgräflerland is best known for two white varieties. Gutedel is an ancient variety introduced to this area over 200 years ago by Margrave Karl Friedrich, a progressive champion of quality winegrowing in Baden. Gutedel had been grown in Egypt for at least five thousand years, and is planted in vineyards from Freiburg to Basel. It is known as Chasselas in France and Fendant in Switzerland. It is a fresh, mild white wine for aprés-skiing in winter and sheer enjoyment in summer. Nobling is a recent crossing of Silvaner and Gutedel, and gives ripe, fruity wines with more body and acidity.

Nature, art and legend

Just minutes southwest of Freiburg (on the B 3) you can explore six small wine villages bordering Batzenberg hill (248 hectares/613 acres of vines) by walking the *Weinlehrpfad* beginning near Schallstadt – there are lovely views. In Oberkrozingen (Glöcklehof), near the pretty spa of Bad Krozingen, art lovers will appreciate the 9th-century wall paintings in **St Ulrich's Chapel.**

Turning towards the Black Forest, you can see the imposing ruins of Staufen castle perched high on a vine-covered slope (Schlossberg). It overlooks the town of Staufen, with colorful houses, historic buildings, and a curious claim to fame: Faust is said to have succumbed to the devil in the Zum Löwen inn on the market square. You can enjoy a glass of wine here and in early August, taste the Markgräflerland wines at the wine festival. The exquisite Baroque church of the **St Trudpert monastery** is worth a detour to Münstertal, a former silver mining center.

Staufen to Müllheim

Sulzburg merits a stop for the **Ottonian (AD 993) St Cyriak Church**, stunning in its simplicity. In Laufen, you can visit an excellent cooperative and a world-famous nursery of perennial plants, especially iris (Staudengärtnerei Gräfin von Zeppelin). Neuenfels fortress ruins are visible as you drive towards Britzingen, where the cooperative has an outstanding wine shop.

Badenweiler's modern spa is set below the dramatic Hohenstaufen castle ruins. The Romans discovered the thermal springs in the first century AD and built extensive baths, which can be visited in the spa park. Baden's oldest wine market (1882) takes place every April in Müllheim, giving visitors a chance to taste many different Markgräflerland wines. The museum in the old town hall in the market square has exhibits devoted to wine and to Adolph

Blankenhorn, a great scientist who devoted his life to improving viticulture and helping small growers (www.markgraefler-museum.de).

Southern Markgräflerland

The Baden Wine Road continues south on the B 3 to Auggen, whose best vineyard is Auggener Schäf. The Auggen Cooperative is a model of ecological viticulture. Just to the south are two villages – Mauchen and Schliengen – that share a fine vineyard called **Sonnenstück**, which is one of the best in Markgräflerland. Schliengen has a picturesque town hall in the moated Entenstein castle. Bad Bellingen too has quite a large vineyard and thermal springs that were discovered during an unsuccessful search for oil.

Schloss Bürgeln, a rococo castle situated back in the hills, offers a good view (www.schlossbuergeln.de). Kandern, nearby, is famous for wine, pottery and pretzels.

The southernmost vineyards of Markgräflerland include the Istein "block," which is a promontory that stands next to the Rhine and blocked it millions of years ago. It is an almost vertical rock about 150 meters high (400 feet) and the area round it has limestone and a myriad of geological layers, which give the vineyard, **Isteiner Kirchberg**, a terroir with extraordinary complexity that is ideal for vines. The **Efringer Ölberg** vineyard is next to it and is another great vineyard. Last but not least, the moated **castle in Inzlingen**, east of Weil, is a wonderful setting, with superb wine and food.

Schwarzwälder (Black Forest) specialties

Kirschtorte chocolate cake layered with whipped cream and cherries flavored with *Kirschwasser*.

Schäufele mit Kartoffelsalat lightly pickled and smoked pork shoulder with potato salad.

Schinken smoked ham.

Wässerle clear, distilled fruit spirits, eg *Kirschwasser* (cherry) or *Zwetschgenwasser* (plum).

Wild game, eg *Rehrücken* (saddle of venison) served with pear halves filled with wild cranberry sauce.

BADISCHER WEIN GMBH

The Bodensee (Lake Constance) is a popular tourist destination.

Zibärtle a rare spirit made from mountain plums.

Other specialties include clocks, wood carvings and pottery. (*Töpferei* is the name for a potter's studio.)

The Bodensee

The Bodensee (Lake Constance) is surrounded by some of Europe's most beautiful scenery. Bordered by Germany, Switzerland and Austria and not far from the Alps and the Black Forest, it is a popular vacation spot, with many recreational opportunities and sights, not least of which is the lake itself. The lakeside promenades are lined with cafés where you can enjoy a panorama of graceful sailboats and windsurfers over a glass of *Seewein* (lake wine). **A boat trip to Meersburg** provides a good view of its medieval townscape and the steep vineyards below the Baroque palace. Steamers also cruise to Lindau, a delightful resort on the lake's eastern edge.

The islands of Mainau (famous gardens) and Reichenau (art treasures) as well as the historic town of Konstanz, are worth visiting, as are the fascinating prehistoric lake dwellings on piles, near Unteruhldingen (www.pfahlbauten.de).

The Bodensee's vineyards, mainly planted with Müller-Thurgau and Spätburgunder vines, are concentrated on the northern shore from Meersburg to Hagnau, the southernmost and highest altitude in Germany.

The lake tempers the climate and reflects the sun's warmth. Most sites face south and are planted on hills of moraine gravel and chalky, sandy loam. At Hohentwiel, near Singen, however, a volcanic cone is the site of the highest vineyards (530m/1740ft). The castle ruins on the top of the hill are a good vantage point.

Bodensee wines are seldom available outside the area, but Meersburg's popular wine festival in September features wines from many towns.

Art treasures en route to Meersburg

In Überlingen's Old Town are **St Nicholas Church**, which has magnificent altars, and the town hall, famous for its Gothic *Ratssaal* (council chamber). The Gothic church with its Baroque interior, and the buildings of the former Cistercian monastery in Salem are worth a detour (open Apr–Nov). The cellars of Max Markgraf von Baden's wine estate are also in the grounds. To see the small wine museum, ask at the wine shop. The estate's wines are served at nearby Gasthof Schwanen. Return to the lake via Mendlishausen. The lavishly furnished church at Birnau is one of the finest Baroque buildings in Germany.

Meersburg

This medieval town is best explored on foot. Walk up the Steigstrasse to the Marktplatz in the upper part of town to see the historic houses, such as **Weinstube Löwen** and Gasthot Zum Bären (both are good places to taste wine). Also of interest are the dungeons and living quarters in the Altes (old) Schloss and the period rooms and stairway by Balthasar Neumann in the Neues (new) Schloss. The outdoor terrace of the café upstairs in the Altes Schloss offers a truly spectacular view of the Bodensee and the Alps. The ferries connect the port with Constance in Switzerland.

The Staatsweingut was

founded in 1803, and is one of the oldest state-owned wine domains of Germany. It is next door to the former riding stables of the palace and has a good restaurant. Its best-known vineyard is Meersburger Rieschen.

MEERSBURG
Weinbaumuseum
(Museum of Viticulture)
Vorburggasse 11. Meersburg. April to mid-Oct, historic casks, old press, coopers' workshop.

WEINLEHRPFAD (WINE EDUCATIONAL TRAIL)
In Meersburg: from near "Wetterkreuz" at eastern edge of town, and there is a vineyard path to Hagnau (5 km/3 miles), with superb views of the lake and the Alps. In Hagnau: vineyard path near Wilhelmshöhe.

Hagnau to Lindau

Baden's first winegrowers' cooperative was founded in Hagnau in 1881. Hagnau, Kippenhausen and Immenstaad mark the end of Baden's vineyards along the lake. Further east, the landscape consists mostly of orchards and fields, although Württemberg claims a patch of vineyards near Kressbronn, and Franken administers the three vineyards around Lindau. The lovely promenade of this island resort is a perfect place to enjoy a glass of Lindauer Seegarten while watching the boats sail in and out of the harbor.

WINERIES & MORE

MALTERDINGEN
Weingut Huber
Heimbacher Weg 19
79364 Malterdingen
Tel: 07644 1200
www.weingut-huber.com

LAUFEN
Privatweingut H Schlumberger
Weinstrasse 19
79295 Laufen
Tel: 07634 8992
www.schlumbergerwein.de

MEERSBURG
Staatsweingut Meersburg
Seminarstrasse 6
88709 Meersburg
Tel: 07532 446744
www.staatsweingut-meersburg.de

WHERE TO STAY AND EAT

Baden-Baden

Röttele's Residenz & Restaurant im Schloss Neuweier (H/R)
Mauerbergstrasse 21
76534 Baden-Baden
Tel: 07223 800870
www.armin-roettele.de
Hotel with 12 rooms. Armin Röttelle's modern Michelin-starred restaurant. Italian cuisine. Superb Rieslings and other wines.

Bühl

Grüne Bettlad (H/R)
Blumenstrasse 4
77815 Bühl
Tel: 07223 93130
www.gruenebettlad.de
Sixteenth century half-timbered house with five rooms. Charming restaurant. Classic and regional cuisine.

Bühlertal

Bergfriedel Hotel (H/R)
Haabergstrasse 23
77830 Bühlertal
Tel: 07223 72270
www.bergfriedel.de
Ten rooms. Restaurant with interesting mix of classic and regional dishes. Great views.

Denzlingen

Rebstock-Stube (H/R)
Hauptstrasse 74
79211 Denzlingen
Tel: 07666 900990
www.rebstock-stube.de
Eight-hundred-year-old guesthouse, ten rooms, friendly atmosphere. Restaurant serves both regional and classic French dishes.

Efringen-Kirchen

Gasthof Traube (H/R)
Alemannenstrasse 19
79588 Efringen-Kirchen
(in Blansingen suburb)
Tel: 07628 942 3780
www.traube-blansingen.de
Hotel with nine rooms. Michelin-starred restaurant, sophisticated cuisine.

Ettlingen

Hotel Restaurant Erbprinz (H/R/W)
Rheinstrasse 1
76275 Ettlingen
Tel: 07243 3220
www.erbprinz.de
Hotel with 119 rooms. Restaurant and *Weinstube* Sibylla. Good regional dishes and pleasant atmosphere. (The town has a

fascinating old town hall, old paper mill and 18th-century palace).

Freiburg

Colombi-Hotel (H/R)
Rotteckring 16
79098 Freiburg
Tel: 0761 21060
www.colombi.de
Hotel with 115 rooms. Restaurant Zirbelstube, classic gourmet and regional specialties. Comprehensive wine list.

Glottertal

Hotel Restaurant Hirschen (H/R)
Rathausweg 2
79286 Glottertal
Tel: 07684 810
www.hirschen-glottertal.de
Forty-nine rooms. Restaurant with traditional Baden cuisine. Also rustic Schwarzwaldstube.

Zum goldenen Engel (H/R)
Friedhofweg 2
79286 Glottertal
Tel: 07684 250
www.goldener-engel-glottertal.de
Hotel (1507) with 14 rooms. Restaurant serves regional cuisine in Black Forest style, as well as modern dishes. Very comfortable.

Heidelberg

Die Hirschgasse (H/R)
Hirschgasse 3
69120 Heidelberg
Tel: 06221 4540
www.hirschgasse.de
Hotel with 20 rooms. Restaurants Le Gourmet (classic cuisine) and Mensurstube (simpler dishes).

Lahr-Reichenbach

Hotel Restaurant Adler (H/R)
Reichenbacher Hauptstrasse 18
77933 Lahr-Reichenbach
Tel: 07821 906390
www.adler-lahr.de
Typical Baden guest house, 21 rooms. Michelin-starred Black-Forest style restaurant with very fine wines.

Inzlingen

Inzlinger Wasserschloss (H/R)
Riehenstrasse 5
79594 Inzlingen
Tel: 07621 47057
www.inzlinger-wasserschloss.de
Hotel with 12 rooms. Gourmet dining in a 15th-century castle.

Neckarzimmern am Neckar

Burg Hornberg (H/R)
74865 Neckarzimmern
Tel: 06261 92460
www.burg-hotel-hornberg.de
Twelfth-century castle hotel with 24 rooms. Restaurant with terrace and grand Neckar views.

Meersburg

Hotel Zum Schiff (H/R)
Bismarckplatz 5
88709 Meersburg
Tel: 07532 45000
www.hotelzumschiff.de
Attractive hotel on Lake Constance. Restaurant with lakeside terrace.

Residenz am See (H/R)
Uferpromenade 11
88709 Meersburg
Tel: 07532 80040
www.hotel-residenz-meersburg.com
Twenty-five rooms, close to the lake. Two restaurants: Casala (Michelin starred, classic and creative cuisine), and Residenz (good regional food).

Staatsweingut Meersburg (R)
Seminarstrasse 4
88709 Meersburg
Tel: 07532 807630
www.staatsweingut-meersburg.de

Müllheim

Alte Post (H/R)
Posthalterweg, on the B3
79379 Müllheim
Tel: 07631 17870
www.alte-post.net
Historic guest house with 51 rooms and a restaurant.

Ortenburg

Edy's Restaurant Hotel (H/R)
Kinzigtalstrasse 20
77799 Ortenburg
Tel: 0781 9 34 90
www.edys-restaurant-hotel.de
Hotel with 12 rooms. Restaurant with international seasonal food.

Sasbachwalden

Hotel Talmühle (H/R)
Talstrasse 36
77887 Sasbachwalden
Tel: 07841 1001
www.talmuehle.de
Twenty-seven rooms. Michelin-starred restaurant Fallert and a Badische Stuben with regional specialties.

Weingarten

Walk'sches Haus (H/R)
Marktplatz 7
76356 Weingarten
Tel: 07244 70370
www.walksches-haus.de

Hotel with 26 rooms in 16th-century house. Gourmet restaurant with classic menus, also *Weinstube*.

Weil am Rhein

Hotel-Restaurant Adler (H/R)
Hauptstrasse 139
79576 Weil am Rhein
Tel: 07621 98230
www.adler-weil.de
Hotel with 23 rooms. Restaurant with classic and regional cuisine.

Vogtsburg

Steinbuck Hotel (H/R)
Steinbuckstrasse 20
79235 Vogtsburg-Bischoffingen
Tel: 07662 91 1210
www.hotel-steinbuck.de
Eighteen rooms. Restaurant with Baden dishes.

Schwarzer Adler (H/R)
Badbergstrasse 23
79235 Vogstburg-Oberbergen
Tel: 07662 93 300

Andreas Laible built this winery himself, made his own bread, and produced fine Durbacher Plauelrain Rieslings.

www.franz-keller.de
Hotel with 14 rooms. Michelin-starred restaurant, closed Feb. Traditional.

Sulzburg

Hotel Restaurant Hirschen (H/R)
Hauptstrasse 69
79295 Sulzburg
Tel: 07634 8208
www.dance-steiner.de
Nine rooms. Michelin-starred restaurant with top gourmet fare, seasonal classic menus and great wines.

30

SAALE-UNSTRUT

VINES HAVE LINED THE SLOPES of the Saale and Unstrut river valleys for ten centuries. Today, Saale-Unstrut is Germany's northernmost winegrowing region, straddling the 51° N line of latitude between Leipzig and Weimar. It is a gentle landscape of hills ringed by forests, poplar groves and broad plateaus. Vineyards and orchards are scattered on the slopes, while corn and wheat fields dominate the flatter expanses. Much of the region lies within the Saale-Unstrut-Triasland nature park, a haven for rare fauna and flora (especially orchids, at Laucha-Krawinkel and Kleinjena-Toten Täler).

Freyburg, Naumburg and Bad Kösen are the main wine centers, but in order to get to know the region, travel on the *Weinstrasse* (wine road). It follows the Unstrut from Nebra to Grossjena, then continues westward along the banks of the Saale and the Ilm to Bad Sulza. Sections of the route are identical with the *Strasse der Romanik* (the Romanesque road), with signposts to historical castles, monasteries and churches. The *Radwanderweg* (bicycle trail) along the rivers' banks, the *Wanderweg* (hiking trail) through the vineyards, as well as trips by boat and train are pleasant alternatives.

No one really knows when viticulture was introduced into this eastern outpost of the Frankish kingdom, but vineyards were first documented in Emperor Otto III's deed of gift to the monastery in Memleben in AD 998.

The forests were *gerodet*, or cleared, (town names that end with -roda reflect this fact) and monasteries and churches were built throughout the region as it was colonized "by the sword and by the plough." Vineyards were necessary to ensure the supply of Communion wine. It was through of the Cistercian monks in particular that

‹‹ The Saale-Unstrut wine region, characterized by unspoiled countryside covered in vineyards, is ideal for family cycle trips.

Querfurt
B250
B180
Eisl
B18
Vitzenbur
Kalzendorf
Reinsdorf
Steigra
Nebra
Karsdorf
R. Unstrut
B180
Wennungen
Memleben
Gleina
Burgscheidungen
Tröbsdor
Kirchscheidungen
B250
Dorndorf
Weischütz
B176
Laucha
Freyb
Zscheiplitz
Bad Bibra
Hirschroda
Balgstädt
Kleinje
Rossba
B250
Altenb
Schulp
B87
Bad Kösen
Eckhartsberga
Kleinheringen
B88
Sonnendorf
Saaleck
B87
Grossheringen
Kaatschen
R. Ilm
Bad Sulza

See
Höhnstedt
B80
randeroda
Rossbach
B91
Reichardtswerben
B176
eroda
Kriechau
Tagewerbe
Burgwerben
Markröhlitz
ödelist
Weissenfels
ena
Goseck
A9
R. Saale
Eulau
Schönburg
burg
B87
B180
N
S
E
W

viticulture thrived here. In 1137 they established a monastery near Bad Kösen and by 1153 had planted vines on the Köppelberg hill – which remains an outstanding site to this day.

By the mid-16th century, there were about 10,000 hectares (24,700 acres) of vineyards in greater Thuringia, including the vineyards of Saale-Unstrut. The centuries that followed were less auspicious for wine. Wars, competition from imported wines and other beverages, as well as migration to better-paid jobs in the cities all contributed to the decline of viticulture that culminated in the arrival of the phylloxera (vine louse) here in 1887.

Much of the German research to combat the dreaded phylloxera was done in viticultural institutions in Naumburg, but it was sad that Germany alone would not allow the grafting of European wine varieties on to American rootstocks, while other countries had already successfully done so.

Today, there are 665 hectares (1600 acres) of vines. The main white grape varieties are Müller-Thurgau (18.49 per cent), Weissburgunder (12.1 per cent), Silvaner (8.4 per cent) and Grauburgunder. The rest consists of lesser amounts of Riesling, Kerner, Bacchus and Traminer, plus the red grapes varieties Portugieser, Dornfelder and Spätburgunder. Limestone and sandstone are the main soil types.

The continental climate here created difficulties, with long, very cold winters and frosts in spring. Grape picking may be cut short by bad weather and frosts in the fall. However, as with the rest of Germany, global warming started to improve the climate in the 1990s.

After WWII, wine growers in this region (part of the Soviet Occupied Zone) were forced to join local farm cooperatives. The quality of the vineyards and wines were lost.

After the Berlin Wall came down, West Germany and Europe started to inject huge sums of money to support and develop the economy. Farm cooperatives were converted to wine cooperatives and some winegrow-

Max Klinger vineyard has great views, holiday homes and a café.

ers recovered their former vineyards. Since then, there has been remarkable progress in viticulture. Today there are more than 50 vineyards as well as 5 cooperatives.

The Unstrut Valley

Memleben was the site of an imperial monastery and a *Pfalz* (palace) that was a favorite residence of King Heinrich I the Fowler (AD 876-936). A visit to the ruins, idyllically set in a garden, and the crypt, make a good starting point for a journey on the *Weinstrasse*. This zigzags across the Unstrut from Nebra, where the valley narrows and tall sandstone cliffs rise up from the water's edge, to Karsdorf, whose chalky soils yield excellent wines. The best vineyard here is **Karsdorfer Hohe Gräte**. From Wennungen to Kirchscheidungen the *Weinstrasse* nestles between the river and woods. The Hahnenberge vineyards line the slopes on the opposite bank, but are not always visible from the wine road.

Between Laucha and Dorndorf – with an interesting bell museum and a center for hang-gliding – the road crosses the river again, skirting the vineyards as it winds to Freyburg.

Historic sites with views

Regal lions adorn the bridge you will cross at Nebra en route to Vitzenburg, where a detour uphill (via the B 250, then the first left turn) to the castle provides a fine view of the valley. At Tröbsdorf, cross the Unstrut to Burgscheidungen. The Baroque palace and its Italian gardens still exude an air of splendor and the view from the terrace is beautiful.

Zscheiplitz offers an impressive panorama of the Schweigenberge hills' terraced vineyards, extending as far as Freyburg and the Neuenburg castle. The 12th-century monastery church and Weissenburg fortress ruins are worth seeing and on the path to the Kalkbrennofen (historic lime kiln) there are lovely views of the meadows and forests in the valley below.

WINERIES & MORE

ZSCHEIPLITZ

Weingut Bernard Pawis
Auf dem Gut 2
06632 Zscheiplitz
Tel: 034464 28315
www.weingut-pawis.de

KIRCHSCHEIDUNGEN

Weingut Klaus Böhme
Lindenstrasse 42
06636 Kirchscheidungen
Tel: 034462 20395
www.weingut-klaus-boehme.de

From Zscheiplitz to Freyburg

Follow the road next to the river to the Eckstädter Turm, a tower that belongs to Freyburg's 13th-century fortifications. This town is the region's viticultural center and the site of its largest wine festival (second weekend in Sep). **Freyburger Edelacker** is the outstanding vineyard here. The Freyburg-Unstrut cooperative (founded in 1934) has some 500 members and is the largest winery in the region, and about half the grapes from the region are fermented and bottled here. The vast Rotkäppchen sparkling winery was founded in 1856 and produces millions of bottles. It has a historic Domkeller with a 120,000-liter carved cask and merits a visit. The beautiful altar and baptismal font in the **St Marien Church**, the **Neuenburg castle** and the **Jahnmuseum**, devoted to the "father of gymnastics," are also of interest.

Blütengrund and Naumburg

Depart Freyburg via the Mühlstrasse and bear right

WEINVERBAND SAALE-UNSTRUT

The Herzoglicher (Duke's) Weinberg on the slopes below Freyburg's Neuenburg castle is today a model vineyard.

at the fork in the road towards Grossjena, Blütengrund and the Fähre (ferry) at the confluence of the Unstrut and Saale rivers. Here you can see monumental reliefs carved into the stone hillside (1722), historic villas and the studio where the artist Max Klinger worked – all set amid the Sonneck site. You can also travel this pretty route on the 1888 boat *Fröhliche Dörte* (two-hour round trip, daily).

From here it's a few minutes to Naumburg, famous for its cathedral with exquisite art treasures, such as the life-sized statues of its patrons. The town square and St Wenzel's Church are also striking in appearance. A detour northeast of Naumburg will enable you to see the vineyards, and historical buildings at Goseck, Weissenfels and Burgwerben that are not on the *Weinstrasse* – to which we now return via the Kleinjena bridge.

The Saale Valley

From Kleinjena to Rossbach and the Saale crossing at Altenburg, the site Steinmeister is on the right, followed by a nearly uninterrupted succession of good sites (Saalhäuser and Schöne Aussicht) all the way. The wine road, however, crosses the Saale to enable you to visit **Kloster Pforta**, a Cistercian monastery from 1137. In 1993 the monastery and its 50 hectares (123 acres) of vines was taken over by the State of Sachsen-Anhalt. It is now called **Schulpforte** and its Romanesque and Gothic buildings merit a visit.

You will pass by the Köppelberg site en route to Bad Kösen, a spa with thermal saline springs. Don't miss the remarkable collection of Käthe Kruse dolls in the history museum in the 12th-century **Romanisches Haus**.

From Bad Kösen the **Weinstrasse** follows the Saale to Saaleck, where you can visit the romantic Rudelsburg (1171) and Saaleck (1050) castle ruins. The best vineyard in this area is **Kaatschener Dachberg**. You can enjoy the trip to the castles by boat (allow two hours). The wine road continues along the Ilm river from Grossheringen, passing by the Sonnenberg site on the opposite heights, to its end at Bad Sulza.

Höhnstedt is known for vines (c. 60 hectares/150 acres) and orchards. Drive north from Freyburg on B 180 via Querfurt to Eisleben, where you can visit the houses where Martin Luther (1483-1546) was born and died: Seminarstrasse 16 and Andreaskirchplatz 7. Then drive east on B 80 and turn left 3.5 km (2 miles) past Lake Süsser See.

The leading *Weingüter* in Saale-Unstrut are **Pawis, Klaus Böhme, Lützkendorf** and **Winzerhof Gussek.**

REGIONAL WINE PROMOTION BOARD

Weinbauverband Saale-Unstrut
Querfurter Strasse 10
06632 Freyburg
Tel: 034464 26110
www.saaleunstrut.com

WINERIES & MORE

NAUMBURG

Winzerhof Gussek
Kösener Strasse 66
06618 Naumburg
Tel: 03445 7810366
www.winzerhof-gussek.de

Weingut Uwe Lützkendorf
Saalberge 31
06628 Naumburg
Tel: 034463 61000
www.weingut-luetzkendorf.de

BAD KÖSEN

Landesweingut Kloster Pforta
(State Wine Domain)
Saalhäuser 73
06628 Bad Kösen
Tel: 034463 3000
www.kloster-pforta.de

BAD SULZA

Thüringer Weingut Bad Sulza
Orsteil Sonnendorf 17
99518 Bad Sulza
Tel: 036461 20600
www.thueringer-wein.de

Vineyards surrounding Freyburg, the capital of Saale-Unstrut. The town has a thousand-year history of winemaking.

WHERE TO STAY AND EAT

Bad Kösen

Landesweingut Kloster Pforta (W)
Saalhäuser 73
06628 Bad Kösen
Tel: 034463 3000
www.kloster-pforta.de
Weinstube in historic monastery. Schulpforte: shop 10AM–6PM.

Himmelreich (H/R)
Bergstrasse 6
06628 Bad Kösen
(Watch for right turn at Lengefeld, west of town.)
Tel: 034463 27391
www.himmelreich-bad-koesen.de
Three rooms, one apartment. Views of the castles.

Schöne Aussicht (H/R)
Ilskeweg 1
06628 Bad Kösen
(Over the bridge).
Tel: 034463 27365
www.schoeneaussicht-badkoesen.de

Freyburg

Gasthaus Pretzsch (R)
Am Anger 6
06632 Freyburg
Tel: 034464 27311
www.gasthaus-pretzsch.de

Berghotel zum Edelacker (H/R)
Schloss 25
06632 Freyburg
Tel: 034464 350
www.edelacker.de
Adjacent to Neuenburg castle. Superb views. Terrace dining.

Hotel Unstruttal (H/R)
Markt 11
06632 Freyburg
Tel: 034464 7070
Historic house with a pretty courtyard.

Zum Künstlerkeller (H/R/W)
Breite Strasse 14
06632 Freyburg
Tel: 034464 70750
www.kuenstlerkeller.de
Historic house and cellars.

Naumburg

Hotel Stadt Aachen (H/R)
Markt 11
06618 Naumburg
Tel: 03445 261060
www.hotel-stadt-aachen.de
Historic house. Restaurant Carolus Magnus.

Zur Alten Schmiede (H/R)
Lindenring 36
06618 Naumburg
Tel: 03445 24360
www.hotel-zur-alten-schmiede.de
Charming hotel-restaurant.
Vitzenburg

Vitzenburg

Zum Unstrutblick (H)
Parkstrasse 3
06268 Vitzenburg
Tel: 034461 23891

Zum Schweizerhaus (H)
Am Weinberg 4
06268 Querfurt OT Vitzenburg
Tel: 034461 22562
www.schweizerhaus-vitzenburg.de

Germany has a centuries-old tradition of barrel carving. This fine example is in the Freyburg cellars of Rötkappchen-Mumm Sekt, Germany's largest producer of sparkling wine.

SACHSEN

GERMANY'S SMALLEST AND EASTERNMOST winegrowing region, Sachsen (Saxony) nestles in the Elbe river basin some 200 km (125 miles) southeast of Berlin and 150 km (95 miles) northwest of Prague. The *Sächsische Weinstrasse* (Saxon Wine Road), the *Elbe-Radweg* (bicycle path) and the *Weisse Flotte*, founded in 1836, the world's oldest fleet of paddle-wheel steamboats, travel along the length of the wine country as they follow the course of the river from Pirna, south of Dresden, to Diesbar-Seusslitz, north of Meissen.

Along this route, a mere 55 km (34 miles), there is an extraordinary number of art and architectural treasures to admire, from historical fortresses to sumptuous palaces surrounded by elaborate parks or gardens. These were financed by revenues from Sachsen's wine and the silver mined in the Erzgebirge (Ore Mountains), and from 1710, the "white gold" produced in Meissen's renowned porcelain manufactory.

Your efforts to seek out Sachsen's vintners and restaurateurs will be rewarded with good wine, food and hospitality second to none. The warmth of their welcome is genuine.

Vines have been cultivated of the Elbtal (Elbe valley) since the 12th century. Here, as elsewhere in Europe, viticulture initially thrived under the Church and the aristocracy. Later, wealthy citizens bought vineyards and built the little "huts" as summerhouses that still dot the landscape.

Viticulture and wine-related jobs were vital to the region's economy. At the turn of the 19th century, Sachsen had over 1600 hectares (c. 4000 acres) of vines. By 1945 only 67 hectares (166 acres) remained and by 2013, it has increased to 462 hectares (1080 acres).

The climate here has been difficult, with long, cold

‹‹ Dresden's Catholic cathedral, the Hofkirche, was largely destroyed by bombing in 1945. It has since been impeccably restored.

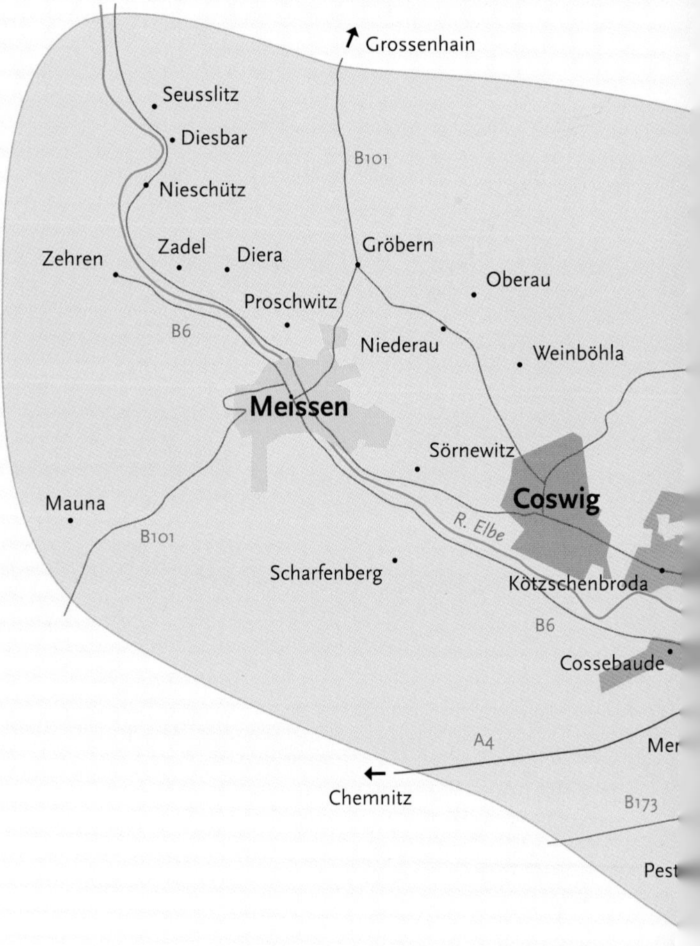
Grossenhain
Seusslitz
Diesbar
B101
Nieschütz
Zadel
Diera
Gröbern
Zehren
Oberau
Proschwitz
B6
Niederau
Weinböhla
Meissen
Sörnewitz
Coswig
Mauna
R. Elbe
B101
Scharfenberg
Kötzschenbroda
B6
Cossebaude
A4
Chemnitz
B173

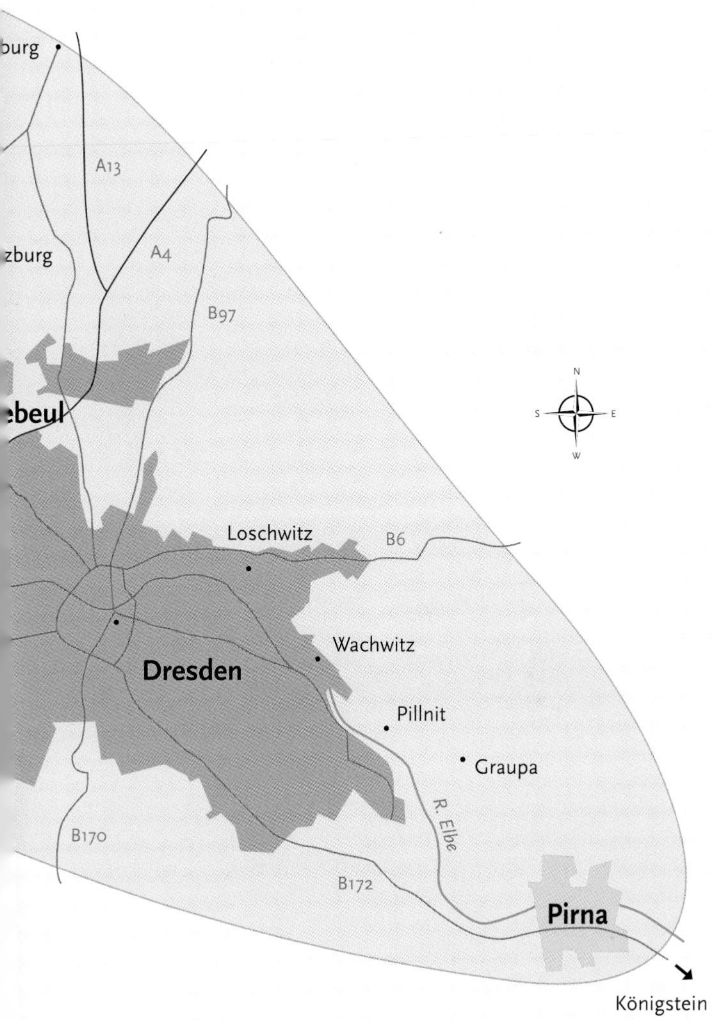
burg
A13
A4
zburg
B97
N
S
E
W
ebeul
Loschwitz
B6
Wachwitz
Dresden
Pillnit
Graupa
R. Elbe
B170
B172
Pirna
Königstein

winters and frosts in spring. Grape picking may be cut short by bad weather and frosts in autumn. However, like the rest of Germany, global warming started to improve the climate in the 1990s. The history of viticulture from the end of WWII in Sachsen is similar to that of Saale-Unstrut. Today, hobby vintners tend most of Sachsen's vines and deliver their grapes to the regional cooperative in Meissen. The State Wine Domain, Schloss Wackerbarth in Radebeul, and Schloss Proschwitz are other large producers.

Terraced slopes

Most of Sachsen's vineyards are small parcels planted on steep, labor-intensive terraces facing south. Weathered granite is the main soil type, with loess or sand deposits in some sites. The rocky soils, stone terraces and sun-reflecting surface of the Elbe all provide warmth, yet an early spring can still be deadly, and there can be frost as late as mid-May.

The main white grape varieties are Müller-Thurgau (18.4 per cent), Riesling (14.5 per cent) and Weissburgunder (12 per cent). Grauburgunder, Traminer and Goldriesling, a Riesling-Muscat crossing, and a local specialty. The main red varieties are Spätburgunder, Dornfelder and Portugieser.

Dresden

Sachsen used to include the largest and most affluent territories of the Holy Roman Empire, such as Leipzig, Meissen, Magdeburg, Wittenburg, Poland and parts of Prussia and Lithuania. It also included Dresden, which became the capital of Sachsen in 1806. However, national boundaries were perpetually changing as a result of a series of wars. August der Starke ("the Strong") was born in 1670 and was Elector of Sachsen. He was also King of Poland from 1697-1704 and again from 1709-1733, the year of his death.

August was passionate about traveling to other cities, oriental feasts (particularly Turkish), Baroque architecture, great picture galleries, music, jewelry of gold and precious gems, porcelain ware, assembling his army of 30,000

The grand entrance of Schloss Proschwitz, near Meissen.

men – and his numerous mistresses.

Because of all these, Dresden was known as "Florence on the Elbe," a cultural center, which today is absolutely unique. The city's small center contains the fabulous Baroque Protestant **Frauenkirche**, the Catholic **Hofkirche**, the **Schloss**, the **Operahouse** and August's glorious **Zwinger palace**. These and other galleries were almost completely destroyed in 1945 but had been miraculously restored over the next 50 years. They are grouped on the south bank of the Elbe river. The sculptor Permoser, the architects Pöppelmann and Bähr, the organ builder Silbermann and Böttger, the inventor of porcelain, are all names you will encounter during your visit.

Wine revenues helped line the royal coffers and by 1500 vineyards were an integral part of the landscape between Dresden and Pillnitz, an area known as the Elbhang. Today, hobby vintners have taken the initiative to restore some of Dresden's viticultural tradition. They have replanted the riverside terraces of two palatial mansions near Loschwitz as well as two parcels of the Königlicher

Weinberg (royal vineyard) in Wachwitz and Pillnitz.

In Loschwitz, you can reach the heights for a good view via two venerable cable cars. Or, in Wachwitz, walk through the royal vineyard on the Panorma Weg and up the steep steps called the *Himmelsleiter*, the "ladder to heaven." Garden lovers can visit the Rhododendrongarten nearby.

Pillnitz

From the Blaues Wunder, the blue suspension bridge at Loschwitz, it is a brief drive to Pillnitz via the *Sächsische Weinstrasse* (Pillnitzer Landstrasse). The street is the site of the *Elbhangfest*, a huge folk festival in late July. A more scenic option is to take an historic steamer from Dresden, arriving near the majestic stairway of Baroque Schloss Pillnitz (about two hours).

Pöppelmann designed the twin palaces with decorative chinoiserie for August in 1721. A 200-year-old camellia is but one of many rarities in the magnificent gardens (www.schlosspillnitz.de). Cross the road and walk past the historical press house (1827) to see another Pöppelmann gem (1725), **the Weinbergkirche**, at the foot of the Pillnizer **Königlicher Weinberg**, which is one of the best vineyards of the area. Gilded grapes decorate its sandstone altar and there are concerts on Sundays. Both the church and the vineyard were restored by local initiatives. A walk along the Leitenweg path at the top edge of the vineyard affords a good view. It begins behind the Weinbergschänke restaurant via An der Schäferei.

Gateway to "Saxon Switzerland"

The *Weinstrasse* loops through Graupa – where Richard Wagner composed *Lohengrin* while convalescing in a farmhouse (now a museum) – before resuming its riverside course to Pirna. Here, at the southern end of the *Weinstrasse*, vines are also being replanted. As you explore the market square and its side streets, look up to see the decorative gables, portals and oriels. The late Gothic **St Marien Church** is also worth seeing. Just minutes to the south the splendid scenery of "Saxon Switzerland" begins.

The Lössnitz hills of Radebeul

Near the Dresden-Neustadt Bahnhof (train station), drive under the railway tracks to reach the *Weinstrasse* (Leipziger Strasse) and proceed to Radebeul. Turn right at Hoflössnitz Strasse and watch for the signs to Hoflössnitz, an historic wine estate. There are concerts, exhibitions, wine tastings and festivals at Hoflössnitz throughout the year.

Research carried out here in the early 1900s was sadly not a success in reviving viticulture in Sachsen, after the havoc wreaked by the vine louse phylloxera, because in Germany it was forbidden to graft vines on to American rootstock – a practice that was successful everywhere else in Europe. In the wine museum you can actually see a vine louse (and wine-related items) as well as remarkable paintings on the walls and ceilings (exotic birds) in the rooms upstairs.

Before visiting western Radebeul, don't miss the historic wine estates and villas on the *Weinbergstrasse* and the **panorama from the Spitzhaus**. Steep vineyards rise up behind the historic houses on the Obere Bergstrasse. From the Volkssternwarte (planetarium) walk to the Jakobstein hut for a superb view of the **Schloss Wack-erbarth** palace at the foot of the beautiful terraced

The city of Meissen with the spires of the great cathedral just visible.

The majestic Semperoper Opera House in Dresden.

vineyards. The Baroque palace, now called Sächsisches Schloss Wackerbarth, was built in 1727 by Graf August von Wackerbarth. It manages 90 hectares of vines and its specialties are Riesling, Grau- and Weisserburgunder, and Traminer – and excellent *Sekts*. A visit to the recently built winery is a must, and all sorts of events take place there. **Radebeuler Goldener Wagon** and **Lössnitz** are the best vineyards here. Also recommended is the scenic path through the vineyards on Zechsteinweg (near Sarkengasse).

Weinböhla and Schloss Moritzburg

From Radebeul the *Weinstrasse* (Meissner Strasse) follows the Elbe to Meissen, but there is a secondary route from Coswig that takes in the old wine towns of Weinböhla, Niederau and Gröbern. Their vineyards, all in the Gellertberg site, were renamed in honor of the 18th-century writer Gellert, a frequent visitor. By 1840, this was the largest continuous vineyard area of Sachsen. However, after phylloxera, the alluvial sandy soils were replanted with asparagus and orchards.

In Weinböhla there is a wine and history trail that starts at the town hall. After the walk, relax over a glass of local wine at the Peterkeller. One other "detour" is recommended – a visit to the castle at Moritzburg, which is 7 km (4 miles) east of Weinböhla. Or, from the Radebeul Ost train station, you can enjoy a 30-minute ride on the historic *Lössnitzdackel* train.

It is to August and his architect Pöppelmann that the palace owes its Baroque appearance and majestic lake setting. The splendid furnishings and impressive collection of hunting trophies make it well worth a visit. Given their passion for hunting, it is not surprising that the Saxon rulers set up a stud farm here. You can see the horses with riders in period costumes at the festive *Hengstparaden* (stallion parades) in September.

The Spaar Hills

The slopes of the Spaargebirge between Sörnewitz and Meissen boast not only the excellent vineyard sites of **Kapitelberg** and **Rosengründchen**, but also very scenic hiking trails. Old vineyard walls and the remains of historic wine estates share the landscape with the woods and vines. Ascend the heights to the **Boselgarten**, a botanical garden, and the vantage points Boselspitze, Juchhöh and Karlshöhe. These afford great views of Old Meissen and, on a clear day, as far south as Sachsische Schweiz.

Meissen – on the right bank

In Meissen the *Weinstrasse* (Dresdner Strasse from Coswig) runs under the railway tracks left of the train station, then turns right into the B 101 (Grossenhainer Strasse). To visit the Meissen Winzergenossenschaft, the regional cooperative and Sachsen's largest producer, follow the B 101 to the left turning into the Bennoweg. The cooperative was founded in 1938.

Today, the co-op's 2500 members cultivate one-third of the region's vineyards and offer a comprehensive selection of wines.

Historic Meissen

Cross the Elbe on the B 101 and park on the river bank to visit Old Meissen, founded in 929, when the Saxon Duke Heinrich, Germany's first king, built a fortress on the Burgberg (castle hill) as a defence against the Slavs. The **Albrechtsburg castle** is its successor. From the second-storey windows of the north wing you can see a vineyard in the Meisa valley, where viticulture in Sachsen was first documented in 1161. The castle was never used as a residence, but from 1710 to 1864 it housed Europe's first porcelain manufactory. The interior vaulting, paintings and draped-arch windows are remarkable (open daily from 10AM).

The other magnificent Gothic structure on the Burgberg is the cathedral, whose origins date from 968, when Heinrich's son Otto, the first German emperor, made Meissen a diocese.

Gems of "white gold"

Descend the Burgberg via the steps to the Burgstrasse to the market square. It is ringed by an ensemble of beautiful Renaissance houses, the town hall and the Frauenkirche, with a 37-bell porcelain Glockenspiel. From here it is a brief walk along the Triebisch river to the porcelain manufactory at Talstrasse 9. A visit to the **Meissen factory** is perfectly organized: you enter the first room and see the basic shaping of the porcelain. Subsequently a series of rooms shows each stage in creating a piece, and everything is explained in detail, and finally there is a shop. The wonderful museum goes back to 1814.

Nearby, in a small memorial church, the **Nikolaikirche,** the unique porcelain figures are also worth seeing.

From Meissen to Seusslitz

Opposite Old Meissen the *Weinstrasse* (Hafenstrasse/Elbtalstrasse) skirts the Bocksberg, a granite outcrop with the Schloss Proschwitz site on the heights, and the terraced Katzensprung site below. The **Katzenstufen** (200 steps) rise to scenic views from the heights.

Before World War II Schloss Proschwitz had been the hereditary palace of Prinz zur Lippe, whose family owned vast lands and forests as well as vineyards. After 1945, the family was expropriated and left for West Germany. Dr Georg Prinz zur Lippe returned after the Berlin Wall fell in 1989. He gradually bought up the palace and the vineyards and invested $10 million to restore the buildings and the vineyards and to build a new winery. The family now owns 90 hectares (220 acres) of vines, as well as an excellent guesthouse by the winery and the vineyards, and produces some of the finest wines in the region.

Where the Elbe bends at Nieschütz the dramatic cliffs of Diesbar-Seusslitz come into view. There is a pleasant walk through the Heinrichsburg site, starting either at Diesbar or at the Schlosspark in Seusslitz (**Seusslitzer Heinrichsburg** is one of the best vineyards). You can enjoy the local hospitality at concerts and festivals in the grounds of the palace or at the family wine estates on the *Weinstrasse* (Meissner Strasse). Or cross the Elbe by ferry for a glass of wine at the **Elbklause** and a splendid view of this idyllic landscape.

REGIONAL WINE PROMOTION BOARD

Weinbauverband Sachsen e.V.
Fabrikstrasse 16
01662 Meissen
Tel: 03521 763530
www.weinbauverband-sachsen.de

WINERIES & MORE

ZADEL ÜBER MEISSEN

Weingut Schloss Proschwitz Prinz zur Lippe (H/R)
Dorfanger 19
01665 Zadel über Meissen
Tel: 03521 76760
www.schloss-proschwitz.de

DRESDEN

Weingut Klaus Zimmerling
Bergweg 27
01326 Dresden-Pillnitz
Tel: 0351 2618752
www.weingut-zimmerling.de

RADEBEUL

Sächsisches Staatsweingut-Schloss Wackerbarth
Wackerbarthstrasse 1
01445 Radebeul
Tel: 0351 89550
www.schloss-wackerbarth.de

WHERE TO STAY AND EAT

Dresden

Hilton Hotel (H/R)
An der Frauenkirche 5
01067 Dresden
Tel: 0351 86420
www.hilton.de/dresden

Hotel Restaurant Pattis (H/R)
Merbitzer Strasse 53
01157 Dresden
Tel: 0351 42550
www.pattis.net
Restaurant, wine lounge and spa. Idyllic setting.

Schloss Eckberg (H/R)
Bautzner Strasse 134
01099 Dresden
Tel: 0351 80990
www.schloss-eckberg.de
Neo-Gothic castle in a riverside park. Great views. Pretty garden.

Meissen

Welcome Parkhotel Meissen (H)
Hafenstrasse 27-31
01662 Meissen
Tel: 03521 72250
www.welcome-hotel-meissen.de

Hotel Goldener Löwe (H)
Heinrichsplatz 6
01662 Meissen
Tel: 03521 4 11 10
www.welcome-hotels.com

Vincenz Richter (R)
An der Frauenkirche 12
01662 Meissen
Tel: 03521 453285
www.vincenz-richter.de
Historic house (1573) with attractive courtyard.

Lippe'sches Guthaus (R)
Dorfanger 19
01665 Zadel über Meissen
Tel: 03521 767673
www.schloss-proschwitz.de

Pirna

Romantik Hotel Deutsches Haus (H/R)
Niedere Burgstrasse 1
01706 Pirna
Tel: 03501 46880
www.romantikhotel-pirna.de
Historic house with lovely garden courtyard.

Hotel Pirna'scher Hof (H)
Am Markt 4
01796 Pirna
Tel: 03501 44380
www.pirnascher-hof.de

Weinböhla

Laubenhöhe (R)
Kölerstrasse 77
01689 Weinböhla
Tel: 035243 36183
www.laubenhoehe.de

This 2011 placard celebrates 850 years of winemaking in Sachsen.

GRAPE VARIETIES

WHITES

Bacchus has a fragrant, slightly Muscat nose and a pleasant softness, especially in wines from Franken.

Grauburgunder (Pinot Gris) is a lovely wine with a distinctive bouquet. It is excellent with many dishes, fine with fish, meat and oriental food. Synonyms: Pinot Grigio and Ruländer.

Gutedel is an ancient variety grown in the Markgräflerland in Baden. It makes a light, pleasant quaffing wine. Synonyms: Chasselas in France and Fendant in Switzerland.

Kerner is a crossing of Trollinger with Riesling. The wine is similar to Riesling, but lacks its complexity and character.

Müller-Thurgau is a crossing of Riesling and another grape variety (nobody seems to be certain which). It ripens early and produces huge quantities of grapes, which is why the resulting wine is weak and sweet. The sooner it disappears, the better. Synonym: Rivaner.

Muskateller is an ancient variety and a delicious light, elegant wine, sweet but not too sweet, that is served on special occasions, such as weddings and birthdays.

Rieslaner is a crossing of Riesling and Silvaner and ripens sooner than Riesling in certain areas to develop Auslese quality.

Riesling is Germany's greatest wine at every level of quality from the finest vineyards. A Kabinett is delicious young and fresh, while a great Auslese will develop for years and last for decades.

Scheurebe has good acidity, a distinctive bouquet and a flavor reminiscent of blackcurrants as a dry wine. As an Auslese and above, it can be a glorious dessert wine and is delicious with blue cheese. It can improve with age and last for 20 years or more.

Silvaner is traditional in Franken and Rheinhessen. The wines are full-bodied, mainly dry, and excellent with food.

Traminer is prized for its hints of roses and spicy character. It is mainly planted in Baden and Pfalz. Gewürztraminer is used on labels to describe wines with greater concentration and richness, as in Alsace. Synonym: Clevner.

Weissburgunder (Pinot Blanc) is a delightful, fresh, dry wine that is particularly enjoyable to drink in summer, especially with fish and cold food.

REDS

Dornfelder is a crossing that yields deep red, full-bodied wines with a rich black cherry fragrance and a fairly tannic acidity, provided that yields are low and the wine is matured in oak barrels.

Lemberger is a speciality of Württemberg. The wines are fresh, racy and full-bodied. Synonyms: Limberger, Blaufränkisch.

Portugieser is an old and prolific variety and the wines are mild and suitable for quaffing. It probably originated in the Danube valley, not in Portugal.

Regent is a very new grape variety. It has immunity to fungus disease and is making many friends.

Sankt Laurent has similarities with Pinot Noir but its origin is unknown. It is quite powerful, deep colored, with sour cherry aromas and flavors.

Schwarzriesling is a mutation of Pinot Noir but it ripens earlier and the wine is lighter and of lower quality. Württemberg has the most plantings. Synonyms: Pinot Meunier, Müllerrebe.

Spätburgunder (Pinot Noir) is the finest red wine grape in Germany. The wines are velvety and full-bodied with a bouquet reminiscent of blackberries. The finest wines are made in the same way as in Burgundy – long fermentation with the skins and long maturation in small *barriques,* before bottling. It thrives in the Ahr, Rheingau, Rheinhessen, Pfalz and Baden. Frühburgunder (früh means early) is an old clone from the Ahr that ripens two weeks or so before Spätburgunder and its wines are very elegant and gentle.

Trollinger is a speciality of Württemberg. Late to ripen, it yields high quantities of light, fragrant wine with a pronounced acidity.

Zweigelt is a cross of Limberger and Sankt Laurent from Austria. It ripens early, is frost-resistant and suited to the climate in Saale-Unstrut and Sachsen. The wines can be enjoyed fresh, like Beaujolais, or matured in oak casks for development in bottle.

GLOSSARY OF GERMAN WINE TERMS

Abfüller bottler.

Amtliche Prüfungsnummer official simple tests.

Anbaugebiet one of 13 specified winegrowing regions in Germany.

Bad town that owns special water wells that are thought to improve health.

Bereich is a vast area of largely flat vineyards with all sorts of vine varieties and is the lowest of the low appellations in Germany now that *Tafelwein* is being abolished. It is mass-produced and sold in supermarkets.

Berg hill or mountain.

Bocksbeutel flagon-shaped bottle used for quality wines of Franken and a few parts of northern Baden.

Burg fortress.

Deutsche Weinstrasse the German Wine Road, which runs the length of the Pfalz region.

Edelfäule noble rot or *Botrytis cinerea*, a fungus that pierces the skins of ripe grapes, thereby causing the water content to evaporate and the grapes to shrivel. The concentrated acids and sugars that remain yield luscious dessert wines, eg Beeren- and Trockenbeerenauslese. *Edelfäule* imparts a honeyed tone to the wine.

Einzellage individual vineyard sites.

Erzeugerabfüllung producer-bottled, ie the grapes were grown and the wine was produced and bottled by one individual or a collective of individuals.

Federweisser milky-colored, nearly fermented grape juice available for only a few weeks during the harvest in fall, when most of the natural sugar has been converted. Good with *Zwiebelkuchen* (onion quiche).

Grosslage vast area of vineyards of up to 50 or more villages. The resulting blended wines are mass-produced.

Gutsabfüllung estate-bottled.

Halbtrocken medium dry style.

Keller cellar.

Kelter wine press.

Lese the picking of the harvest.

Oechsle scale developed in the 19th century by Ferdinand Oechsle to measure how much sugar there is in the grape before fermentation.

Prädikat a guarantee of high quality of German wines based on German wine laws.

Schloss castle or palace.

Sekt sparkling wine. (*Sekt* bA is made entirely from German grapes).

Strausswirtschaft wine shop in a grower's home, where for four months of the year he can sell his own wines (no others) with light food or snacks. Look for a *Strauss* (wreath) hung over the door, or, in Württemberg, a *Besen* (broom).

Trocken dry style.

Weinbaulehrpfad educational path through the vineyards, signposted with information about growing conditions, grape varieties, work in the vineyards, etc.

Weingut wine estate.

Weinkellerei winery that buys grape must (to make wine) or wine from a grower, and then bottles and markets the wine.

Winzer vintner, wine grower, wine maker.

Winzerfest wine festival. The German Wine Institute publishes an annual calendar.

Winzergenossenschaft cooperative of wine growers who deliver their grapes to a winery that will make, bottle and market the wine.

WHERE TO E-MAIL, WRITE OR CALL

CANADA

Wines of Germany – Canada
2 St Clair Avenue East, Suite 1206
Toronto, ON M4T 2T5
Tel: (416) 637 2044
www.germanwinecanada.org

GERMANY

German Wine Institute
Gutenbergplatz 3–5
55116 Mainz
Tel: 06131 28290
www.germanwines.de

UK

Wines of Germany
c/o Phipps PR
17 Exeter Street
London WC2E 7DU
Tel. 020 7759 7405
www.winesofgermany.co.uk

USA

German Wine Information Bureau
950 Third Avenue, 7th Floor
New York, NY 10022
Tel: (212) 994 7523
www.germanwineusa.com

WINE TOUR ORGANIZER

VinTour Wine Experiences
Gut Schnellenberg
21339 Lüneburg
Germany
Tel: 04131 2209860
www.vintour-weinreisen.de

PUBLIC HOLIDAYS

1 Jan, Good Friday, Easter Monday, 1 May (Labor Day), Ascension Day, Whit Monday, 3 Oct (Unity Day), 25–26 December. (Check locally about other, regional holidays.)

SAMPLE E-MAIL/ LETTER TO AN ESTATE (WEINGUT)

[Sender's name, address, telephone number, email address and the date.]

Sehr geehrte Damen und Herren,

ich habe in *A Traveller's Wine Guide to Germany* über Ihr Weingut gelesen und würde es gerne kennenlernen. Wäre ein Besuch am [date] um [time] Möglich?

ich reise allein/Ich reise nicht allein. Wir würden

gerne mit insgesamt [total number in party] Personen kommen. (Delete where not applicable.)

Bitte benachrichtigen Sie mich kurz per Brief, e-mail oder Telefon, wenn mein Terminvorschlag ungünstig für Sie liegt. Herzlichen Dank für Ihre Bemühungen im Voraus.

Mit freundlichen Grüssen
[signature]

Dear Madam/Sir,

I have read about your wine estate in *A Traveller's Wine Guide to Germany* and would like to visit it. Would a visit on [date] at [time] be convenient?

I will be traveling alone/I will not be traveling alone. We are a party of [number] persons in all. (Delete where not applicable.)

If the suggested date and/or time are not convenient, would you please be so kind as to notify me by letter, e-mail or telephone? Thank you very much for your help.

Yours sincerely,
[signature]

WINE AND FOOD IN GERMANY

The opportunity to sample the local wines with regional cooking is one of the greatest pleasures of traveling through wine country. Since the nineties, the new generation of creative chefs has helped dispel Germany's "sausage and sauerkraut" image. These masters of light, contemporary cuisine prepare both traditional and original recipes with seasonal, local ingredients selected at the peak of freshness. They use modern culinary techniques, which call for a reduction, rather than the addition of heavy, thickening agents, to prepare light, flavorful sauces.

German wines are well-suited to the trend of lighter eating and drinking. They stimulate and refresh – rather than dull – the palate. Both dry wines and relatively sweet Kabinett and Spätlesen wines complement many foods. Auslesen and above are a superlative way to end a meal.

DINING IN GERMANY

Here are a few basic terms related to eating out in Germany:

Frühstück breakfast

Mittagessen lunch: served from 12PM to 2PM.

Abendessen dinner: served from 6PM to 9:30PM.

Gaststätte, Gasthof, Gasthaus Restaurant. Weinstube, Winzerstube, Winzerkeller, Gutsschänke, Gutsausschank, Strausswirtschaft pubs: all mean roughly the same thing and serve wine

Ruhetag closed

Geöffnet ab (time): open as of (time).

Stammtisch table reserved for regular guests, usually indicated by a sign. Avoid the embarrassment of being asked to leave the table. Ask for another table, and it is common to share a table if a restaurant or pub is full.

Die Karte, bitte The menu, please.

Die Rechnung, bitte or **Zahlen, bitte** The check (bill), please.

Trinkgeld the tip, almost always included in the price. It's normal to "round up," eg if the bill comes to EUR34,20 you pay EUR35,00. *Auf Wiedersehen* (good-bye) is said as you leave the restaurant or pub.

THE MENU

Karte/Speisekarte menu

Tageskarte menu of today's specials

Aal eel

Beilagen side dishes

Bratkartoffeln fried potatoes

Ente duck

Fisch fish

Fleisch meat

Forelle trout

Gans goose

Geflügel poultry

Gemüse vegetables

Hähnchen/Huhn chicken

Hauptgerichte main dishes

Hecht pike

Kalb veal

Kartoffeln potatoes

Kartoffelnbrei or -purée: mashed potatoes

Käse cheese

Klösschen/Knödeln dumplings

Lachs salmon

Lamm lamb

Leber liver

Nachtisch dessert

Nudeln/Spätzle noodles

Reis rice

Rind beef

Salat salad

Salzkartoffeln boiled potatoes

Schinken ham
Schwein pork
Seezunge sole
Speise/Gericht dish
Steinbutt turbot
Suppen soups
Vorspeisen appetizers
Wild game
Wurst sausage
Zander pike-perch

DRINKS

Getränke beverages
Weinkarte wine list
offene Weine wines sold by the glass
Flaschenweine wines sold by the bottle
Saft juice (*Apfelsaft* apple juice)
stilles Mineralwasser non-carbonated mineral water

INDEX

Page references in *italic* type indicate illustrations